Creating a Business-based IT Strategy

UNICOM Applied Information Technology

Each book in the series is based upon papers given at a seminar organized by UNICOM Seminars Ltd. The reports cover subjects at the forefront of information technology, and the contributors are all authorities in the subject on which they are invited to write, either as researchers or as practitioners.

1 **Fourth-Generation Systems**
Their scope, application and methods of evaluation
Edited by Simon Holloway

2 **Evaluating Supercomputers**
Strategies for exploiting, evaluating and benchmarking
Edited by A. van der Steen

3 **Failsafe Control Systems**
Applications and emergency management
Edited by Kevin Warwick and Ming T. Tham

4 **Computer Vision and Image Processing**
Edited by Anthony Barrett

5 **The Distributed Development Environment**
The art of using CASE
Edited by Simon Holloway

6 **Software Quality and Reliability**
Tools and methods
Edited by Darrel Ince

7 **Open Systems for Europe**
Edited by Tony Elliman and Colston Sanger

8 **Hypermedia/Hypertext**
And Object-oriented Databases
Edited by Heather Brown

9 **Software for Parallel Computers**
Edited by R. H. Perrott

10 **Object-oriented Programming Systems**
Tools and applications
Edited by J. J. Florentin

11 **Object-oriented Design**
Edited by Peter Robinson

12 **Software Reuse and Reverse Engineering in Practice**
Edited by P. A. V. Hall

13 **Parallel Processing and Data Management**
Edited by P. Valduriez

14 **Creating a Business-based IT strategy**
Edited by A. Brown

15 **Executive Information Systems and Decision Support**
Edited by Clive Holtham

Creating a Business-based IT Strategy

UNICOM

APPLIED INFORMATION TECHNOLOGY 14

Edited by **A. Brown**
Lecturer in Operational Research,
City University Business School, London

CHAPMAN & HALL
London · Glasgow · New York · Tokyo · Melbourne · Madras

Published by Chapman & Hall, 2–6 Boundary Row, London SE1 8HN

Chapman & Hall, 2–6 Boundary Row, London SE1 8HN, UK

Blackie Academic & Professional, Wester Cleddens Road, Bishopbriggs, Glasgow G64 2NZ, UK

Van Nostrand Reinhold Inc., 115 5th Avenue, New York NY10003, USA

Chapman & Hall Japan, Thomson Publishing Japan, Hirakawacho Nemoto Building, 6F, 1–7–11 Hirakawa-cho, Chiyoda-ku, Tokyo 102, Japan

Chapman & Hall Australia, Thomas Nelson Australia, 102 Dodds Street, South Melbourne, Victoria 3205, Australia

Chapman & Hall India, R. Seshadri, 32 Second Main Road, CIT East, Madras 600 035, India

First edition 1992

Printed in Great Britain by St Edmundsbury Press Ltd, Bury St Edmunds, Suffolk

ISBN 0 412 45910 8   0 442 31643 7 (USA)

A catalogue record for this book is available from the British Library

Library of Congress Cataloging-in-Publication data available

∞ Printed on permanent acid-free text paper, manufactured in accordance with the proposed ANSI/NISO Z 39.48-199X and ANSI Z 39.48-1984

Contents

CONTRIBUTORS

Ann Brown, Lecturer in Operational Research at The City University Business School, has experience of both the strategic and management issues that arise when developing the use of IT within an organization. She lectures on both the subjects of business strategy and the management of IT at MBA level. Her research interests include the impact of IT developments on business strategy.

David Norman, editor of the International Management Advantage briefing Papers & Book reviews and visiting lecturer at both Management Centre Europe in Brussels and The City University Business School, is a management consultant on business management issues.

David Axson, Gunn Hackett & Markos, was until recently a manager at A.T. Kearney Management Consultants. He combines business and consultancy experience in information technology and operations.

John Swift, Director of Management Consultancy, Hoskyns Group plc, has many years' experience as a senior executive in operational management at a number of international companies. His functional responsibilities have been wide ranging and include organization strategy, organizational development, the effective and strategic use of information in the business and the management of change.

Paul Raimond, Senior Lecturer in Business Policy at The City University Business School and Head of the Division of International Business and Export Management, is a Chartered Accountant with considerable consultancy experience in strategic planning. He worked for some time as a strategic planner for a multinational company.

John Freestone, Managing Director – Catering, Dairy Crest, joined Dairy Crest as Sales Manager in 1981 following a career in sales and marketing spanning over 20 years. He was appointed to manage the newly formed Dairy Crest Catering business in 1986, progressing from Sales and Marketing Manager to Managing Director.

Gregory Hackett, Principal at A.T. Kearney Management Consultants, combines business and consultancy experience in information technology and operations.

Kit Grindley, Professor of Systems Automation at the LSE, and Price Waterhouse Consultants, is the editor of the *Information Technology Review* published by Price Waterhouse.

Iain Perring, Partner, Mindworks, has many years' experience in the IT industry and in information consultancy. Mindworks specializes in information strategies and the development of more effective IT support services within organizations.

Leslie Willcocks, Director of the Centre for the Study of Use of Information in Management at The City University Business School and executive editor of the *Journal of Information Technology*, has worked for many years in IT in all three areas of research, consultancy and training. He has published books on systems design and the human and organizational issues of using IT.

Veronica Symons, Senior Management Services Officer at Leicester City Council, has published on her research into multiple perspectives in information systems evaluation.

Frank Land, Professor of Information Management at the London Business School, spent 15 years in the British computer industry before joining the LSE. His main research interests include the impact of information technology on organizations and their employees, a subject on which he has a number of publications.

Pat Griffiths, has a wide-ranging experience in the application of information technology to industrial problems. She is one of DCE's foremost exponents of Strategic IS/IT Planning – consulting and lecturing to many organizations. She has co-authored two books on the subject.

Clive Holtham, Bull HN Professor of Information Management at The City University Business School, worked as finance director joining the Business School. He has extensive experience in managing and using information technology. His research is centred around the top management use of IT and the application of IT for strategic advantage.

Marco Kapp, Kapp & Partners, has over 20 years' experience in data processing, telecommunications and office systems. He directed the £1m European Security Study, the results of which he co-authored. Subsequently he established and directed the European Security Forum, an initiative that has attracted some 70 member organizations from 12 European nations.

Brian Davis, Resource Director, Nationwide Anglia Building Society, was responsible for bringing together the two societies' (Nationwide and Anglia) technologies when they merged in 1987. He was appointed to the Board in 1989 and his current responsibilities include technology.

Hugh Macdonald, ICL (UK), has been in the IT industry for over 30 years. He was the ICL sponsor representative for five years on the 'Management in the 1990s' research programme at the Sloan School of Management at MIT and is now with the ICL group consulting subsidiary IT Partners Limited.

Chris Yapp, Senior executive program ICL (UK), has been working for three years on using the output of the MIT 'Management the 1990s' research programme within ICL and with ICL's clients.

David Kaye, has over 30 years' experience in management consultancy, much of it spent as a partner at Anderson Consulting (Arthur Anderson & Co.). He started their strategic consulting practice in London. He is the author of 'Gamechange: the impact of IT on corporate strategy and structure'.

Henry Green, Head of Research and Development Group of The Treasury Division, Hill Samuel Bank Ltd and Visiting Professor at Imperial College, is currently involved in developing long-term strategic planning for risk management and treasury operations.

Part One

Introduction

1 Creating an IT strategy

A. Brown
City University

1.1 AIMS OF THIS BOOK

Despite general agreement on the immense potential of IT to improve performance at all levels of business, there is fundamental accord that its contribution so far has been disappointing. The claims initially made for IT have vastly outstripped actual performance. Contributor after contributor to this book confirms the current widely held view, that investment in IT for the UK has not yielded the benefits expected of it. The return on the money spent, by any measure, has been poor. The outstanding examples of IT being used for competitive advantage are still relatively few. In the ten years since the first examples appeared, there have been comparatively few successful imitators.

The lack of an IT strategy within most organizations, or the poor formulation and implementation of such strategies, is seen as a very significant contributor to the current malaise.

The future consequences of inadequate IT strategies look even grimmer. Where advantage is to be gained from the effective utilization of IT, the magnitude of the benefits available means that those organizations that first achieve mastery dominate the market. Organizations that fail to master IT will be at a progressive disadvantage.

This book is concerned with the creation of effective, implementable IT strategies. It is about the process of IT creation. It does not seek to identify in any systematic way the various ways that IT can support and enhance business activity in general, although a variety of case examples are described. We take the view that organizations of any size must think more systematically and coherently about how they use IT. We consider the issues involved in attempting to create an IT strategy and seek to suggest ways of dealing with the various problems raised.

The contributors are a diverse group from industry, consultancy and academic institutions, with a wide range of experience in the application of IT.

1.2 CORE MESSAGE

Many organizations are attempting to move from the use of IT in isolated applications within individual functions to a more integrated approach. This places a premium on establishing how IT can best be used to support the current business strategy of the whole organization. For an organization to achieve such an effective integrated approach to the use of IT, two major steps are required – far more time, sophistication and resource needs to be put into the development of the IT strategy and the organization must be prepared to institute radical change. This book investigates the ways in which organizations can improve their IT strategy planning.

However, the point is made time and again that effective strategies require a revision – almost certainly a radical revision of the current way of carrying out the business. Jobs will need to disappear, new jobs will be created, organizational structure will change, the culture will need to change. The analysis carried out here assumes that such changes once understood can be made. The mechanism for making such changes is left to another book.

1.3 STRUCTURE OF THE BOOK

There are four major sections, of which the next three deal with conditions as they appear to be at present for many organizations in the UK. In the last section, Part Five, contributors look to the future.

In Part Two existing practice with respect to the creation of IT strategy is explored. Some of the problems raised in Part Two are investigated in greater depth in Part Three. The contributors to Part Four offer various methods for the creation of an IT strategy.

Part Five comprises five papers, all of which are concerned with what organizations could achieve in the future, by exploiting the potential of IT to the full.

1.4 CURRENT APPROACHES TO IT STRATEGY AND BARRIERS TO IT STRATEGY CREATION

One framework from 'the MIT Management of the 1990's research programme' explained by K. Hugh Macdonald and Chris Yapp in Part Five allows us to put much of the current concerns (and hence the contributions to the next three sections) into context.

Organizations are seen as moving through a number of levels in their use of IT. The starting point is usually the localized use of IT within isolated business functions (level 1). At this stage the use of IT is largely unrelated to the overall business strategy of the organization and the aims are cost reduction and efficiency increases. IT applications are independent (K. Hugh Macdonald's term) of the strategic context and can be implemented with reasonable success by the IT professionals together with the local management concerned.

As organizations move to level 2 a different picture emerges. This is when some form of internal integration is attempted. Typically a common IT platform is installed and the organization seeks to gain advantage from the integration of IT facilities across divisions and departments. Applications that align with the organization's overall business strategy begin to offer the greatest value-added potential. The most valuable applications are then dependent (Macdonald's term) on the organization's overall business strategy, and the need for business management to be involved in their development becomes paramount. The increasing urgency of a number of other problems can be seen to flow from this development. IT soaks up more resources (human and financial), spawns applications that are far more complex to identify and describe and begins to impact at many levels and in all parts of the organization in a more radical way than previously. The evaluation of the benefits and costs of new IT systems and their implementation becomes a more complex affair. Unsurprisingly we see calls for more time, resources and sophistication of analysis to be devoted to these activities. Effective communication between IT professionals and business managers becomes imperative and we see the perception emerging that such communication is difficult if not impossible under current conditions. The involvement of top management is an absolute necessity and we see the perception emerging of how difficult this could be to achieve.

Most of these problems are identified by the first three contributors to Part Two (David Norman, David Axson and John Swift), as highly pertinent to the current situation of many organizations. The evidence of these three authors suggests that many organizations are at a stage where they need to make just such a move towards the integrated use of IT as described above, but are finding it difficult to do so. Paul Raimond describes in more detail some of the extreme ill-effects observed when organizations fail to align information systems to business strategy. He highlights the need for some way to regularly reassess IT strategy to capture the effects of a company's changes to its business strategy, and suggests some ways of doing this. John Freestone's description of the successful development of an innovative use of IT to support a new business venture at Dairy Crest, comes as a welcome contrast to the more pessimistic comments of the previous four contributors!

Of the perceived barriers to creating an effective IT strategy, five are discussed in greater depth by contributors to Part Three. These are:

- The problems of describing business process for transfer to IT – inappropriate automation.
- The culture gap between IT professionals and business managers.
- Evaluation problems.
- Implementation problems.
- Top management lack of involvement in IT strategy.

1.4.1 Inappropriate Automation

One manifestation of the misalignment of IT with business strategy is inappropriate automation. David Axson and Gregory Hackett describe some of the examples encountered in the financial sector. They establish that automation is no panacea and is only likely to yield serious benefits when combined with a careful study of the business process to be automated and a willingness to change such process if necessary.

1.4.2 The Culture Gap

If business managers and IT professionals cannot communicate, collaboration between them will be difficult. Yet collaboration is becoming more urgent every day as the need for corporate IT strategy emerges. The failure to develop a common language between IT professionals and business managers is analysed by both Kit Grindley and Iain Perring. These authors offer some fascinating insights into the causes of the problem. Kit Grindley is more pessimistic that Iain Perring on the potential for solving it. Iain offers the experience of his group in training IT professionals to understand business issues. He describes how his group handle such training and their belief in the importance of such work.

1.4.3 Evaluation

Inaccurate evaluation of costs and benefits leads to poor investment decisions. IT projects have a long history of unrealistic appraisals. Traditional investment appraisal methods emphasize tangible benefits measurable in cash terms. This can lead to an underestimate of intangible benefits and a reluctance to consider longer-term consequences. Both of these qualities have not only been important characteristics of IT projects in the past but will grow in significance in the future. Leslie Willcocks considers that too little effort has been put into evaluation in the past and sets out to offer ways of improving current practice. He gives a wide-ranging review of both the problems of cost and benefit evaluation and appraisal techniques. He then analyses recent work on both areas and suggests how they can best be used in practical situations. He ends by making an interesting suggestion that regular evaluation should be regarded as one of the ways in which a company learns about IT.

1.4.4 Implementation

An IT strategy that is difficult if not impossible to implement is of little value. Two writers are concerned with implementation, Veronica Symons and Frank Land. Veronica Symons supports the general view that applications are increasing in potential value. She points out that while the scale and type of the impacts that an IS system has on an organization may be critical to successful implementation, little effort is devoted to its measurement. She emphasizes the importance of gaining user acceptance of new systems. However, no move to gain such acceptance can be made until we know how they will be affected by new developments. She proposes a systematic method of assessment of the impact of IT projects on an organization, which can be applied at the planning stage. Frank Land extends the discussion by proposing guidelines on what steps are necessary for the implementation of an individual IT project. These guidelines are the outcome of a research project that looked at the way a sample of companies actually implemented a number of IT projects.

1.4.5 Top Management and IT

Top management involvement in IT strategy planning is seen as crucial by the last contributor to this section (the editor Ann Brown). When a corporate IT strategy is needed, top management must take responsibility. No one else can. The major changes required for the effective use of IT when an organization reaches this stage, can only be initiated successfully by top management. Her paper explores their changing role with respect to IT and hence what type of IT education programmes would be of value to them.

1.5 ORGANIZING TO CREATE AN IT STRATEGY

The previous sections established the increasing complexity of IT strategy formulation. Contributors to this section discuss ways of overcoming some of the problems posed, to develop an effective, business-based IT strategy. Their proposals therefore are of particular relevance to organizations reaching for the integrated use of IT.

Pat Griffiths sees the alignment of IT with business strategy as the central issue. She starts with the process by which an IS/IT strategy can be derived from consideration of the business strategy. She is principally concerned to obtain a portfolio of applications which can then be classified using McFarlane's four-way model of support, core systems, strategic systems and high potential systems. The paper contrasts the characteristics of these four types of application and shows how such activities as the development of IT strategy need to vary from type to type.

While Clive Holtham is equally concerned with the alignment of IT with business strategy and vision, he considers a wider range of problems than Pat Griffiths. His four-element model incorporates people, their skills and commitment, IT implementation as well as those elements that Pat Griffiths concentrates on: IS applications and business vision/strategy. The problems of impact and implementation therefore become part of his planning procedure. He is concerned that a balance is achieved between these four elements. In this he comes closer to the views of contributors to Part Five. The last part of his paper deals with the detailed steps required to produce a strategy and what should be included in the strategy documents.

Organizations that come to depend on IT can be unpleasantly surprised by the consequences of breakdown. As IT applications ramify, dependability tends to reduce. An IT strategy that failed to consider the implications of the addition of equipment and applications to overall system reliability would store up serious trouble for the future. Marco Kapp analyses the scale of the current problem. His central point is that the use of IT has at present outstripped the means to keep risks contained. As a result, considerable efforts are being made at international level to establish appropriate procedures. However, Marco Kapp suggests that organizations can individually improve their position, and uses his extensive experience in the analysis of systems reliability to outline how to do it. This cannot be achieved without time and effort. But, as he concludes, 'In the IT age, if you want systems that will keep your business up and running, you have to put in the effort up front to make sure they won't let you down when you most need them'.

Brian Davis gives an interesting account of how Nationwide Anglia organizes to ensure that IT strategy is planned and aligned with the business strategy. Like all building societies, Nationwide is clearly well down the path to the integrated use of IT and deeply dependent on IT. It is from his description that we begin to understand the constraint that existing investment in IT represents for those organizations that have been using IT for some period of time.

1.6 FUTURE REALITIES

All contributors to this section look beyond the current situation. They are concerned with achieving a far more creative and effective use of IT. The first and last contributors propose ways of assessing an organization's position in order to compare with others' achievements and to identify future direction.

In the first paper, by K. Hugh Macdonald and Chris Yapp, some of the key ideas of the management of the 1990s' research programme on IT strategy are explained. A core concept is that of a classification of IT usage into five levels based on the degree of business transformation involved. Only organizations that have successfully mastered the second level (of integration) are likely to be able to jump to one or all of the remaining three levels, where IT begins to extend the organizations' strategies. At these levels the interdependence of all parts of the organization becomes of increasing significance.

In the earlier sections of this book, IT strategy is predominantly discussed in relation to business strategy. K. Hugh Macdonald and Chris Yapp would argue that this is appropriate only up to level-2 applications (i.e. where most organizations probably are at present, according to the evidence of the initial papers). We begin to see that the idea of developing an IT strategy in some senses apart from, although dependent on, the organization's business strategy must be abandoned when IT begins to extend the organization's strategies through enabling new ways of doing business (levels 3-5). A more holistic view of the company is needed, in which IT is seen as one constituent of a functioning whole. Business strategy, organizational structure, management process, people and roles together with IT must act in concert. IT itself increases this interdependence. Changes in one factor must trigger changes in one or all of the rest and vice versa, if the organization is gain the full benefit.

In the second paper, K. Hugh Macdonald develops a model for strategic alignment designed to handle these more complex conditions. His approach differs from those proposed previously (in Parts Two and Four) in a number of significant ways. It is a dynamic, iterative process that in theory need never completely stop. It embraces all factors thought to be important, currently those listed above. The alignment of IT with business strategy is but one part of this process. The effect on organizational infrastructure and process is therefore explicitly considered in this model. The process is perfectly general so that changes in the prime factors for example could easily be accommodated.

David Norman ends the book with a view of the future, in which mass production is obsolete and where the 'lean' company dominates the market. He offers a framework for the analysis of an organization's development, which concentrates on business process. His description of the five main ways to reconfigure business establish the magnitude of the change he foresees. All five are currently being practised albeit by few companies. Perhaps he, more than any other contributor, underscores the central importance of business strategy and company organization. IT is seen as valuable but its potential limited by the extent of the business redesign.

The remaining two contributors (Henry Green and David Kaye) discuss future problems and possibilities.

Henry Green's paper divides evenly between problems and future trends. He looks at a number of unresolved issues that affect IT strategy planning and offers ways of dealing with them. For example, he offers a model of how the three main contributors (the CEO, the IT professionals and the user departments) to such plans could interact. He also considers the implications of a number of trends. He forecasts for example that IT will eventually be so freely available and so easy to use that the only question of strategic import will be what needs to be done with it.

David Kaye concentrates exclusively on his vision of an organization that has all possible information freely available to everyone. He calls this having an Open Information capability. His organization of the future will be able to deliver service of an unparalleled quality. It will be able to offer products tailor-made to each individual's requirements. He does strike a more pessimistic note when he comes to discuss the changes that will be necessary to achieve this vision!

All contributors to this section unite in the view that the potential, but as yet unrealized, value of IT to many organizations is enormous. It follows that those that fail to make the appropriate changes in a reasonable time-scale will face overwhelming competition from those that do. There is every reason to expect that such competitive pressure will come from abroad if it does not develop at home.

Part Two

Current Approaches to IT Strategy

2 Why information strategies fail

D. Norman
DNA Management Group

Ironically, despite massive investment and immense strategic importance, information technology (IT) (Norman, 1991) has failed to live up to its promises. The inability of IT to deliver tangible business benefits and a sustainable competitive edge stems from widespread misalignment of business and IT strategies, poor understanding of business needs, extravagant claims for competitive advantage, and a disregard for people, change and organizational issues.

2.1 STRATEGIC MISALIGNMENT

The inability to align business, information and organizational strategy is both widespread and serious. The alignment process is shown in Figure 2.1. Whilst symptomatic of a wider malaise, the simplistic and rigid misapplication of business strategy concepts have played their role in the abject failure of IT strategies. Seductively conceptual frameworks, such as the BCG growth/share, 'Boston box' or 'farmyard' matrix, largely conceal the enormous complexity of detailed and insightful analysis required to understand the real business dynamics which underpin them. Furthermore, business portfolio techniques are poor at organizing data and developing systems.

2.2 INADEQUATE UNDERSTANDING OF BUSINESS NEEDS

Dogmatic complacency in reliance on a single technique, the tyranny of structured proprietary methodologies and the inability to surface strategically significant applications, are at the root of a poor understanding of business issues and needs.

The narrow 'User needs analysis' or 'critical success factors' capture users' perceived perspectives on business issues as a basis for formulating information requirements. The approach ignores independent business assessment and consensus about future strategic opportunities. Executive Information Systems requirements are still largely, and erroneously, identified in this way. Proprietary methodologies are designed to identify traditional information management requirements in areas like accounting and planning. Generally they ignore or are inadequate in identifying information which supports or shapes competitive strategy (Wiseman, 1988) or redraws market boundaries (Cash, McFarlan and McKenney, 1988). Structured methodologies used for systems design which model complex data flows and entity relationships are poor in dealing with business strategy issues and largely neglect organizational strategy, implementation and change management issues.

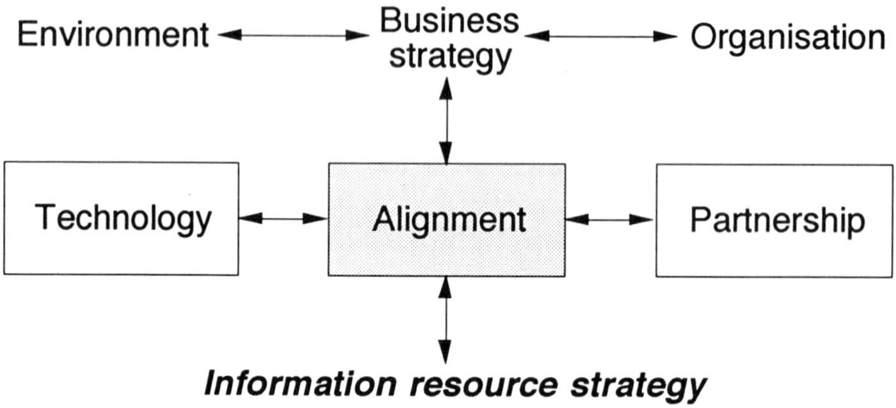

Figure 2.1. The alignment process

2.3 THE COMPETITIVE ADVANTAGE SNAKEOIL

Even greater damage to the credibility of IT strategy was created in the mid-1980s by a wave of industry 'hype' promising unrealistic competitive benefits from computer technology. Suppliers did not even have to goad gullible users into making inappropriate procurement decisions since they both expected to share in the impending glory of more sales or faster promotions. The backlash was predictable and severe. Successful war stories of American Airlines SABRE, Thompson's TOPS and McKesson's Econoscan precipitated this trend. Large and sustained investment in IT is a precondition for doing business in many industries like financial services, airlines and retailing. Whilst there are very real and sustainable opportunities for competitive advantage applications, like those used by Benetton, Baker Perkins and Allied Dunbar, the persistent use of inappropriate and partial methods may impart fleeting advantages or even, competitive *dis*advantages.

2.4 THE COMMUNICATIONS VOID

The resolute failure to develop a common understanding between IT professionals, business managers and their departments has reached crisis point in many firms. The inability to monitor user expectations and accommodate changing information requirements for projects persistently delivered late and over budget only aggravates the situation. Furthermore, poor cross-boundary cooperation, tenacious patronage of project milestone sign-off rituals and political manoeuvring are serious impediments to smooth relationships. Modest initiatives such as placing a few IT people into business units have been adopted. A case of too little, too late. The search for business and strategic value from IT continues unabated as the jury remains out on the latest 'value for money', 'benefits quantification', 'downsizing' and 'hybrid manager' initiatives which aim to restore IT's strategic credibility.

2.5 PICKING THE RIGHT METHOD IS CRITICAL

Over the past few years a torrent of intellectual energy has been channelled into developing new information management strategy techniques. Published frameworks which aim to align or match investment priorities in IT with the real needs of the business are arrayed along two dimensions in Figure 2.2. Only about one-third of the more widely adopted foundation techniques, identified by name and author(s), are shown. The business/technology continuum reflects the primary orientation of the techniques. Business includes financial, competitive and customer strategy tools whereas Technology mirrors the IT platform and systems applications portfolio status of, say, customer databases, supplier Value Added Data Services and Executive Information Systems. The vertical axis scale shows the estimated contribution or value of each technique in information management strategy formulation.

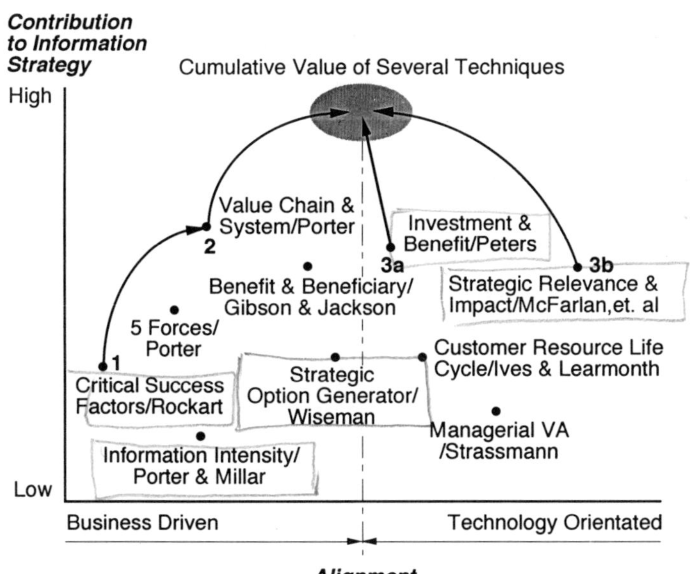

Figure 2.2. The best information strategies use several techniques

Whilst many practitioners rely on a single technique, a vastly superior information management strategy can be tailored to suit individual corporate strategic information requirements through a 'roll-out' combination of several techniques. See for example a simple framework derived from several techniques, e.g. 1, 2, 3a and 3b. A successful information resource strategy uses the appropriate permutation of alignment techniques, a relevant systems design methodology and an implementation approach supported through an adaptive organizational culture.

2.6 RELATIONSHIPS MATTER MORE THAN TECHNIQUES

Implementation can only succeed by forging cordial relationships or 'partnerships' between IT professionals and business managers within an adaptive culture, see Figure 2.3. This requires a common language and value set, professional respect and mutual trust engendered through management development, champions and multi-disciplinary teams. 'Partnership' is required at all stages from strategy formulation and applications surfacing through to systems design and project management to implementation. Richard Walton (Walton, 1989), argues that successful implementation needs operational alignment and user ownership, mastery and commitment.

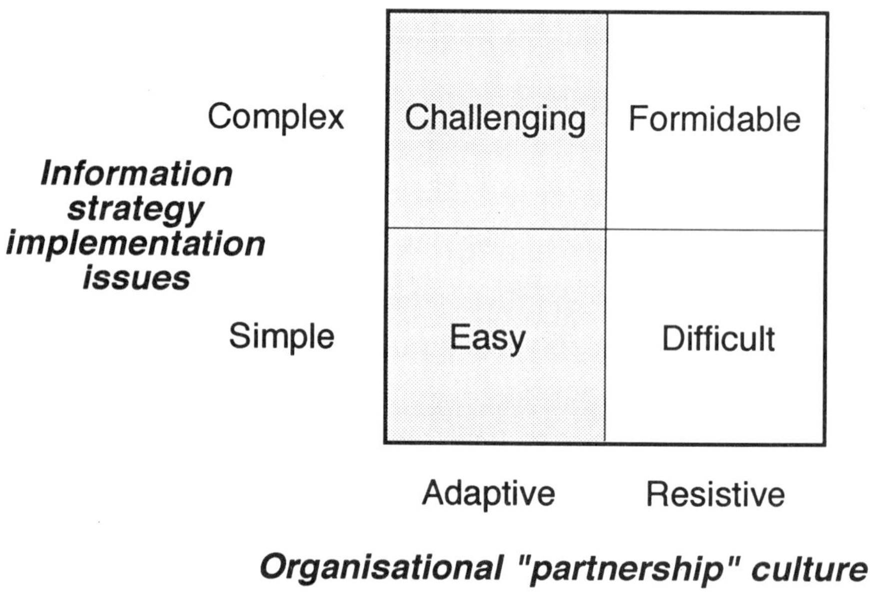

Figure 2.3. An adaptive 'Partnership' culture is essential for successful implementation

There are many examples of strategically successful information systems used by firms like Otis Elevators, GE, Akzo Coatings, American Express, W. H. Smith and many others. Accelerated performance improvement in information resource capability is mandatory for those firms playing catch-up, and invaluable for those who want to stay ahead!

A simple five-stage method using some of the ideas discussed in this paper can help. It guides firms purposefully through the maze of business, competitive, technological and organizational complexity required to develop an effective information resource strategy. By incorporating relevant operational issues and constraints, this intensive process deals with the crucial practicalities of implementation, culture and 'Partnership' and sets clear priorities for action.

REFERENCES

Cash, McFarlan and McKenney, (1988) *Corporate Information Systems Management: The issues facing senior executives*. 2nd Ed. Irwin.

Norman, D. (1991) Information Technology and Information Systems are used interchangeably and, are defined as all the computer and networked based technologies used to support the modern firm.

Walton, R. (1989) *Up and Running: Integrating IT and the organization*. Harvard Business School Press.

Wiseman, C. (1988) *Strategic Information Systems,* Irwin.

3 Role of strategy in maximizing IT benefits

D. Axson
Gunn, Hackett & Markos

3.1 INTRODUCTION

How important is an IT strategy and do organizations really need one? Many senior managers question the value of IT strategies, particularly as years of late delivery, budget overruns and unrealized benefits have engendered a very cautious approach to technology investment. Achieving tangible results in terms of added value remains one of the major management challenges.

Much attention focuses on the relationship between business and IT strategies and the successful translation of business requirements into operational systems. However, many organizations still struggle to understand the true purpose of an IT strategy and the practical steps required to translate strategy into action. A major survey by A.T. Kearney (1990) of IT effectiveness indicated that many senior managers are deluding themselves about their organization's ability to use IT successfully.

This paper explores some of the quantitative and qualitative evidence, sets out the characteristics of successful users of information technology and considers the issues which need to be addressed in formulating effective IT strategies.

3.2 THE FAILURE TO REALIZE VALUE FROM IT

Measuring success in IT has always been an area of great debate. However, as investment demands continue to increase, senior managers are less tolerant of vague qualitative assessments of value. Recent surveys confirm this opinion; however, few have attempted to apply objective measures of success in using IT. A.T. Kearney's (1990) survey did make such an attempt. Based upon the responses of over 400 companies across all industry sectors, the survey attempted to identify the characteristics of successful and unsuccessful users of IT. The criteria attempted to set realistic benchmarks and addressed the scope of use of IT, the success in implementing and controlling IT and the organizational impact of IT. Specifically, these were that:

- IT must be used in at least half of the potential areas of the business, and must be seen to have had an important impact on the business.

Intranet can achieve this

- At least half of all projects must have been completed on time and at least half within budget.
- Expected benefits must have been realized for at least half of all projects and exceeded in one case.
- Some element of organizational change must have accompanying IT implementation.

The most revealing result was the wide gulf between management perception of success and the objective facts. Subjectively, over 67% of all respondents considered their companies to be successful users of IT. However, when the above criteria were applied only 11% of companies passed on all counts. The absence of objective measures clearly limits management's ability to define strategy, manage implementation and measure the effectiveness of IT investments.

Similarly, only 23% of companies satisfied the on-time and to-budget criteria, or – expressed another way – fewer than one in four companies is capable of delivering half or more of its IT projects on time and to budget. An unsatisfactory performance by any measure.

The gap between perception and reality has two possible explanations. Either management are incapable of measuring IT success or they have very low expectations of IT investment. In reality, the truth is probably somewhere in between. Why is such poor performance the norm and what do successful users do differently?

The Kearney survey provided further support for earlier research by Earl (1983), Grindley (1985) and Galliers (1986) regarding the keys and barriers to success in the use of IT. As Figure 3.1 shows, the major factor in IT success is people. Technical considerations, while remaining important, are not the key determinants or the key barriers to success. Management, IT staff and users are critical to the effective use of IT, with top management support being the most important. Successful companies actively consider the relationship between investments in human resources and investments in technology. Similarly, they recognize that IT cannot be considered in isolation from business operations. Some organizations such as Barclays Bank have gone further and expanded the senior IT position to that of director of all IT and service businesses recognizing the all pervasive nature of technology.

The biggest barrier to success is seen as the quality of user staff. When taken with the earlier research by Grindley (1985) and Galliers (1986) which highlighted the absence of clear business plans and lack of commitment to change as the key barriers, the importance of clearly communicated, business-based IT strategies is apparent. Establishing the link between business and IT strategies greatly enhances an organization's ability to use IT effectively.

The survey identified four further common characteristics of successful users of IT. Firstly, they continually look to invest in the value-adding areas of their business while minimizing the investment in purely administrative activities. The need to add incremental value through investment is seen as critical. Examples of success which focused on adding value include American Airlines who have achieved significant competitive advantage through investment in the SABRE reservations system

(Hopper, 1990).

Secondly, successful users are more likely to have developed a formal IT strategy and are twice as likely to make their IT strategy fully interdependent with the business strategy. As Steiner and Teixeira (1990) identified '...implementing new technology without thinking about new business approaches will probably produce average results at best'.

Thirdly, successful companies are twice as likely to try to measure the return on their investment and are much more likely to use a range of different measures to determine the impact technology is having upon the business. As technology pervades almost all areas of business it is no longer seen as acceptable to simply measure success in terms of reduced headcount. More sophisticated measures attempting to measure the value from investment are increasingly used. Evaluation in terms of perceived quality, customer satisfaction ratings or tangible external costs such as the impact on interest and financing charges are all used.

As the use of technology moves more to the management of information and the provision of service, value cannot only be measured in terms of reduced headcount or cost. However, for a number of years benefits have been expressed in terms of vague, qualitative assessments such as 'improved service' or 'increased flexibility'. This is not acceptable; successful managers of IT do not tolerate such imprecision as investment demands increase. They demand clear evidence of the tangible results that investing in technology will deliver.

Finally, successful users maintain accountability for IT at senior levels within the organization. Increasingly, this is at board level (over 50% of all companies) while less than 5% of successful companies delegate responsibility more than one level below the board. The emergence during the 1980s of 'technology literate' CEOs such as John Reed at Citicorp and Sir John Harvey-Jones at ICI demonstrate the growing value of executive level IT expertise.

These characteristics of success allow some conclusions to be drawn about typical IT management styles (Figure 3.2). It is clear that successful companies not just successful users of IT must adopt an anticipatory approach to IT management through accountable, responsible and suitably qualified people.

3.3 CAUSES OF DISSATISFACTION

Consider the following three quotes that illustrate the position in which many senior managers find themselves.

1. 'I have no problems with the IT strategy that has been prepared except that I am not sure it is right for our business.'
   (Group Managing Director, UK publishing company)

2. 'I see ever more evidence that the ability to create technology with fantastic potential greatly outstrips our ability to use it effectively.'
   (Senior Vice President, Asian Finance Group)

3. 'Combine a selection of financial applications with our new IBM family and you have the perfect business solution for your requirements.'
(IBM marketing brochure, 1990)

Firstly, a very senior manager fails to recognize that IT strategy is wholly dependent upon business strategy for its success. The view that IT strategy is something that can be developed independently of the business is all too common and fatally flawed.

Secondly, many managers feel unduly pressured by the fear of being left behind by the advance of technology while unable to see how it can benefit their own business. This highlights the classic scenario of technology solutions looking for problems. Unfortunately, technology suppliers often offer little assistance as the third example illustrates. Technology vendors see their hardware and software products as the complete answer to business needs. This only compounds management's confusion in trying to match the technology available to the true needs of the business.

At one international trading company in the mid-1980s, the question 'What are your requirements?' was answered by the managing director offering a glossy brochure from a leading hardware manufacturer and saying 'Everything that is in here.' It was only after much closer examination and discussion that the true requirements became clearer– the hardware supplier did not even make the shortlist!

Unfortunately, for many organizations the decision-making process is equally simplistic and the systems are implemented. It is only when users try to operate the system that it becomes clear that the sleek sports car promised in the sales literature is really a 16-ton truck. This goes a long way to explaining the dissatisfaction felt by businessmen about the contribution IT has made to the business.

However, senior managers do not escape unscathed; the lack of rigour applied to IT investment appraisal contributes to many poor decisions. Senior management frequently make technology investment decisions with little or no realistic appraisal of the true benefits that can be realized. The approach that technology is important and therefore we must invest is all too prevalent. However, there is no correlation whatsoever between the size of technology investments and successful investment. It is not the amount spent, but how it is spent that is important.

Businessmen routinely take major investment decisions relating to product launches, the establishment of new delivery channels and company acquisition and divestiture, supported by clear analysis of the financial implications. Yet many IT investment decisions completely ignore such analysis. At a Scandinavian bank, a $25 million IT investment decision had been given preliminary approval until a clear expression of the financial impact was provided (Figure 3.3). It rapidly became clear that the business simply could not afford the investment demanded at the level of risk associated with the project.

Equally common is the criticism that systems are constraining the business, as the following exchange illustrates.

CEO of UK bank: 'The latest budget has introduced a new tax-exempt savings account (TESSA). All our competitors will be launching their products in the next few days. When can we get ours into the branches?'

Marketing Director: 'Well, we have the specifications for the product, our advertising agency is working on the campaign, all we need to do is price the product and we are ready to go.'

IT Director: 'Unfortunately our banking system cannot cater for the gross payment of interest, the system is programmed to always calculate interest net of tax. It will take three months to make the necessary changes and then to test the new application. Until then we simply cannot handle the account.'

An unfamiliar tale? Unfortunately not, this reflects the true position in which one bank found itself after the UK Chancellor's 1991 Budget. The result was a three-month delay in delivering the product and thousands of potential customers lost to competitors.

It is unacceptable for business strategy to be constrained or dictated by technology. In markets characterized by increasing competition and declining margins the speed of product innovation is radically shortening the time available to bring new products to market. In setting business strategy, management needs to be aware of the potential problems they may face and the impact upon future freedom of current decisions. For example, few companies have the luxury of throwing out all their existing systems and starting again from scratch. There is a need to recognize the past investments made and the large installed systems and knowledge base that exists when considering the way forward. It is not always possible to embrace the latest technology without undermining past investments.

The growing importance of information technology based upon its rising share of total business costs, increasing impact upon business operations, growing importance for maintaining competitiveness, and increasing uncertainty over how to measure performance, all contribute to unease in the board room. Problems arise when top management devote too little time to technology issues either through lack of interest or more often through lack of understanding. At one European bank which had invested over $100 million in systems, the top management team had never met to discuss technology issues. As a consequence, when a major overhaul of all systems became critical, none of the management team felt able to make a decision. A series of 'make do' upgrades resulted which increased running costs and progressively reduced performance.

Frequently, IT strategy is developed in isolation from the business and there is a lack of commercial investment appraisal of IT projects. Consequently, powerful central IT functions develop which are remote from the business and overly concerned with technical considerations such as the latest software engineering tools or the newest database technology. Frustration amongst users increases and the barrier between IT and its customers increases. More tangibly, there is excessive growth in

IT staffing and costs and the lead time for system delivery seems to increase while the quality of management information fails to improve.

This trend is usually followed by moves to break the power of the central function by trying to increase its accountability to the business units. Transfer pricing of IT services, service level agreements and outsourcing are techniques commonly used. However, this can only work if business unit managers actually understand how to manage technology and can make a positive contribution to the development of the IT strategy. After years of indifference or neglect this is often not the case. The following case study helps to illustrate how one organization addressed these issues and implemented the systems that the business really needed.

3.4 CASE STUDY: BARING BROTHERS, TREASURY AND TRADING GROUP

During the mid-1980s, Baring Brothers, one of the premier UK merchant banks, began to re-appraise the way in which its back office operations were being supported by IT. During the previous few years the size of the bank's systems department had grown dramatically, including a large number of semi-permanent contractors and consultants. In addition, a major feasibility study was being undertaken by an outside software house to develop a functional specification for a new system to support the Treasury and trading activities of the bank. This encompassed all foreign exchange and money market business together with the rapidly developing Eurobond and derivatives markets.

By August 1985, the study had been in progress for six months and had already incurred significant costs. To date, the outputs had been restricted to some preliminary functional design documents. Progress was slow and business unit managers were becoming increasingly frustrated at the demands made on their time by the project team and the lack of tangible outputs. The feelings of frustration were compounded as the bank was experiencing two major operational problems. Firstly, the Eurobond settlement department was drowning in a sea of paper due to an enormous increase in trading volumes which accompanied the 'bull' market of the mid-1980s. Secondly, the records for the cash and the securities portion of each trade were held on different computer systems. This made reconciliation very difficult and the production of accurate and timely management information a manually intensive exercise. Consequently, pressure was mounting from business management to find a quick and effective IT solution to solve the immediate business problems.

The impetus for making change was the appointment of a new finance director. Anxious to get to grips with the organization, he spent much of his first few weeks with the bank's Internal Audit Manager, tapping the latter's broad knowledge of both the practices and personalities of the bank.

The Internal Audit Manager was in the ideal position to provide a non-technical appreciation of the problems the business was experiencing as he combined a sound knowledge of the whole business, with access to and acceptance by, all the key executives. While not having an IT background he did have a good understanding of business operations and was not afraid to ask the simple questions of technical experts such as why, when, how and how much. More importantly, he kept asking them until a satisfactory answer was forthcoming.

Given the growth in the size of the DP function, particularly its costs, and the problems of bond settlements, both of which were of immediate concern to the Finance Director, considerable thought was given to the alternatives to a long-term bespoke development project.

Upon studying the scope and terms of reference for the Treasury and trading system feasibility study it became obvious that there was a mismatch between the objectives of the IT study and the real needs of the business. Closing this gap was essential since the risks of the bespoke project failing to deliver on time or to fully satisfy business needs were high. However, senior management had little experience or understanding of managing large-scale systems projects across the organization. The ability to evaluate IT investments as an integral part of the business management process was relatively underdeveloped. This was not wholly surprising given the stage of development the bank had reached. In fact, this is still a common problem today for many organizations. Barings learned their lesson early and have benefited as a result.

The bank's use of technology had grown slowly from the introduction of batch-based systems in the early 1970s (some of which were still operational) and IT had a relatively low profile within the organization. While it was clear that the development of a bespoke system was not in the bank's best interest, it was essential that a realistic and viable business case was put forward if progress was to be made. The Finance Director and the Internal Audit Manager made such a case by demonstrating the ability to solve the immediate business problems quickly and effectively. At the same time they showed that a package solution could provide a proven foundation for the development of systems which would be capable of supporting a wide range of the bank's business for a number of years to come. The combination of tangible benefits to the business, certain delivery and known costs provided a very powerful argument for making the correct business decision.

Nine months later in June 1987, for an investment of around £1.5 million which was below initial estimates, the core accounting and settlement system, and the bond processing modules were operational. Over the next two and a half years, capabilities for handling UK government securities (gilts), foreign exchange, money markets and a range of derivative instruments were added. All utilized the core system and built upon the existing IT investment. Apart from the new software and incremental purchases of hardware, no major new investments were required.

For Barings, the benefits of effective IT investment which met short- and long-term business needs were significant:

- The provision of comprehensive and accurate management information allowing for more timely decision-making.
- Improved ability to cater for market volatility. The combination of improved systems support and a decline in gilt and Eurobond trading volumes following

the 1987 stock market crash allowed the bank to achieve significant reductions in staffing levels while maintaining both accuracy and efficiency.

- The removal of IT as a constraint on business. No longer were management faced with a settlement and accounting function which simply could not cope with increased levels of business.

- Breaking the cycle of the need to replace existing systems whenever a new product was developed. The core system provided the base for incremental investment in IT over time.

There were three keys to making the change work at Barings:

1. Ensure the IT objectives fit with the business needs

The arguments put forward by the IT specialists for a bespoke development were threefold.

- Requirements Fit. No package system can precisely meet the bank's.

- Competitive Advantage. Development in-house could potentially deliver significant competitive advantage– even generating revenue through subsequent sales of the system.

- State-of-the-art. The project would utilize state-of-the-art design techniques and technology resulting in the most advanced system available in the London market.

However, none of these recognized the true needs of the business. There was no mention of reduced costs, improved productivity or enhanced service levels. The requirements fit argument failed to recognize the immediate problem, the bank's bond settlement department simply could not process the business. Delivering a known 80% solution in nine months was a far more attractive proposition than a possible 100% in four years.

The competitive advantage argument while initially attractive, missed the point. Barings is a bank not a software house, the skills of management are in banking not in commercial software development. Secondly, the history of attempts to translate bespoke systems into generic packages is painful.

Finally, the use of state-of-the-art technology was not a key issue for the bank, reliability offered far more benefit than any perceived technological leadership that may have been gained.

What this project demonstrated was the initial failure to match the benefits of technology to the true needs of the business. It was only when the Finance Director and the Internal Audit Manager became involved that the link was made and the real needs of the business became clear.

2. Treat technology investments in the same way as other investment propositions

The approach to evaluating technology investments should be identical to evaluating any speculative business venture. It should not be devolved to the technology function in isolation as is often the case. The many examples of marketing-led products which manufacturers can't produce (the foul-tasting smokeless cigarette from R.J. Reynolds) or of engineering/design-led products which marketeers cannot sell such as the Sinclair C5, provide ample evidence of the need to integrate all elements of a business in the decision process. IT is no different.

The scale of technology investments and their impact upon the business dictate that senior management understand and participate in the decision-making process. All too often managers fail to get to grips with the practical issues associated with technology projects for fear of exposing their lack of technical knowledge. This is the worst disservice they can do to their organization.

3. Develop individual commitment to change

It is vital not to underestimate the importance of individual commitment to achieving real change. To effect change project champions need the confidence and support of their superiors to build the vital link between the true needs of the business and the requirements of IT systems.

The environment at Barings was such that the presentation of a sound analysis of business needs supported by a clear review of the options available made the decision process easy. However, up until that time the understanding and involvement of key decision-makers was limited, which caused problems in delivering appropriate technology solutions. The involvement of business people with the trust of senior management and, equally important, access to senior management is crucial.

Finally, the rewards can be high. Barings has continued to achieve real productivity and cost improvements in its operations. The system continues to serve the business well and has been progressively developed and expanded to handle a wider range of instruments. On the people side, the Internal Audit Manager is now a Director, responsible for a division of the bank's business.

3.5 IMPERATIVES FOR IT STRATEGY FORMULATION

Technology now pervades all areas of business, however, many organisations find that the substitution of labour by technology is replacing variable costs with fixed costs. Therefore, the need to ensure value from IT investments is critical. The recognition of business imperatives in IT strategy formulation underpins this process. Today, management are concerned about fundamental business issues such as:

- Cutting out less profitable services.

- Adding higher value-added services.
- Improving the measurement of profit and risks.
- Only serving attractive customer segments and modifying distribution channels accordingly.

Attempts to improve productivity and profitability increasingly focus on the reallocation of resources, the aim being to move people from administration and cost-incurring tasks to revenue-producing activities. Technology is the key to this change. For example, American Airlines sees the future as building technology platforms not developing applications (Hopper, 1990). This is translated into two key commercial principles which drive projects.

- Projects must have quantifiable hard savings through improved productivity.
- IT projects must be implemented as an organization initiative, not a technological one.

This clearly recognizes the need to integrate IT strategy and planning into the business and presupposes that IT strategies accurately reflect the requirements of the business strategy. The implications for IT strategy are fourfold:

- Business strategy will define technology imperatives.
- Business planning will drive IT planning.
- Strategy drives practical implementation.
- The commercial impact of IT underpins the planning process.

To illustrate the relationship between business and IT strategy, consider the matrix in Figure 3.4 which shows how a major conglomerate may view its portfolio of businesses. Each individual business units value as a standalone entity is compared to its contribution to the overall group. Based upon the results of this analysis, a clear, strategic direction may be set. The implications for IT strategy are clear, particularly in terms of the degree of centralization and integration or the consideration of outsourcing specific IT services.

Secondly, technology planning and business planning are linked on three levels (Figure 3.5). Understanding this concept helps to ensure that the potential value of technology is recognized at all stages in the planning process. This helps in maximizing the potential benefits to be gained and in making senior management explicitly aware of the opportunities and threats posed by technology.

Thirdly, successful organizations look at technology investments in terms of their impact upon profitability. Figure 3.6 shows a situation where a business was misdirecting its investments, by relating IT investment to the number of customers by type. It failed to recognize that 12% of its customers generated 57% of its profits and that it was consistently under-investing in the area where the potential to add value was greatest.

Finally, many organizations fail because of their inability to translate strategy into practical implementation. However, the link between strategy and individual projects is explicit (Figure 3.7). Business strategy drives IT strategy which sets the framework for developing technical standards. For example, if the business strategy calls for a 'Hanson'-like structure of largely autonomous individual business units but with strong central financial control, the technical standards will need to accommodate the necessary networking and communications to support such an infrastructure.

The IT strategy also defines the projects the organization must undertake. Options for satisfying these needs can then be assessed and the commercial case evaluated. It is here that many projects fall down. No businessmen should accept a project proposal unless there is a valid commercial case.

Starting with a cost-benefit analysis (Figure 3.8), there is then a need to compare the benefits of a project to the business strategy to ensure the overall objectives of the business are being satisfied. If the answer is no, it is necessary to review alternative options. If the answer is yes, one must ask if it is a viable economic investment. If yes, the project is commercially justified. However, if the answer is no, it is necessary to ask one further question. Is the investment a commercial necessity?

For example, when the Financial Services Act (1986) in the UK came into effect it radically changed the regulatory framework of the securities industry. One of the major requirements was the need to monitor continually and report daily individual holdings of various securities. For many companies this was only possible through the modification and development of computer systems The failure to comply with these new regulations would prevent a business from operating; therefore, regardless of whether the investment could be justified in economic terms, it was a commercial necessity.

Establishing a viable commercial case is essential: all too often the reasons put forward for technology projects are based upon the technology, not the benefits to the business. Frequently, IT specialists cite the use of state-of-the-art technology or employment of the most advanced design and development methods as the reason for undertaking a new project. This is akin to saying that the reason for building the Channel Tunnel was because some exceptionally advanced tunnelling machines had been developed. Senior management must demand that a commercial case is expressed in terms of the tangible results that will be delivered to the business. As with tunnelling machines, IT is a means to an end, not an end in itself.

3.6 CONCLUSION

Few people disagree about the importance of linking IT strategies to business strategies. However, what is frequently lacking is the ability to translate fine words into concrete action. This position is unsustainable as IT costs as a proportion of total business costs continue to increase. The development of practical IT strategies supported by realistic and commercial IT investment appraisal will determine success in the use of IT. Demonstrating a tangible contribution to improved business performance will become the key criteria for directing future IT investment.

REFERENCES

A.T. Kearney (1990) *Breaking the Barriers– IT Effectiveness in Great Britain and Ireland.* A.T. Kearney, London.

Earl, M.J. (1983) Emerging Trends in Managing New Information Technologies. Oxford Centre for Management Studies, research paper 83/4; reproduced in N. Piercy (ed), *The Management Implications of New Information Technology*. Croom Helm, London, 1986.

Grindley, C.B.B. (1985) *Information Technology Strategy Studies*, Price Waterhouse, London.

Galliers, R.D. (1986) IT Strategies Today: The UK Experience, in *Information Management– The Strategic Dimension*, M. Earl (ed), Clarendon Press, Oxford.

Steiner, T.D. and Teixeira, D.B. (1990) *Technology in Banking*. McKinsey & Company, USA.

Hopper, M.D. (1990) Rattling Sabre– New Ways to Compete on Information. *Harvard Business Review*, Volume 68, Number 3.

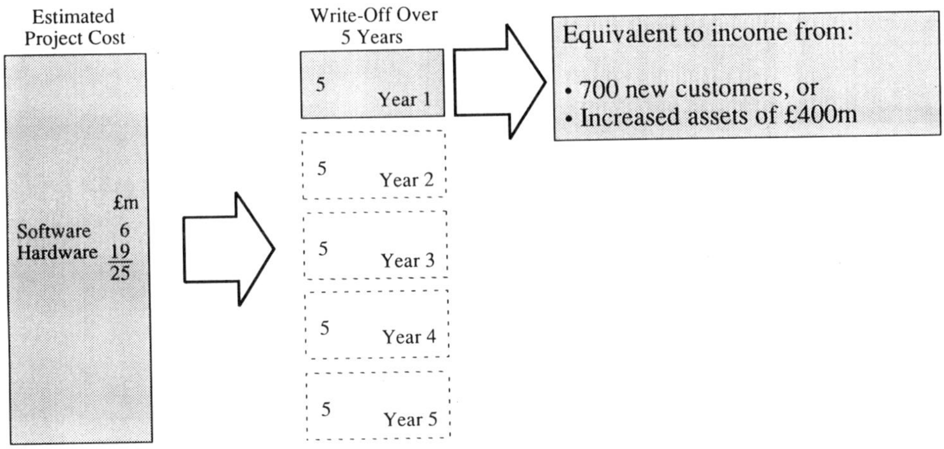

Figure 3.1 Expressing IT investments in commercial terms is essential

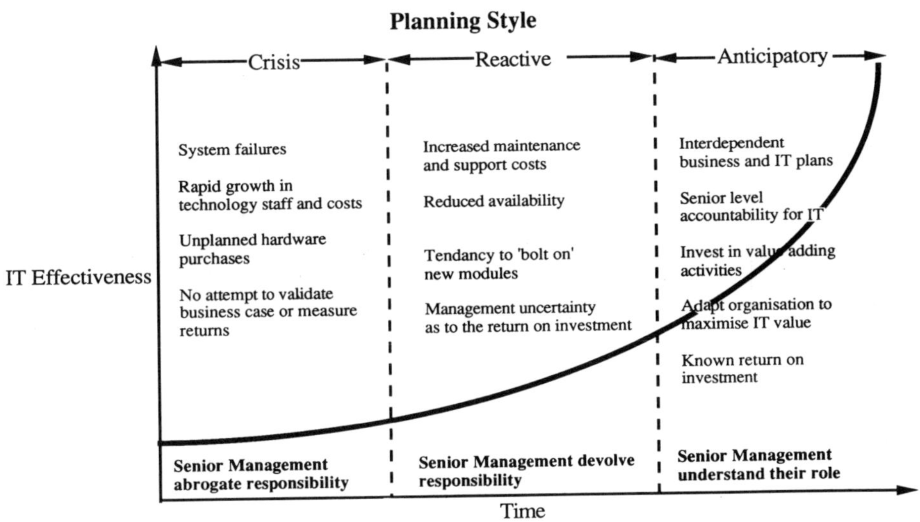

Figure 3.2 Crisis management

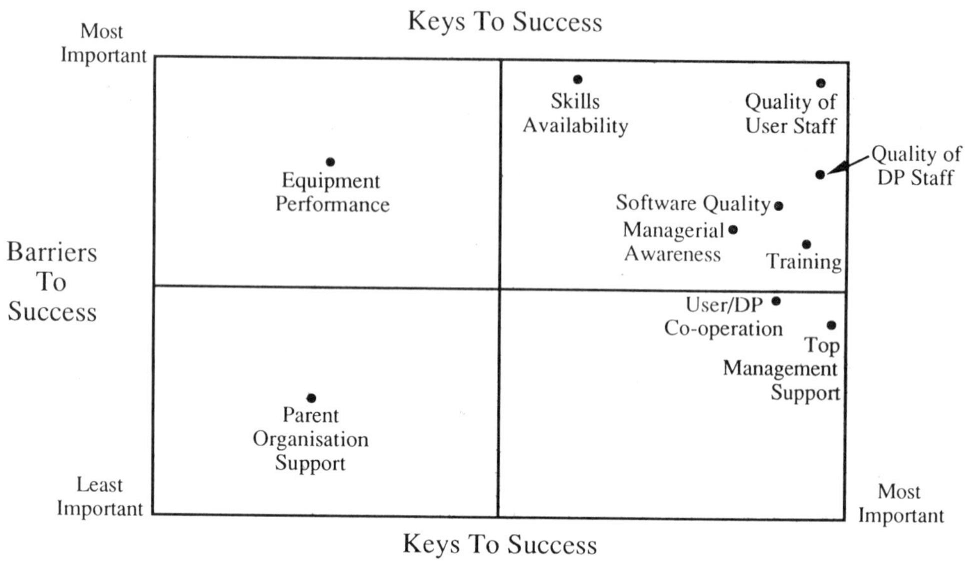

Source: Breaking The Barriers, A.T. Kearney

Figure 3.3 success in IT is a people issue

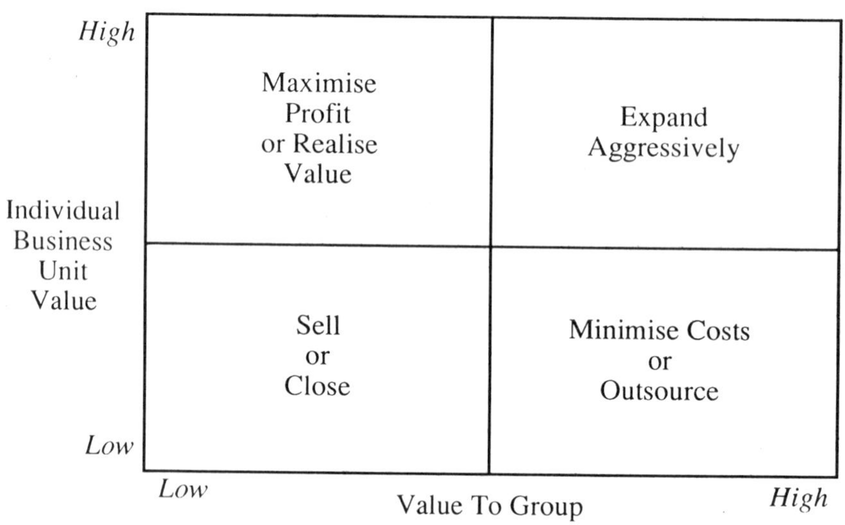

Figure 3.4 Business strategy defines technology imperatives

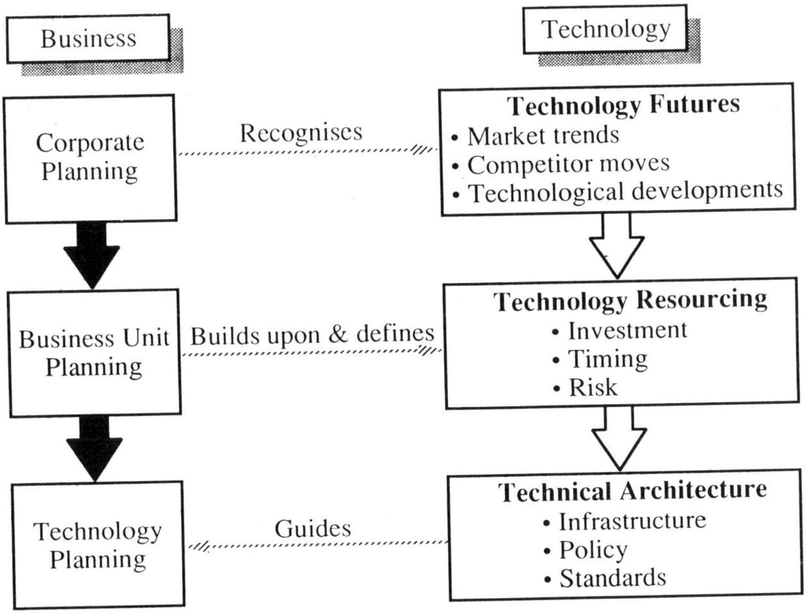

Figure 3.5 Linking technology planning to business planning

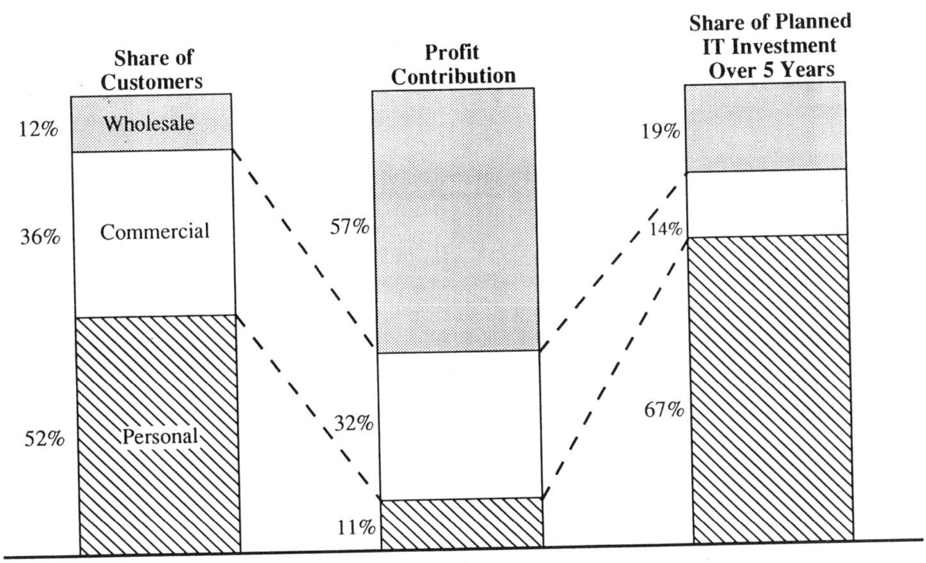

Figure 3.6 Getting the balance right

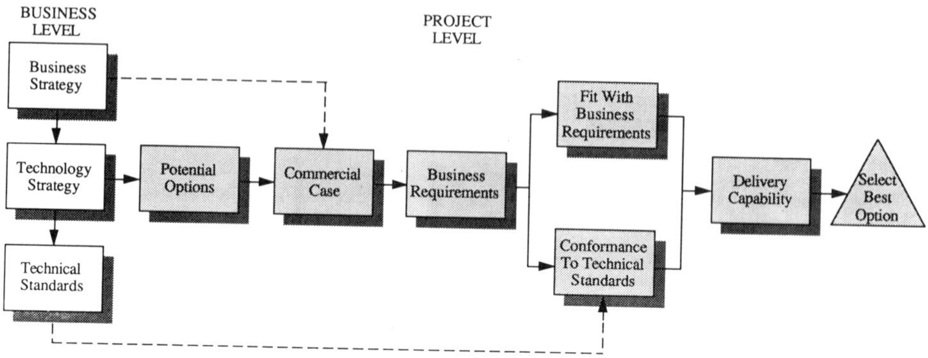

Figure 3.7 Translating strategy into action

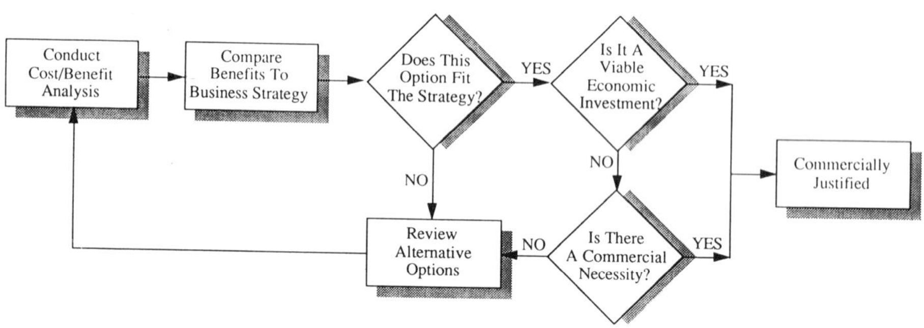

Figure 3.8 The commercial case must hold

4 Making IT happen successfully – a consultant's view

J. Swift
Hoskyns Group plc

4.1 INTRODUCTION

4.1.1 One New Thing after Another

I am sure we would all agree that the history of IT has been characterized by one new thing after another – a continuous stream of new technologies, techniques, tools and methodologies. Moving into the 1990s the pace of development would appear to be accelerating rapidly, with the increasing convergence of what have hitherto been regarded as separate technologies and now the significant rate of progress towards *'open-systems'*, bringing the welcome prospect of increased choice, flexibility, supplier independence and ease of connection.

Alongside these developments in IT has been a succession of new business and management concepts, techniques and tools, many of which have become over-laid onto the IT scene. Management gurus are now big business and there is certainly no shortage of learned papers, seminars and books providing a readily available store of distilled wisdom on every conceivable aspect of business management, including of course IT.

This plethora of developments – all valid in their own right – has created for many executive and management teams what they regard as a bewildering set of issues, thoughts, ideas and choices – and a good deal of *'cerebral indigestion'*!

In these circumstances it is easy for companies to lose sight of the basics, perhaps to get *'hooked'* on rather glamorous projects and high-flying ideas, and to forget simply what IT is all about.

4.1.2 From Perspective to Action

What I will be putting forward to you in this paper is that future success with IT is dependent on three things:

- Adopting a *'new'* perspective on IT and getting away from being driven primarily by technology and technologists.

- Identifying and overcoming the barriers to progress which exist in any company in relation to IT.

- Getting to grips with each aspect of what I shall call the *'total'* Information management environment of a company.

These are all practical issues which Hoskyns has found to be the key in helping companies, large and small, achieve a radical turn-round in their IT scene.

Addressing these issues requires, amongst other things, a fundamental re-alignment of IT in companies, significant changes in the focus and style of the IS and IT service function and the development of a new breed of business systems professional working at the interface between the business community and IT.

4.2 GETTING THE RIGHT PERSPECTIVE

4.2.1 Total Information Management

I'd like first of all just to return to a few basics and put it to you that the real *'field of play'* is the *'total'* information management environment of a company. This can be pictured as follows:

- The gearing of information management to the real needs of the business – now and for the future – a complete alignment with business and organization strategies.

- The effective organization and management of those business processes which achieve the complete throughput of the business and through which the company trades and communicates in its market place.

- The professional management of information and systems which drive and service the processes of the business and enable performance to be managed.

- The effective exploitation of technology.

- The delivery of quality IS and IT services.

- The development and operation of effective and efficient business systems, which in turn, contribute to the effectiveness of business processes and thus to improving the productivity, competitiveness and performance of the business itself:

  – a *'virtuous circle'*.

In other words, IS and IT within the context of *'total'* information management.

Now for some observations on this *'field of play'* from our work with companies, large and small.

4.2.2 Total Inter-dependence

Clearly between all of the six key elements of the total information management environment there is complete *'inter-dependence'*.

Success with IT is dependent on *'getting the complete act together'*. To be successful you cannot simply put all your focus on just one or two of the elements. Every one tells a story of potential strength or potential weakness.

'Your success with IT will be a function of your weakest link in this complete chain'.

We find that many companies do lack the clear perspective that *'total information management'* is the field of play and there is too little understanding of the key elements and their relationships to one another. In the midst of all today's sophistication, a company's lack of success with IT can be as basic as that.

4.2.3 Supply v. Demand Orientation

'Traditional DP' has been driven very much from a supply-led perspective.

The issue facing most companies is how to get a reversal in this scene. A *'demand-led'* approach driven, not by what people say they want, but by business and organization strategies, the processes required to run the business effectively, the information and systems required to drive these processes, etc.

An approach which puts business and businessmen *'in the driving seat'* rather that technology and technologists.

4.2.4 Technology as a Key Enabler

On the other hand, in some businesses the exploitation of certain aspects of technology will, in itself, be a key determinant of business and organization strategy and may radically impact the nature of the business, its ways of doing business and its ability to use information for positive advantage. We have seen this in the financial services industry, in travel and certain areas of manufacturing and distribution. Without exploiting technology, *per se*, things simply would not have been possible.

There must therefore be an element of *'chicken and egg'*.

'You can't effectively exploit IT without a clear understanding and articulation of the strategies of the business and its organization and a complete alignment of IS/IT with business strategies.'

'You won't recognize the potential opportunities offered by IT without an awareness of its capability, potential application and investment justification in the context of the above and without keeping up-to-date on relevant developments.'

4.3 BARRIERS TO PROGRESS

Barriers to progress with IT exist in virtually every company. Overcoming these barriers is an essential precursor to establishing an environment within which one can make progress. Experience shows that strategies, plans, technologies, etc., however valid, well thought out and sophisticated, will be frustrated unless certain attitudinal barriers are *'unlocked'* right from the outset.

I would now like to share with you what we typically find in companies.

4.3.1 The View from the Business Executive

When we go in to work with companies who state they need to improve their use of IT, we often find the attitude of the business executives towards IT can be pictured like this:

- Right at the front of their minds is the current business climate characterized by increasingly fierce competitive pressures, expanding markets, continued cost escalation and pressure on margins, a greater rate of change than most of us have experienced throughout our business careers and less predictability in the patterns of change, in many industries increasing regulatory requirements and impositions, skills shortages and demographic changes which are likely to lead to considerably increased levels of turnover in the mid-1990s.

- Most executives still regard DP (or whatever they call it) as an overhead – a burden – and not necessarily a force for profit. Like all overheads they want it to be fitter, leaner and better.

- On the other hand, most executives now realize that IT does offer real business opportunity, evidenced by the growth and breadth of application seen in business and in society at large, in the home, bank, shop, etc. It is all around us and surveys, like a dripfeed, keep dropping onto our desks daily, telling us we must embrace IT or we'll be out of business.

- On the other hand, most executives have some very genuine concerns about IT:

  - The practicalities of making it happen successfully.

  - A bewildering array of choices in the market place – all of course taking us to the promised land!

  - Most executives have had some bad experience with DP and, rather like being dropped on your head when a child of two, if someone comes to pick you up you like that again, you *'tighten-up'* and are very wary indeed.

- A feeling that, whatever they say, at the end of the day DP deliver what they want to deliver. *'They've got a stranglehold on us'*.

- But perhaps the biggest issue of all is that of IT discomfort. Most executives don't have a clear picture of what IT really is. They find it difficult to articulate and be sure, if executives don't have a clear structure and can't readily articulate any subject, they won't get their hands around it and manage it like any other key resource in the business.

We run various boardroom events and we have found that whenever we have put this picture to boards of directors, all of them have indicated that it is *'them to a tee'*. When we then ask them to *'weight'* each of the bubbles, *'IT discomfort'* always comes *'Number 1'* in terms of what they see as their main barrier to progress with IT – strategic or otherwise.

4.3.2 The View from the IS Executive

If we then look at the scene from the perspective of the IS executive or IT director (whatever he or she is called):

- He is now receiving a much wider range of demands than ever before, increasingly in more highly specialized areas. It was OK when he was just serving the accounts department but now he is being drawn into areas like Computer Integrated Manufacture (CIM), EPOS, EFTPOS, etc., areas often beyond his experience, bringing increasing pressure on priorities and potential conflicts.

- Maintenance of existing DP systems is absorbing 70/80% of his resource - basically just to stand still.

- Many of the systems are outdated either because the business has moved on apace since the system was developed or technology has advanced.

- Then there are the newer things – the integration of DP/OA/telecoms, the convergence of technologies (data, text, image and voice) and the issues and opportunities which stem from these developments.

- He faces skills shortages, not just in relation to the newer things but also in relation to the old – for one thing is certain, IT professionals don't see their careers benefiting from being tied-down on old systems and old technologies.

- Then he has the conundrum of wanting to encourage *'do it yourself'* but without creating *'unilateral declarations of independence'* and losing control.

- But perhaps the biggest issue the IS executive faces is the presentation of issues to the business community in terms which will switch them on and gain their involvement and commitment, whether at a strategic, management or operational level. This is the biggest issue that keeps emerging from IS executives in private discussion.

So here we have the business executives with real discomfort about IT and IS executives with great discomfort about bridging to the business and these two pictures clearly represent the main barriers to progress. They are the barriers to that *'Partnership'* between the business community and IT professionals so essential to dynamic development. In overcoming some of these barriers, three things we have found practical and successful.

4.3.3 Boardroom Workshops

Getting boards away for one or two days to really think through the issues and what they are going to do about it.

- Starting off with a *'confessional session'* based on an honest appraisal of the issues above.

- Incorporating education and helping to structure thinking on key issues.

- Going through a business-led information systems planning process and getting them to relate it to their business.

- Addressing the *'making it happen successfully'* issues.

- Creating a business-orientated awareness of the structure and strategic directions in IT.

We often find this is the first time the board have seriously got together as a team to really think things through clearly and openly. Again, I stress this is not limited to just the smaller companies.

4.3.4 Action-centred Teamwork

Next, cutting out the dead hand of thick reports and specifications. Thick reports don't transfer knowledge and understanding. Executives sign-off to get the damn thing *'off the desk and out of sight'*.

We find what we call *'action-centred'* workshops far more effective and motivational in getting understanding and commitment at all key stages of a project from concept right through to delivery. People will contribute, people will get involved, people will be prepared to receive education if they can really *'feel'* the dynamism, sense the teamwork and can see that it is an integral part of achieving *'a real live end result'* in the business to which they can relate.

4.3.5 Focusing on the Business End

At first, get the focus on business : organization : information. Deliberately relegate technology and get good cerebral thinking from the business end.

When executives feel comfortable about business and organizational issues and when they have thought through the structure, content and flow of the information required to drive their key business processes and trading relationships in the market place, then they will more readily embrace the concepts and practicalities of technology.

4.4 GEARING IT TO THE BUSINESS

4.4.1 A Practical Process

Gearing IT to the real needs of the business and aligning IT with business and organizational strategies does require a very practical planning process. However, there does tend to be a lot of *'hype'* about strategic Information Systems planning and it is important to keep right at the forefront the real purpose of the process which is to:

- Identify opportunities.
- Evaluate potential investment levels and pay-offs.
- Help determine priorities from a business point of view.
- Produce a practical plan.
- And it can't be a practical plan if it doesn't incorporate all those things which will get developments to deliver what is required, on time and on cost with built-in quality.

If the process does not clearly and directly address all of these issues, the chances are that you have gone off in some form of *'academic whirl'*.

We do find companies who do get *'hooked'* on the application of a methodology or practice of a particular technique or tool and lose sight of the key business objectives.

No methodology, technique or tool, however good, can of itself create a successful strategy – this will depend on the quality of thinking which it stimulates. As with everything else, at the end of the day, there can be no substitute for good quality minds, experience and objectivity, i.e. **PEOPLE**.

4.4.2 Creating Partnership

Above all a strategic Information Systems planning process must get everyone *'singing off the same hymn sheet'* :

Business Executives
Managers
IT Professionals
Staff

Having referred to the gap between the business community and the IT community earlier on, I have to say that we find just as many gaps between business executives, their managers and staff. Particularly in the area of middle management where, with senior executives becoming clearer on IT opportunity and staff becoming more computer literate, managers can begin to feel very squeezed-out and this of course is not helped by publications broadcasting that IT can enable you to cut out multiple levels of management almost at a stroke!

4.4.3 Homing-in on Business Opportunities and Priorities

Central to strategic Information Systems planning is the task of picturing and articulating the strategy of the business and its organization in such a way that you can identify opportunities and priorities.

This requires an approach, which takes both an outward and an inward view of the business, its strategy and organization – a definition of the business, its market positioning, competitive structure, key performance criteria, success factors, goals, customer and supplier characteristics, etc.

In using this analysis to home-in on opportunities and priorities for IS and IT development, we have found the *simpler* approaches to be the most effective in this area. It is very easy to become overcomplicated and algorithmic.

Principally, we seek to create a *'business impact'* matrix which helps highlight the *'hot buttons'* of the business.

Whether you are a manufacturer, distributor, solicitor, banker, insurance broker, restaurateur, consultant, you have a *'throughput chain of key processes'* which achieve the complete throughput of your business.

The first step in creating the matrix is to establish a clear picture of this chain and then seek to identify what we term *'business impact values'* under six headings:

- Everybody is concerned about *cost*, where in the chain are the processes which proportionally add most to the final cost delivered into the market place?

- Which processes really lever your *sales performance* in the market place?

- Which processes most impact the achievement of *factors key to the success* of the business now and for the future?

- Which processes will make most contribution to *competitive opportunities and threats*?
- Where do you anticipate significant *change*? Where are the change imperatives?
- Where in the chain do you have significant *risk* in relation to people, intellectual property, financial exposure, etc.?

4.4.4 Justifying Investment

Addressing the *'hot buttons'* in this matrix and identifying potential returns to the Business is the key to doing two things:

1. Identifying opportunities where IS and IT can make a real contribution and have a real impact on what is important to the business.

2. Setting-up the basis for proper investment justification.

I don't know how you find it but a lot of our clients do a *'Cost v. Benefits'* justification, i.e. it's going to cost £200,000, now, how can we trump up enough benefit to equal £200,000 and 1? They openly admit that in all honesty that's how they do it!

This *'Business Impact Value'* approach leads to *'Benefits v. Cost'*, i.e. an identification of what benefits you are trying to drive at **before** identifying the costs associated with delivering improvement.

It represents a fundamentally different and more practical approach to investment justification.

Many are looking for the magic thermometer which you can stick somewhere and it will do the investment justification equation for you. There is no such thing, but we find that *'getting the focus on benefits first'* often sheds a much clearer light at a much earlier stage compared with the other way round.

4.5 THE EFFECTIVE ORGANIZATION OF BUSINESS PROCESSES

Turning now to the effective organization of business processes, the *'watch phrases'* are:

'Don't be automating if you should be eliminating'

'Don't automate inefficiency and ineffectiveness'

In most companies, the processes of the business are *'as they have grown-up to be'* rather than necessarily *'as they really ought to be'*, they've been shaped by tim and history and all the built-in inefficiencies that this tends to bring. You might be interested in what we find a very common picture in companies:

- If you look at the total activity of a company, only about 20% of what is done are activities which directly achieve the throughput of the business, i.e. people actually buy, make, sell, move and deliver.

- 60% of the total activity are support activities of which:

  - 30% are essential, i.e. nobody will despatch and deliver unless a sales order is processed, nobody will pay you if you don't generate an invoice, etc.

  - 30% are discretionary – market research is a good example. We do it because we believe in it but the business wouldn't stop tomorrow if we didn't do it.

  - 20% of all activity in many businesses shouldn't exist – it only exists because *'we've always done it'* or *'we've always done it this way'*.

The first message is that, if you don't picture the processes of the business *'as they really ought to be'* or *'as they've got to be for the future'*, then the chances of automating inefficiency and ineffectiveness are very high. The concept of systems re-engineering is starting to receive increasing prominence in management publications and is at the heart of this issue – really thinking through from scratch the total organization of a business process as it ought to be.

The second message is that, in companies which have gone from say 20 personal computers to 200-odd PCs in a couple of years, when we have surveyed their usage for clients, we have found the vast majority of applications to be addressing *'discretionary'* and *'shouldn't exist'* activity – people producing colour graphics for breakfast, tea, lunch and dinner with no beneficial impact on the performance of the business at all!

Why is this? Well, two things:

- Firstly, the people associated with these activities tend to have discretionary time and they enter the computer business as a compensation for the rather dull, unglamorous routine of the supporting act!

- Secondly, IT professionals do like people who have time for them! People at the sharp-end are running like hell to achieve the business, others are running like hell to support them. IT professionals find it very difficult to nail them down and, often when they do, they are rude to them. So they gravitate to the kinder climes of those with the time.

This illustrates the vital importance of having an effective IS strategy targeted on those issues key to the success of the business, preventing what we see as a natural drift into areas of personal interest and whim.

4.6 BUSINESS SYSTEMS DEVELOPMENT

The success of companies with IT in the future hinges crucially on the function of business systems development. A function which helps to create quality demand for IS/IT geared to the real needs of the business and ensures IS/IT develops and delivers what the business really needs, on time, on cost and as a natural and integral part of the overall organization of the processes required to drive the business.

When assessing with companies the reasons for failure in the development and operation of IS/IT systems, there seems little argument, either in the business community or amongst IT professionals, that the following propositions pin-point where things really do go wrong:

'MORE SYSTEMS DEVELOPMENTS FAIL THROUGH INADEQUATE ENGINEERING OF THE ORGANISATIONAL AND MANAGEMENT ASPECTS OF THE SYSTEM THAN POOR HARDWARE AND SOFTWARE'

'WHERE HARDWARE AND SOFTWARE DOES FAIL, IT IS OFTEN CAUSED BY INADEQUATE UNDERSTANDING AND ARTICULATION OF THE REAL REQUIREMENTS IN THE FIRST PLACE'

'OTHER CAUSES OF FAILURE ARE:-

- **INADEQUATE PROJECT MANAGEMENT OF ALL THE ACTIVITIES INVOLVED IN DEVELOPMENT**
- **POOR MANAGEMENT OF CHANGE'**

Companies, large and small, are struggling to establish success in business systems development. Yet no IS development methodology that I have so far seen truly addresses the need for all aspects of organization development to be addressed in parallel with the IS/IT systems development cycle, with project management embracing the total scene. Neither do IS development methodologies adequately address *'management of change'* and the premium management and organizational skills required in this area.

In other words, the emphasis of our current approach to the systems development cycle is not in tune with what are rated as the most important ingredients for success or, from the other perspective, the common reasons for failure.

4.6.1 The 'Total Organization' Approach

What do we mean by *'total organization'*? Well, we picture it in this way. If you say that here in our organization we have a business process which is really productive and competitive, I bet you've got three key ingredients:

1. The process is tightly geared to the business, its success factors and direction, i.e. it's not ploughing its own furrow in a rather disconnected way, its role and responsibilities are clearly defined.

2. The process has been engineered *'as it ought to be'* and not *'as it has grown up to be'* and the essential functions and tasks within it have also been clearly defined.

3. It has the right quality and blend of all elements of organization required to carry out those functions and tasks.

4.7 THE NEW BREED OF BUSINESS SYSTEMS PROFESSIONAL

This brings us on to the *'new breed'* of business systems professional to which I referred at the beginning. What are the abilities required in this person?

- The ability to address the ***total*** organization of business processes as described above.

- To take approaches which are *'top-down'* business-driven, organization-led and people-centred and which follow the total information management approach.

- To be clearly regarded as being *'on the business side'* and to have credibility and empathy with business executives and managers.

- To be able to educate and train as an integral part of the development.

- To run action-centred workshops and task teams.

- To totally project manage organization development in tandem with IS development.

- To understand and orchestrate the management of change.

- To consult, market, sell and potentially manipulate.

- To be the vital bridge between the business community and management services professions in any specialization contributing to a study or development, e.g. IT professionals, O&M, OR, human resources, etc.

In our experience, although not exclusively so, this animal is more likely to come from the business than from IT or the *'traditional'* management services specialities.

One of my clients looks for what she describes as *'restless young tigers'* – not *'reckless'* but *'restless'*, dissatisfied, eager for responsible change and with the political savvy and experience to organize it.

We see in a limited number of large companies, *'high flying'* executives being *'rotated'* through the business systems development function as an essential part of their development path.

Whatever the source or the route, the new breed of business systems professional is becoming an essential cog in the wheel of success with IT.

5 The destructive power of information systems

P. Raimond
City University Business School

5.1 INTRODUCTION

Much is currently written about creating 'competitive advantage by taking a strategic, business driven approach' to information systems design (Meyer & Boone, 1987). This we are told can lead to 'extraordinary returns on investments and improved competitive edge' (ibid). 'Strategic uses of information are greatly affecting the profits of corporations and increasingly will become a key to corporate survival" (Martin, 1984). The Association of Information Technology has as its central aim 'the development of a body of knowledge about the use of IT in business organizations for the achievement of organization goals'.

That is the sunny side of the picture. It plays an equally powerful role in thwarting the achievement of organizational goals. That too has to be recognized if the science of IT management is to progress. Some of the visionary claims for the potential of IT are so enthusiastic that one would feel obliged to shout Alleluliah! were it not for the scepticism induced by working in real companies with their existing systems. The prophets and visionaries of the IT movement are in the difficult position of Moses. They have been to the mountain. They have looked over and seen the Promised Land. Meanwhile back at ground level it is Monday morning in the desert and the camels won't start. The donkeys are causing trouble. Moses who is supposed to sort these things out has gone off for a walk with his head in the clouds. When he returns he wants to talk about visions and the Promise of what lies ahead if only the camel drivers would see it his way. Moses and systems designers are met with occasional cynicism.

When companies first began computerizing their information systems, or their accounting systems which is what they really were, the coming of the computer was hailed as the coming of the Messiah. Companies whose accounting systems were a mess hoped that the computer would solve everything. In time it became apparent that if your system is a mess the computer will simply give you your mess a lot quicker. In another chapter of this book Leslie Willcocks talks about the difficulties of justifying the cost of investments in IT. Part of the reason is that managers being asked to spend money have long memories. Some of them remember previous large capital expenditures on computers which resulted in DP managers coming to board meetings with heaps of printout a metre thick. As a result of a very large investment in information technology, operating managers had less comprehension of what was going on in their company than they had previously. At that point they understood clearly the difference between information and data. They had acquired a data processing system when what they wanted was an information system. According to Meyer and Boone (1987), '... the potential investment in office automation in the next few years is likely to match all that has been spent on corporate data processing'. That level of expenditure will require close attention to investment justification. Chastened by previous experience, that justification will have to start with a consideration of information needs, not from a consideration of available technology. A retrospective analysis suggests that too much of the past investment in IT has led to further costs rather than benefits. Some of the cost-benefit analyses that were used to support applications for capital expenditure might with the benefit of hindsight be usefully supplemented with a cost-cost analysis.

5.2 SYSTEMS OF STRATEGIC MISINFORMATION

IT managers are beginning to take on one of the functions of the accountant as the 'provider of information'. That includes the role as provider of wrong information. Not inaccurate information but the wrong information presented with meticulous accuracy. When there is a gap, a dissonance, between the way things rationally should be and the way they are in practice, that dissonance is often first captured in business anecdotes and humour long before learned observers notice it and catalogue it. So it has been with the accountant's information systems. Rationally the accountant's information systems have been designed to produce the right information 'in the right place for a given organization to match the requirements of the current business environment'; a brief more recently adopted by IT managers (JIT editorial, March 1990). The accountant's emphasis is on factual, objective, logical, accurate information. That the reality in practice sometimes differs from that lofty ideal is captured in many humorous anecdotes. On one occasion I had the pleasure of introducing a new finance director to his fellow directors. I had only said 'Mr Cratchett is a Chartered Accountant ...' when someone quipped: 'Quick. Lock him up before he does any damage'.

There is the tale of the hot air balloon that lost its way. Seeing a lone figure walking his dog across a cornfield the balloonists landed to ask him where they were. 'You are in a hot air balloon in a cornfield,' came the reply. After they had lifted off again, one balloonist casually remarked to the other, 'That man was a Chartered Accountant.' 'How can you tell?' asked his companion. 'The information that he gave us was perfectly accurate and utterly useless. That masterly blend of accuracy and irrelevance gives them away every time'.

Prompt recording of irrelevant information is not a practice exclusive to accountants. Marketing departments often show themselves adept at monitoring the markets that used to be important and competitors who have ceased to be the major threat. There is a British public company which used to be the market leader in shirts. Its competitors were the other British shirt manufacturers. Over a period of many years the company had developed a sophisticated market intelligence system which allowed it to know in advance what designs, colours and materials its competitors would be bringing to the market six months before they reached the shops. The information system was based on a complex network of family connections, indiscretions, club memberships, interlocking elites. The ties to the retail outlets were equalled tightly knit and long established. In time the British competitors lost market share to imports. British manufacturers who had been dominant became minor competitors in decline. The company's information system went on monitoring the fashion changes of the British shirt manufacturers, ignoring the imports which were now the dominant force in the market. The traditional gentleman's outfitters lost market share rapidly to boutiques and own-brand retailers such as Marks & Spencer. The company's information system stuck loyally to monitoring its old outlets in the market which had since died. This British public company, having once been the leading name among shirt manufacturers, no longer makes shirts.

5.3 A STRATEGY IS A PLAN FOR THE FUTURE

Designing an intelligent information system is not simply a matter of automating a company's existing information flow. It must instead be concerned to provide the information essential to support the intended future strategy to compete against the future competitors and in the markets which the company wants to be in the future. To automate information systems developed in past years runs the major risk of 'hardwiring' the company into the past, making change more difficult, and putting blinkers on its awareness of where its markets, customers and competitors are going. As an information strategy it is about as sensible as driving a car by looking only through the rear window. How many British companies whilst declaring that 'our home market is Europe' know very little about their European competitors, target markets, customers, and everything about the UK? To achieve their planned strategy they will need to know about conditions in Europe, their intended future market. The relevant question for the design of their information system is: how do we tell them what they need to know. It is not relevant nor helpful to design an expensive system to tell them what they already know about markets which will cease to be their main concern. That would be an expensive investment in a blindfold.

The British clearing banks are investing massively in new Executive Information Systems (EIS) designed to tell them where they make profits, on which products, in which markets. The current phase will tell them what profits they made in the past – past year, past month, on the products they have now. It will not tell them about the products which they should be developing now for their rapidly changing competitive markets. Whilst it is essential in any strategic plan to have an accurate understanding of where we are now, that is only the prelude to deciding where we want to get to, and what we have to do to get there. In that respect the clearing banks current investment in EIS is probably only phase one and the relatively easy part. The development of a forward-looking strategic information system will take longer. Some companies have found it easier to install a backward-looking strategic information system, but rather less valuable.

5.4 STRATEGIC CHANGE

The developments in IT strategy in the UK clearing banks are part of a larger process of strategic organizational change with very far-reaching consequences. The banks have been faced with deregulation and an influx of new foreign, aggressive competitors, with new products and new ways of doing business. The UK banks are having to respond with new products and new ways of doing business. Old patterns and customs are ceasing to be appropriate. They have had to bring in new people, develop or acquire new skills, dispense with some people and skills which no longer meet the changed requirements. Changes in information requirements and in organizational structure have become necessary. In the old days of a year or two ago, the major management decisions were made at the centre and cascaded down in a centrally controlled fashion. Each level of the hierarchy had its discretionary limits, the amount they could lend without seeking higher authority. Each customer had an agreed borrowing limit. If any customer overstepped that limit the local banker had to explain the reason to his immediate superior in the hierarchy. In stark contrast the branch banker is expected to go out and sell, to be close to the customer, to encourage them to borrow, albeit wisely. Branch bankers are expected to demand products and services from their head offices, not wait for instructions from them. The competitive market has changed. Therefore the banks' competitive strategy has changed. That has forced the banks to change organizational structure from central hierarchical control to a more devolved structure where control is closer to the customer. That change in the nature and direction of control requires change in the nature and directions of flows of information. It means change in essential skills and in personnel. It implies change in culture. Much of the wide-ranging change has provoked resistance and discomfort, as well as challenge and opportunity. One hears branch bankers complaining 'If I had wanted to be a salesman I would not have been a banker'. Another banker observed 'in the old days the closest thing we had to a market information system was the golf club. Market intelligence was knowing when to lose a game'. In this case, as in many cases, the design of a strategic information system is an integral part of a larger change in competitive strategy and structure in response to changing market and competitive conditions. It may be accompanied by changes in skills, people and culture. To design a strategic information system without having first understood the competitive, strategic and organizational changes of which it is an integral part would be to run the risk of installing an irrelevant information system. The cost to the company is likely to be far greater than the initial capital investment.

The destructive power of an information system can undermine every department of its host company. The impact on personnel and industrial relations is often particularly dramatic. One of London's leading shops experienced its first-ever general strike as the result of a plan to computerize its tills. Computerizing the tills and giving each item purchased a code number was intended to produce an up-to-the-minute record of which items were selling well, which slowly, how each department was performing, and to give instant details of stock levels. That is how the computerization plan was perceived by senior management and by the data processing department. Seen from the sharp end it had other effects. Its first effect was to change the entire power structure of the organization. Traditionally the buyer had been the prima donna of each sales department. His or her role was to roam the world for treasures and bring them back for the customers of the London shop. The folklore had traditionally been 'If you can buy right, you can sell right.' Post-computerization, the key decision-making power would shift from the buyer to the central management. The print-out would show which items were selling fast. That would trigger a command to order another thousand of them.

The key players, the prima donnas around whose expertise the stores reputation had been created, saw their skills being devalued. They had the power to hit back. And they found willing allies in the sales staff.

The second effect of the plan to computerize the tills was to raise the scare of draconian redundancy plans. The EPOS (electronic points of sale) system required a large capital investment in computer hardware and software.

In order to win board approval that capital investment had to be justified with cost savings. The requisite cost savings were found by projecting staff cuts. The staff cuts plan was leaked. Rumblings arose. Training in the new technology was scant. Fears and suspicions grew. The DP department fell behind schedule. The DP department took to working behind closed doors to avoid interruption. Departments who would have to bear the brunt of operating the new systems could no longer communicate with the DP department to explain their needs, nor even to find out what was going on. The day scheduled for the introduction of EPOS became instead the day of the first-ever strike in the shop. Introduction of the system was postponed *sine die.*

5.5 RETURNING DESIGN FAULTS

While researchers have to hunt for good examples of IT systems which give their companies a competitive edge, every IT professional knows of several examples such as those cited above where the information system has demonstrated its power to destroy, disrupt and divert the organization which it serves. As IT systems take over the provision of information for the whole organization they acquire the partial information systems previously guarded in the operating departments such as marketing, personnel, finance. These come complete with their own inconsistencies, illogicalities and incompatibilities. The central information system gathers all these together and adds its own to them. The way in which it does this seems not to be random. There are patterns which recur whenever IT professionals' conversation turns to exchanging horror stories about IT systems which went wrong.

If we can identify where information systems commonly go wrong, where the system either by its design or its implementation has a detrimental effect on its host organization, that should bring us one step closer to reducing the destructive power of some information systems.

5.5.1 Up-to-date Information to Serve the Strategy that we Abandoned Long Ago

When an organization decides to make a major strategic change it is obliged to make supporting changes in most of its operating sub-systems, including its information system. Otherwise the old sub-systems will hold the old strategy firmly in place. The planned change will not occur. For example, a new approach to the market may require new people with new skills. If the existing staff are not retrained and the new direction is not adequately communicated to them, they will carry on in the same old way of doing what they have always done.

The same applies to information systems. A change of strategy may create new goals, new performance requirements and new ways of measuring performance.

The new strategy may be designed to take the organization into new markets with new competitors and different competitive offerings. It is precisely these matters that the information system should be reporting on. Unless one has an adequate understanding of the organization's strategy and its competitive position one cannot properly design an information system to support that organization's strategy. As the organization's strategy and competitive situation change so must the information system.

Creating the new information system to support the new strategy is no easy task. Consider the problems facing the IT managers in the UK National Health Service. Government proposals will require units (hospitals, area health authorities) to operate in effect as profit centres buying services from each other. That will require information to be organized on a profit-centre basis which it has not been previously. Services, such as kidney operations and tonsillectomies, will have to be costed and priced so that the NHS internal market can work. Resource allocation decisions are likely to be problematic. Given a fixed budget, how are the managers of an area health authority to decide between doing a kidney operation or a heart operation when both patients need treatment and the budget will not cover both? Information exists to serve a purpose. If you do not know what that purpose is, you cannot provide the correct information to serve it.

The current NHS information system was designed to serve the old style NHS. It was designed piecemeal as needs arose. It was not designed to serve the new strategy current in government thinking. Indeed, as one Health Service manager recently put it, it sometimes seems that the NHS information system was designed not to serve the new strategy. It does not collect and analyse information on a profit centre, internal market basis. But without information available in this form the new strategy may well prove inoperable.

The National Health Service may be an easy example since it is large, problematic and well known. But the same time lag between strategy and information provision exists in many companies. To see whether the same debilitating condition exists in one's own favourite company one needs only ask a few key questions:

(a) What is the competitive strategy of this company
What is special about what it is offering?

Why should anyone buy from this company rather than from its competitors?

(b) What are the critical success factors in this business? What do we have to get right in order to win the sale?

(c) Does the information system support this competitive strategy, this cutting edge, as well as it should?

Let us take some current examples from successful enterprises. The high street banks for example, Lloyds, Barclays, NatWest and Midland, are endeavouring to become more sensitive to their customers' needs. Instead of their traditional centralized approach the banks are trying to devolve much decision-making to the branches where the bank interfaces with the customer. The idea is that the branch banker will understand the customers' needs and call off the requisite package,whether it is tax planning, pensions, insurance, or company finance from regional head office. Does the branch banker have the requisite information to operate this strategy? From personal experience it seems that happy state may not have been reached. Branch bankers do not universally have the knowledge of pensions, insurance and corporate finance to understand their customers' needs or to advise them on the relative merits of what is available.

As a further example the UK building societies now aim to compete against the high street banks for personal customer accounts. One element of their strategy, their competitive edge, is that they will give customers access to their money on Saturdays which some banks do not. Here the information technology is in many cases directly thwarting the building societies' professed strategy. Many customers who try to withdraw cash from a building society on a Saturday morning have found that the information system cannot cope with the heavy demand. Customer accounts cannot be called up on the VDU. Current balances cannot be ascertained, so cashiers refuse to permit cash withdrawals. Irate customers have even been told to come back on Monday when there is less demand.

Until the building societies sort out their IT problems, they will be unable to put their strategy into operation. Their potential competitive edge is lost until such time as they have the information system in place to support it. The existing information system seems to have been adequate for the old strategy.

In these cases the problem has arisen because the information strategy is out of phase with the competitive strategy. The competitive strategy has been changed but as yet the information system has not been changed to support it. The branch banker has all the information which he or she needs to operate the past strategy. He knows the credit limits of his customers, his own discretionary limit, and what to do if he wishes to exceed that limit. He has been thoroughly trained in using the old information in pursuit of the abandoned strategy. Now the competitive strategy of the bank has changed.

Provision of the newly necessary information to the point where it will be used becomes an urgent necessity. Once that information is available on site, it will quickly become apparent how much retraining is needed before the available information becomes useful and used.

A change to a new competitive strategy will usually require the creation of a new system of information to support it. In turn that will necessitate a retraining programme before the people at the sharp end are able to use the new information to implement the new competitive strategy. Perhaps in an ideal world all three phases would happen together. But in practice there are time lags. The process of change beginning with competitive strategy, leading to information provision leading to retraining is often time lagged and may require a number of years to be completely effective.

5.5.2 Structure as an Impediment to Strategy

Information is closely bound up with the structure of an organization. Organizations are divided up into departments for example by product or by country so that we can monitor and control them in those units. In effect we structure our organizations in a particular way in part because that allows us to organize our information around the division and departments we create. Take a monolith like ICI.

Knowing the total sales of ICI is useful perhaps only once a year at the time when the annual report is prepared. It is more useful to the management of ICI to know how the sales of a particular product are progressing. So the totality of ICI information is divided up by product. In this way we can know not only what ICI's total cost and total revenues are, but more usefully we know what profit or loss was made on each product. Gathering information on a product basis is made easier if the company itself is organized into product divisions. If the group is organized in some different way, shall we say by country for example, it may be more difficult to pinpoint what is happening to a particular product. Our subsidiary in India sells 300 products and makes an overall profit. Our subsidiary in France sells several hundred products and makes a profit. Some of these products are made in other countries and transferred to the sales company at a price which minimizes the global tax burden. The net effect may be that we carry some loss-making products for years without being fully aware of it. The way we have chosen to structure our organization and to organize our information is concerned with control. If we wish to focus on controlling our activities in India, France, etc., country by country we structure our operating and control information on the basis of national subsidiaries. That may not tell us very much about the performance of a product which is sold in seventeen countries and manufactured in others. The way we structure our organizations and organize our information is a matter of choice. No choice is likely to serve all ends optimally.

An international group which structures itself into a series of national subsidiaries may find that its structure impedes it from undertaking multinational ventures. A classic example of this is a well-known business school which has campuses in several countries. Each country has a national director responsible for a national budget. However, the business school's competitive edge, the thing which makes it special, is its internationalness. It produces managers who are international, not just Frenchman who have been abroad and returned more chauvinistic. How do you ensure that the French professors do not just teach their students French accounting for example while the German professors teach parochial German accounting and insular British teach British insularity? Very simple. Make the British, French and German professors work together. Make the Faculty international so that they can teach the students to be international. It seems fairly obvious, given that is what the school is supposed to be about. But the organizational structure gets in the way. For German, French and British Faculty to work together to create shared international courses requires that they get together occasionally. How does the national director react to that? His Faculty – employed nationally to teach nationally – wants to disappear to another country outside his control. He is accountable for the national budget. The Faculty wants to spend money not on the national operations but by going outside the country. Friction mounts. In effect the business school has designed an information and control system and structure ideally suited to impede its own competitive strategy.

The giant Philips group used to be the best known example of matrix organization. Philips is now dropping the matrix organization. As one Philips director explains: 'We used to think that the matrix structure would give us creative conflict. It gave us conflict'.

It makes no sense to say to a manager 'we will measure your performance, reward you, fund you according to this set of criteria, but really we want you to do something else entirely'. And yet strangely it happens.

A major international computer company is organized into national subsidiaries. It has major problems in serving a multinational client which wants completely compatible information systems whether it is in Teesside or Dacca. The computer company has had to create an additional organization outside its normal organization structure in order to serve one multinational client. Presumably it will go on creating new organization structures afresh.

The business school with campuses in several European countries had great difficulties finding one computer company who could supply compatible personal computers and software to all its European locations and invoice centrally. Certain computer companies said to be international could not supply compatible kit to Spain, Germany, UK and invoice the lot to France. They were organized nationally not internationally.

The banks are running into the problems of trying to offer an international service in the single European market whilst remaining organized on a national basis. If you have a bank account in the UK, try cashing a cheque in France to see the problems remaining.

Market changes lead to strategic change which in turn lead to structural change which necessitate changes in information systems. The changes to both market and strategy also change the requirements for information.

Design of strategic information systems has to be understood in the wider organizational context of market strategy, and structure. Otherwise the strategic change is thwarted by the old structure and rendered inoperable by the old information system.

The plethora of organizational changes may be unsettling for the people in the organization. It may provoke discontent, resistance, underground warfare, casualties. These are the same people who will have to generate the new information system and change their ways to do so. The information system will only work if the people choose to make it work. Installing a new system requires selling it to the people who will have to generate it. Strategic planners have already discovered that writing the plan is relatively easy. The hard part is making something happen. The same lesson applies to strategic information systems.

5.5.3 Information for the Introspective

Much of the information provided to the management of a company by its regular information system is introspective, concerned with the internal workings of the company. Many a system reports in precise detail the sums spent on stationery in the past month but does not notice the new product with which a key competitor is preparing to capture a large chunk of the market. That is perhaps part of its inheritance from Accountancy. It is the equivalent of attempting to drive a car having regard only to the internal indicators: fuel gauge, speedometer, temperature, mileometer but never looking out of the window to notice the outside world.

For some managers the information most crucial to the successes and survival of their organization is not provided by their corporate information system. If they want to know how their competitors are performing, or what changes are just beginning to be felt in the market they have to set up a special project team to go and find out. Or wait until they show up on the company's internal indicators in the fullness of time when they have been translated into declining sales and below budget performance.

Information systems are often stronger on introspection than on monitoring the competition and the environment; coping better with the housekeeping than with competitor intelligence, telling us how we did last year with the products we already have, not helping us to see what products we should be preparing for next year.

What information does one really need to run a company? Stafford Beer offered a useful classification of the necessary information in his Viable System Model (Beer 19). It still serves as a valuable checklist. Beer suggests that there are five levels of information system involved in any company, or indeed in any viable organization.

System One is the information required for day-to-day operations. Take as an example a restaurant: a customer arrives, is directed to a table, order taken, passed to kitchen, and so on. Eventually the customer, served and satisfied, pays the bill and departs. The completed operation has depended on the flow of accurate information; from customer to waiter to kitchen back to waiter ... eventually to cashier.

System Two is an anti-oscillation device. If several waiters are all doing their System One job of serving customers to the best of their ability there is the risk that the kitchen will resemble a rugby scrum as all waiters attempt to get their customers' food first. Some simple device is needed to restore order. One such device that works well is a spike on which orders are stuck. The chefs pull the orders off the spike and deal with them in the order in which they are received. First come, first served. System Two anti-oscillation devices exist in most organizations. In a university or school the timetable fulfils this function. Each teacher has his or her class to teach and needs a classroom. Were it not for the timetable they could spend their entire lives competing and negotiating for use of the classrooms. Such devices are hugely important when they fail. A business school in the north of England had a room-booking system which broke down and made courses inoperable.

System Three takes an overview of the operations of the business. In the restaurant example it is the restaurant manager who not only keeps a watchful eye on the serving of meals and customers today, but also ensures that the restaurant will be in good condition to continue operations tomorrow. He keeps a beady eye on the waiters, quality controls the food and service delivered, he also attends to stock levels, advertising, etc., and covers for holiday absences.

System Three is concerned with keeping the existing business running successfully as it is. It assumes without question that there will continue to be a potential demand provided that the company can continue to attract it and serve it well.

Systems One, Two and Three are essentially introspective.

System Four looks outward beyond the organization. It is concerned to know what is happening in the outside world which may impact upon the organization. In the case of our restaurant many factors may impact upon it. The forecast closure of the steelworks which is the largest local employer could remove much of the disposable income of the restaurant's client group. Plans for an out-of-town hypermarket may draw away shoppers from the town centre who are presently a source of lunchtime trade. Few restaurateurs monitor such events adequately. They are too busy running the business to worry about things that may never happen.

Beer observes that System Four is the area of information which is most often weak. It is a common observation that small businesses often operate as though they had a local monopoly. Many of them do have a local monopoly but it is very local and entirely dependent on the continuation of a precise set of circumstances which give them a living. Frequently they are not even aware of what that set of circumstances is. Until it disappears. One of the most dramatic instances of a firm relying on a set of circumstances which then disappeared is a firm in the forestry business. Over the years the firm had diversified into all manner of timber products. But its core business on which all the rest depended was the management of woodland estates, that is of agricultural land on which a crop of timber was growing over a period of many years. The viability of that core business was largely dependent on one clause of UK tax law, the old Schedule A of the Income & Corporation Taxes Acts. There were substantial tax advantages for wealthy individuals investing some of their income in woodlands. On that one circumstance the large group of companies depended. Then the tax law was changed to remove the tax advantages.

System Five is what Beer calls the Brain of the Firm. Its function is to take in information from the introspective Systems One, Two and Three, and from the outward looking System Four, and being in possession of the full facts, to make wise decisions about what to do. In practice many firms have a weak System Four and lack adequate decision-making methods for System Five. As Beer observes, given a good crisis the top management comes crashing down and gets involved in System Three.

Beer's Viable System Model is a useful diagnostic tool particularly, in terms of information systems though it has wider applications. It can be used to identify gaps in corporate information and intelligence. Frequently gaps are in System Four, awareness of the significant changes in the outside world, and in System Five where there is a paucity of decision-making models, criteria and capability.

Systems One to Three, information for introspection, are usually present. The Beer model's effectiveness as a diagnostic tool for information management was recently apparent in a Midlands Polytechnic. System One, the teaching of students, was reasonably effective, with information marshalled in a form of courses syllabuses, student assessment, course evaluation and review. System Two, timetabling and room booking, had collapsed under the conflicting demands of a multitude of courses. The Polytechnic was under pressure to generate funds from revenue-earning courses, but was unable to do so because it could not be sure of having appropriate rooms available even though room occupancy was not high. The amount of executive time expended on the timetable and room-booking problem was colossal, the anger it generated intense.

System Three, the management of the teaching departments and supporting departments, was amply staffed, perhaps to excess. System Four, the monitoring of the relevant environment was largely non-existent. All executives' jobs were concerned with day-to-day operations, regular repeat business. No one was specifically responsible for watching out for major discontinuities or turbulent external conditions. The government requirement to plan for a ten per cent and a twenty per cent cut in budget caught them unprepared. When the ten per cent cut came the Polytechnic had no decision-making procedure for deciding what to do about it. It had never happened before so they had not previously needed a mechanism for dealing with it. In Beer's terms System Five, the system which takes in information from the external environment (i.e. System Four) and the internal environment (Systems One to Three) and decides what to do about it, was largely non-existent. There was no means of deciding how to cut funds by ten per cent. There was no set of agreed priorities about which activities could be reduced or jettisoned. No alternative sources of funds cultivated for use in emergencies. No contingency plans. Having no means of deciding where the cuts should fall, the Polytechnic eventually decided that all should suffer equally, everything was cut by ten per cent. The diagnosis of the information system read:

System One: present.
System Two: inadequate. Needs remedying.
System Three: present in large numbers.
System Four: absent.
System Five: absent.

In the Polytechnic as elsewhere the model was a very powerful tool for identifying why the organization was in trouble and why it would be in trouble again in the future. The endemic weakness could usefully be seen as a weakness in information management.

The power of the Viable System Model is a diagnostic tool for information system design. It also uses the diagnosis of the information system to reflect on the structure and the strategy capability of the organization highlighting strengths and weaknesses. Information and organization are mutually interdependent.

5.6 IN CONCLUSION

Potentially and in an ideal world information systems would be designed 'for the achievement of organizational goals' (JIT, 1990). It seems less than logical to design them otherwise. And yet in practice we are all familiar with numerous examples of information systems which have been designed with no consideration of organizational goals. Several examples have been mentioned to illustrate particular points. Claims that the 'strategic use of information are greatly affecting the profits of corporations' are only tenable in so far as the strategic information systems have been designed in full awareness and in harmony with the strategy, structure and competitive environment of the company. In cases where the strategic information system is designed without adequate regard to the strategy and structure of the organization, particularly to planned strategic change and the reasons for it, the information risks being an impediment. The company cannot be managed optimally if the information on which it relies is inadequate or wrong. In such a case the cost of the capital investment may eventually be exceeded by the cost of the destructive power of an ill-designed information system.

REFERENCES

Ackoff, R (1981) *Creating the Corporate Future*, Wiley, New York.

Beer, S (1990) *Diagnosing the Systems for Organisations*, Wiley, London.

Davenport, T, Hammer, M, and Metisto, T (1989) How Executives Can Shape Their Companies' Information Systems. *Harvard Business Review.*

Handy, C (1990) *The Age of Unreason.* Arrow, London.

Kilman, R (1989) *Managing Beyond the Fix.* Jossey Bass, San Francisco.

Martin, J (1984) *An Information System Manifesto.* Prentice-Hall, New Jersey.

Meyer, D and Boone, M (1987) *The Information Edge.* Holt, Rinehart and Winston, Toronto.

Prahalad, C and Hamel, G (1990) The Core Competence of the Corporation. *Harvard Business Review.*

Raimond, P and Eden, C (1990) Making Strategy Work. *Long Range Planning*. Vol. 23, No. 5.

Strategor (1988) *Strategie, Structure, Decision, Identité*. Inter Editions. Paris.

6 A strategic response to a competitive threat at Dairy Crest

J. Freestone
Dairy Crest

6.1 INTRODUCTION

In an economic environment where for the majority of industries, volumes, selling prices and the cost of capital are all under pressure and where costs and competition continue to increase, new creative strategies and their implementation are often the deciding factors between winners and losers. In most instances, the winner is the one with the strongest competitive strategy, coupled with the vision, drive and commitment who also has the flexibility to implement change!

This is the case history of such a situation in a major food manufacturing company. It explores how the restricted markets historically available to the company were expanded. It shows how the use of IT enabled the company to develop a business strategy to bring about an association with other businesses, creating a venture to combine the skills of the company and the associates, re-balancing the business and expanding it, so that additional products could be sold to a wider range of customers. This also provided the opportunity for additional volume and improved margins. It outlines the analytical process adopted, the difficulties encountered by a manager and his team in developing the process that ultimately led to an innovative solution and the implementation process that enabled the objectives to be achieved in a cost fashion. It also shows how this was accomplished without loss of control or of interaction with the end purchaser and without any reduction in the standards of performance achieved by the company.

The case illustrates how the fundamental principles behind the creation of an innovative business concept were woven together with the business format franchise idea, the coupling of the skills of the company, the strengths of selected distributors and the adoption of IT, to underpin the solution into a successful business strategy. The development of an appropriate IT system solution was not accomplished without problems – the reader will also find in the following sections how these were overcome.

6.2 THE BUSINESS SITUATION IN 1985

6.2.1 The Company

With an annual turnover of £1.14bn per annum, Dairy Crest Ltd are one of the top ten largest UK food manufacturers. They produce cheese and butter products and their many brands such as Country Life, Clover Spreads, Willow and Lymeswold Cheese are well-known household names in the market place. Dairy Crest also operates one of the largest transport fleets in the UK, collecting milk daily from over half of the country's 31,000 farms, processing much of the milk collected and delivering it daily to the consumers' doorstep.

Dairy Crest inherited the information technology of the 1960s in many of its sites, through the acquisition of a competitor's factories in 1979. In the early days of the company's history, the prime objective was to manage the business efficiently, whilst looking ahead, creating a strategy for the business and ensuring that the necessary DP facilities were there to support the business. As a result, the company management primarily focused on the management of the business; anything that detracted from it was considered extraneous as resources were scarce.

6.2.2 The Strategic Background

Total volume in the UK food industry has been static over many years. Growth has come from innovation and major brand development in the retail market, which is dominated by five or six major retailers. The available margins are small and the cost of developing and launching any major new product is substantial and is coupled with a high risk of failure. In the search for additional markets, the company identified an opportunity for increasing volumes and improved margins in the food-services or catering industry. This sector had been growing consistently at over 6% per annum and projections showed that this growth would continue.

The catering market has a turnover of £6bn. Despite being only 14% of the size of the retail market, it includes 300,000 delivery points, ten times the number in the retail market.

Caterers, who generally have limited stockholding facilities, have a requirement for more frequent and smaller deliveries than the traditional retail markets served by Dairy Crest. This requirement, for a frequent small drop service, was a major barrier to expansion as far as the major supplier companies are concerned.

Like most chilled-food manufacturers, Dairy Crest possessed a large drop distribution capability designed to serve the retail trade and deliver products to major wholesalers nation-wide. The drop size and the number of deliveries demanded by the catering market was totally outside its capability.

6.2.3 Dairy Crest Organization (1985)

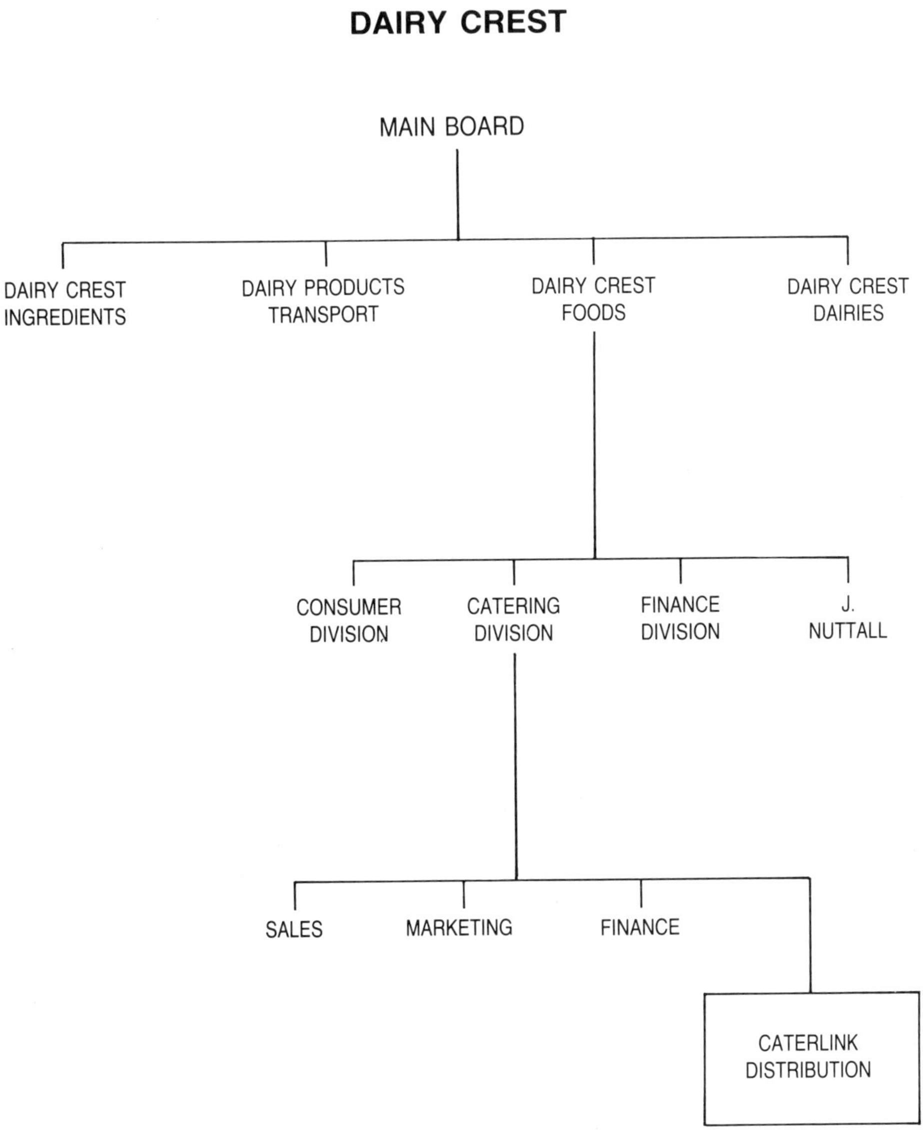

6.2.4 Available Options which could be Readily Understood

The usual four options were considered:

(1) Organic Expansion:
Developing an in-house small-drop distribution capability, by expanding the existing distribution operation.
This was too expensive and was associated with high operating costs and high risk.

(2) Acquisition:
Acquiring another business capable of performing the required tasks, or entering into a joint venture or a cooperative relationship with another business capable of undertaking these activities.
The available margin was not sufficient for two participants.

(3) Third Party:
Contracting the required tasks to a third party.
The available margin was too small to cover the operating costs and there was no third party available anyway!

(4) Do Nothing:
This was not acceptable to the managers or to the company.

All of these options were discounted but the requirement to serve the market remained. The search was now on for some other means of meeting the catering market requirements.

6.2.5 A Strategic Response – Why not Consider an Unconventional Option?

A structured strategic analysis was undertaken; this was designed to define the opportunity in some detail, determine the requirements, identify the means by which they could be met, the resources and investment needed and the payback from the investment and to consider the risks.

Time was taken to identify the lowest risk approach and the least capital-intensive method of serving this customer base.

The need for a structured approach was clear. Dairy Crest used the EMSTAR PROBLEM MANAGER for this task. This approach is based on a systematic, step-by-step process which enables a manager and his team to:

- Scope and define a problem.
- Pin down the root causes; establish alternative ways of resolving the key issues/root causes.
- Resolve such issues in a creative manner using the team's resources.

- Undertake an option analysis in a methodical manner.
- Evaluate rewards and risks.
- Select the most productive, feasible, viable and cost-effective solution.
- Gain the management's commitment to the proposed solution.

Using the EMSTAR PROBLEM MANAGER approach, the core objectives were identified and the alternatives evaluated.

Franchising has long been an established way of delivering fast food to consumers. Successful companies such as McDonalds and Wimpy have operated franchises for many years. They provide the consumer with an identified brand and uniform standards of quality and service, which are indistinguishable from company-owned operations. In this way, franchiser and franchisees have expanded their business and increased their profits in a way that would not otherwise have been possible. For many of these businesses, the risk capital and management would not have been available for other traditional methods and the costs of controlling such a vast and rapidly expanding international operation would have been prohibitive in the formative years.

The solution identified involved the following:

- The idea of putting together a 'comprehensive service package'.
- A novel creative concept of triangular relationship between customers, distributors and Dairy Crest.
- The franchising/licensing concept.
- IT as a basis for implementing the concept.
- A suitable organization with appropriate control mechanisms.

Dairy Crest had traditionally enjoyed good relationships with a number of independent small wholesalers or distributors located throughout the country. These local distributors were set up to make small-volume deliveries within a restricted geographic area.

Individually they could not serve national catering customers. The distributors' standards of performance were variable and they lacked the sales and marketing capability to handle major national purchasers. The strategic analysis showed that individually they possessed local capabilities that were required, but they lacked the broader competencies which were available within Dairy Crest.

By combining the skills of the two parties, in particular the product competencies and procedures in Dairy Crest, with the local care and attention found amongst the distributors, it was considered possible to meet the needs of the major catering customers and obtain competitive advantage.

Under the scheme envisaged, the 'concept and the method of working, including the IT system software' created by Dairy Crest would be licensed by Dairy Crest to selected distributors who would become the scheme licensees. These distributors would continue, under normal arrangements, to buy dairy and other products from Dairy Crest. Dairy Crest would find major customers in the catering industry and negotiate with them, on behalf of the scheme, to list agreed products so that the licensee distributors could take orders from the branches of these customers and supply them with agreed products, making small-drop deliveries as necessary and issuing priced delivery notes to the branches ordering the listed products.

Orders would be captured by the licensee distributors using the licensed software. They would periodically transmit copies of the order and invoice data in an approved IT media to Dairy Crest so that the required monthly collation, statement submission and money collection from the customers' head offices could be processed at the centre. In turn, the licensee distributors would get the payment for their invoices from Dairy Crest.

In essence, the Scheme Strategy, from a business and commercial point of view, was to offer precisely what the target market required:

(1) By establishing a link between the wholesalers, i.e. the distributors, Dairy Crest and the major customers.

(2) By planning for central negotiation to be undertaken by Dairy Crest with the major customers' head offices.

(3) By the distributors taking responsibility for local order capture, the distribution and the deliveries to the branch offices of the major customers.

(4) By the distributors invoicing to all the delivery points with notification to Dairy Crest.

(5) By Dairy Crest presenting statements to and obtaining payment from the head offices of major customers.

(6) By Dairy Crest developing the necessary computer link and software for the co-ordination of the entire operation of this venture.

It can be seen from the previous paragraphs, that this scheme depends on the licensee distributors performing certain functions and Dairy Crest performing certain complementary roles besides the normal supplier/distributor relationships. It was vital that all parties performed to agreed standards of performance – otherwise the risk of failure of the whole scheme would become prohibitive.

A special purpose-built IT solution/software forms an integral part of the scheme and this has to fit in with the procedures/practices not only of Dairy Crest but also the selected distributors.

Dairy Crest saw this as a way of creating a national delivery capability that would meet the needs of all the parties. It could be up and running within one year and, most importantly, it could be developed and controlled to meet the needs of the target customers.

After some deliberations, the decision was taken ... 'go for it'. Dairy Crest adopted the solution based on the franchising/licensing concept coupled with IT to develop its strategic response to this challenge.

6.2.6 Practical Implications of Adopting this Approach

This achievement was a daunting task. The adoption of strict rules and procedures and a commitment to adhere strictly to the scheme discipline, resulting in a dramatic change and control, were required if the operation was to acquire a leading edge and achieve success.

There was no precedence for such a system either within Dairy Crest or outside; several loosely-knit organizations had tried to achieve similar results, but had always failed to provide a uniform standard of performance, quality and customer service as demanded by the customers.

Purchasers of major catering organizations had experienced difficulties concerning accurate and uniform pricing and with the variable standards of performance provided by these operations.

The new scheme was called Caterlink Distribution and it was decided to set up a pilot scheme as soon as it was practicable to do so. In the early stages, it was decided to set up a special Caterlink Business Unit to administer it.

To meet its objective, the new Caterlink operation had to have the ability to handle over 4,000 transactions per week from its first day of operation, almost as many as Dairy Crest with its multi-million pound turnover! To achieve these objectives, strong procedures had to be implemented. Account registration on the product catalogue and nationally agreed prices had to be automatically and strictly controlled. All participants had to be focused on the end-user requirement of a good, controlled and regular service.

Invoices and other administration had to provide the data that was required by major customers; they had to be accurate, and most importantly this documentation had to be provided with the goods at the time of delivery, so that it created a competitive advantage by simplifying the administration and control for major purchasers. As all this had to be achieved with participating distributors spread across the country, each holding stocks of some 1,200 line options, there was a very clear need for automatic controls.

The scheme had to be costed and draft business plans developed to show how a licensee distributor would benefit under various local conditions with different drop sizes and volumes of business in the initial period and subsequently. The proposal had to be presented to the distributors collectively, individually and severally according to the particular preferences of the potential distributors. This is an obvious requirement of any scheme of a franchising type.

6.2.7 Caterlink SCHEME in Diagram

BUSINESS ACTIVITIES AND DATA FLOWS

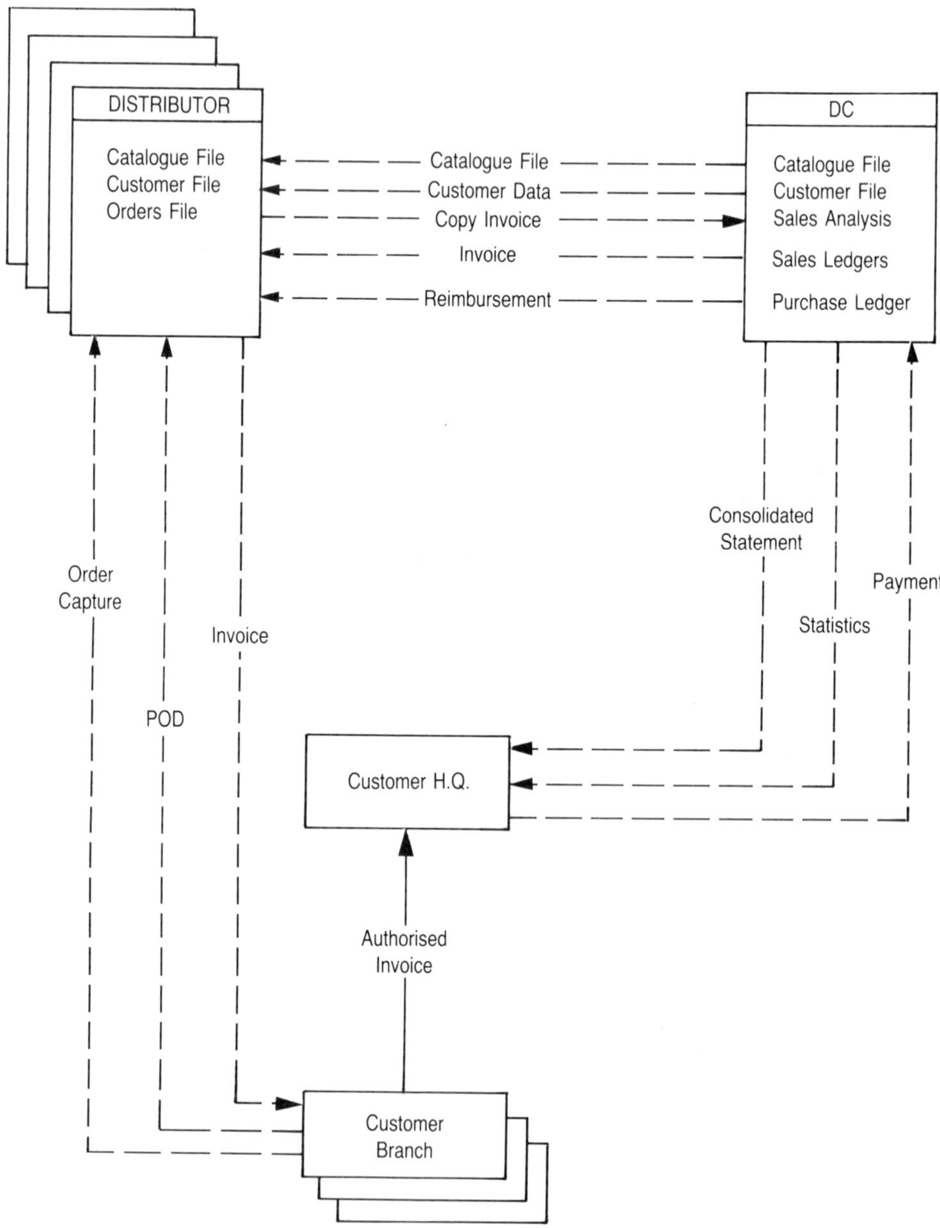

6.3 SOLUTION AND IT PROBLEMS ENCOUNTERED

6.3.1 The Systems Question – How would the Objectives be Achieved?

In terms of strategy, the IT strategy of Dairy Crest centred on the needs of the company as a whole. It did not have room for meeting the needs of a small entrepreneurial venture such as the one envisaged. Moreover, in the views of those in charge of DP, the scope of any existing IT strategy would have to be radically modified, with the natural consequence of diverting the company DP resources from the main tasks. It was decided, after some considerable deliberations, to approach the IT requirements of this part of the business as a separate exercise – in any case this involved taking into account the IT situation of the potential licensee distributors. The systems used within Dairy Crest and the potential licensee distributors were all different and a detailed survey of the installations had to be conducted.

The need for good documentation, systems, procedures and communication was clear, but how would they be created, who would create them and, of course, what did they encompass? What equipment and capital would be required to perform such an activity?

It was desirable, indeed essential, that a low-cost solution should be achieved, but one was not readily available. It had to be created. Was the management time, will and commitment, available for such a task?

As the scheme was itself a new venture, without any model to base it on, of course it involved high risk for Dairy Crest, which in turn meant that the start-up investment was of necessity limited. A low-cost pilot scheme was required to prove the operation. However, even this had to be rigorous in its procedures so that it could provide the service required and could evolve to support the full volume and requirements of the scheme for the future.

Resources were restricted, knowledge limited, experience non-existent.

The Caterlink Computer system was conceived as two linked components:

(i) A central system at Dairy Crest Caterlink Business Unit, an IBM PC-compatible machine operating an accounts software package capable of processing the licensee distributors' invoices receivable and the amounts reimbursable by Dairy Crest, whilst maintaining a database of sales analyses, customer and product information, matching payments against receivables.

(ii) Remote systems at each of the licensee distributors, IBM PC-compatible machines operating an invoicing software package to handle invoicing – priced delivery notes.

The system developed would also take account of the necessary financial and management controls required by the distributor organizations and Dairy Crest.

There was also the requirement of integrating this system with Dairy Crest's own financial control systems which were part of the central data processing facilities at the head office.

6.3.2 The Development of an Implementable Solution

To create business plans, stimulate other people, explain procedures and create commercial agreements and convince customers is all part of the modern manager's activity; he has skills and past experience relating to these problems; he has precedents on which he can draw.

After creating the initial business plan, the commercial agreements that underpin the scheme were developed, negotiations with distributors completed and the operation manuals created and, of course, the customers obtained, but the development of the support technology, the interactions within the business and the connection with the much larger parent business, was not so easy.

The majority of experienced managers have developed their career without the 'hands-on' experience of modern information technology. They have come to it late in their commercial lives, and even when encouraged to use it, find that it is provided in a ready-made and finished form, with set procedures created by others; IT personnel on the other hand are often focused on their own skill areas and are restricted in their commercial vision; if these circumstances are not recognized and overcome, the combination can prove a barrier to joint effectiveness.

The requirement for a significant interaction and high volume of administration made the use of 'state-of-the-art' technology a procedural necessity, but the implementers of the plan, who were largely commercial managers, lacked experience or knowledge of this type of activity and because the scheme itself involved new ideas, the IT managers who were consulted could not often assist in the strategic development that was essential in developing the systems and procedures.

Initially the in-house IT department was approached for assistance, but they were fully occupied in developing what to them were major IT initiatives for the parent company. They were unable to apply themselves to the development of this innovative and high-risk system, particularly when staff resources were scarce.

The only alternative for undertaking the development and development work was to look at an external agency. One was selected and briefed. Within weeks flow charts, diagrams and plans were to be seen everywhere, there was frantic haste and new words were added to everyone's vocabulary.

Like any large organization, the interface with other parts of the business is an essential ingredient for the success of any major project. Intercommunication was vital, so the documentation was circulated internally, comments were sent back and the detailed debates, not on strategy but on the detail, seemed endless.

The demands for further detail and information, constant requirements for re-evaluation and further consideration meant that the project began to grow and become uncontrollable. The newness of information technology, within the organization, meant that everybody had an opinion which they wanted to exercise. This was a change to explore, it was innovative and therefore interesting, everyone had a view regarding it!

The external consultants that were employed in the project had not anticipated such rigorous debate, junior consultants were soon operating outside their experience, errors were made but were lost in the enthusiasm and general momentum of the scheme. The result was an ever-increasing burden placed on the operating managers, who were controlling this project in addition to their principal tasks and, at the same time, trying to learn and understand the complexities associated with modern information technology.

The unique nature of the development created stresses and strains for everyone involved. The scheme being unique, with commercial aspects outside the current operations of a large food company, meant that the principles and concepts were often new, so how could the relevant knowledge exist within the company?

The scheme involved developing and building relationships with third parties and required systems that spanned their independent business units, this was itself a new departure for a major company.

The differing systems used within the businesses, in particular in the information technology departments, created additional problems. The stringent demands of the MODUS procedure (a phased discrete methodology for systems development) were eventually moderated, a different consultant, more experienced and with improved communications skills, was appointed and clearer and more specific guidelines were produced. Simplicity and common sense, coupled with a willingness to learn, were replaced by sterile analysis.

Following the newly developed procedures, better communication lines were established with other interested areas, the procedures began to yield results.

The sponsoring manager again controlled the project. Care was taken to ensure that the jargon often associated with information technology and marketing was replaced by commonsense language so that everybody fully understood the project, not in the technical sense, where there were plenty of experts available, but commercially. There was no need to understand ASCII or Fourth Generation computer language, as long as one understood that the output from the computer was related directly to the input!

The skills and sophistication that resided in small distributors within the scheme were again recognized by large company managers. These were harnessed to the project and procedures were simplified. These smaller businesses were found to be administratively very capable, very adept at adapting their systems and very rapid in responding to demands of change. They were able to be much more flexible than the major company. With this more flexible approach by all, results were obtained.

6.4 THE RESULTS AND LESSONS LEARNED

6.4.1 The Results in Summary

The initial pilot involving two licensee distributors helped to iron out many problems, but the speed with which customers had to be taken on imposed a strain on the capability for a while. There was the inevitable delay due to a variety of causes mentioned above – the fact that the central Data Processing Department did not help much contributed to the delay.

The two distributors chosen were very helpful. Much care had been taken in the choice of these pilot partners.

The one significant competitor did not have the unique combination of competitive advantages which Caterlink had. Dairy Crest was conscious of possible competitive reactions, therefore much care was taken always to keep a step ahead of the competition.

Eventually a decision had to be made to take on other distributors as the business demanded. For competitive reasons a slow gradualist approach could not be adopted.

The concept and capability has now been installed in fourteen distributors. Caterlink now operates nation-wide, it supplies some 3,600 delivery points with products from several manufacturers, each week. It has a £15m turnover after only three years of operation and has achieved every one of its goals and is expanding its turnover at 30% per month. Operational accuracy levels in the field of invoicing and reporting are quite amazing and significantly ahead of those achieved by its prime competitors. It has paid back handsomely.

6.4.2 Lessons Learned

Before any project is commenced it is essential to ensure that the objectives of the operation are fully analysed and the risks evaluated and shared by managers so that commitment can be established. Also a champion must be found and empowered to act.

It is essential that all development procedures are fully documented and that everyone involved is regularly updated on relevant aspects. Constant communication in the team is vital. Only by operating in this way can it be ensured that everyone understands the objectives and the process and the project status. For some reason, project management routines are ignored in projects that are innovative or where there is no precedent. It is often assumed that commercial managers will understand ... too often they don't.

Experience of modern information technology used in such a project is also essential. Care must be taken to ensure that emotions that create tensions in a project, such as fear or lack of trust, are managed. Remove the complexity, cut the jargon, share the methods, recognize that some areas of the business have a commercial need to move faster than others, recognize individuals but foster the team.

Be prepared to ensure that managers are not constrained in any project where innovation is needed and commercial rewards are available. Ensure that they feel that they have sufficient authority and rewards. All too often, success has many fathers; but there should be no shame or loneliness in failure. Managers must acknowledge this risk at the commencement and minimize it during the progress of the project.

It is also likely that the skills and operations of others will go unrecognized; this is often the case when large operations look at small businesses. Like the distributors in Caterlink, small does not necessarily mean unskilled, nor is large always cumbersome. Dairy Crest has proved in its strategic response to a major opportunity that large can be flexible and innovative and small can be efficient and skilled.

6.5 IT STRATEGY IMPLICATIONS FOR CATERLINK DISTRIBUTION

6.5.1 The Future

Caterlink harnesses the flexible energy and enterprise of small companies, operating with the procedures and strength of a large parent, into a unique operation capable of performing activities that were impossible for the individual parties. It is a unique use of Information Technology without which it could not have been achieved.

Having established its commercial advantage, the scheme has the opportunity to expand further, sales will increase from £15m to £30m plus, over the next three years.

A valuable asset has been created for the company and one that allows penetration of new markets, providing as it does, a low-cost method of controlling externally-based personal or independent companies. It could, for example, be used to develop a national or international network of distributors or service engineers, capable of providing a uniform standard of support or service to a pre-agreed price or time.

There are no geographical barriers to its application, the principle could even serve multinational companies. Because of the information technology involved, it can indeed, be truly international.

6.5.2 Change

In the developed economies of the Western world, the 1980s and 1990s have been a period where the economic environment has been such that, in the majority of industries, volumes and prices, together with the cost of capital, have been constantly under pressure. With costs constantly escalating and competition becoming ever more aggressive, competitive strategies and their implementation have been the deciding factor between winners and losers.

In the majority of instances the winner has been the one with the strongest strategy, coupled with the commitment and flexibility to implement change. However, perhaps for the first time, this strategic change has not been limited to the direction of the business but has included the way of managing technology to provide solutions which reduce the pressures on the financial and operational requirements of the business, in short the management of IT.

This is a case history of such a situation and the experiences of a manager in a major food manufacturing company. It explores how the restricted markets, that were historically available to this company, were insufficient to sustain its growth and shows how they were expanded by the use of the available information technology so that products could be sold to a much wider range of customers. They were, in turn, able to provide the additional volume and additional margins that were required to cover the cost of change. It explores the initial analysis that lead to this innovative solution and outlines the implementation processes that enabled the objectives to be achieved cost effectively, without loss of control and with constant interaction with the in-purchaser, all without any reduction in the standards of performance achieved by the company in the supply of its products to the target market.

Part Three

Creating an IT Strategy, Barriers and Pathways

7 Financial sector IT investment – money down the drain?

D. Axson and G. Hackett
Gunn, Hackett and Markos

7.1 INTRODUCTION

Over the past decade, banks and insurance companies have invested millions of pounds in computer and communications technology which promised to sharpen operations into a key competitive weapon. However, many senior managers express growing dissatisfaction with the benefits gained from technology and frustration at the ever-increasing investments demanded.

In 1990, Andrew Buxton, managing director of Barclays Bank, revealed that the bank's huge outlays on computers (£550 million in 1990) were failing to bring down costs proportionately. As a result an executive level IT board was established and a revised strategy aimed at delivering the required cost reductions implemented. Such dissatisfaction with the value gained from technology investments is all too common a feeling for senior management. Managers are very uncomfortable since they have great difficulty in identifying the real value of IT investment to their business.

This is not simply a failing of users; as one Asian banker put it, '... it is not just we bankers who have the difficulty [in using new technology for business benefit], but I find hardware and software vendors equally at a loss'. The struggle to translate the enormous technological advances made in recent years into real improvements in service, competitiveness and profitability is proving very expensive. Perhaps the major technological challenge facing companies in the 1990s is simply to translate technology investments into measurable improvements in the size and quality of earnings through improved productivity.

The charge that many technology investments have simply automated existing inefficiencies has some merit. The promised improvements in productivity have proved elusive. The most noticeable impact upon business has been in terms of capacity not service.

- As many as 80% of UK financial institutions fail to realize expected returns from at least half of their IT projects (AT Kearney, 1990).
- Studies by the American Quality and Productivity Center show that in the banking and insurance sector the effectiveness of labour and capital utilization is lower than it was ten years ago.

- Service quality, although difficult to measure, is generally perceived to be declining.
- Operating and administrative costs – driven to a large extent by technology costs – continue to spiral upwards. During the five years to 1990, technology spending by UK financial institutions increased by over 20% per annum, yet cost-to-income ratios remained static at best.

This paper explores some of the evidence by looking at the financial services sector, one of the most conspicuous consumers of technology over the last 20 years.

7.2 IT INVESTMENT IN THE FINANCE SECTOR

Since the early 1970s automation has exploded. IT budgets have grown by around 20% per annum and, in 1989, total expenditure by the UK finance sector on IT was £3.9 billion or an average of £4,400 per employee (VNU Business Publications, 1990). In the US the comparable figure is $7,700 per head which is more than five times the amount that US industrial companies invest annually in new plant and equipment.

Yet despite such massive investments the results have been disappointing. One of the main reasons is that companies have relied too much on the perceived competitive advantage to be gained. Financial institutions invested in technology in the hope of leapfrogging their rivals using competitive barriers, improved service levels, technology-based products and services, and lower staff costs. However, for many organizations investment has been a competitive necessity rather than a competitive weapon. For example, consider the viability of a provider of checking accounts who cannot offer customers access to a network of automated teller machines (ATMs). While developing an ATM network may have given some competitive advantage ten years ago, it has now become a competitive necessity. The same is true of many other technological innovations in the service sector such as automated airline reservation systems and computerized motor insurance quotations.

The opportunities for competitive advantage are transitory and lie in the application of technology to serve customer needs not in the technology itself. The experiences of Concorde in the late 1960s and Sony in the 1990s with digital audio tape (DAT), indicate that technology alone is not sufficient to ensure commercial success. However, the absence of effective IT systems can severely handicap competitiveness as two UK banks have found. In 1990, the Royal Bank of Scotland admitted that, 'We are under very severe pressure from other banks whose computer systems are more sophisticated than our own and, indeed, around 10% of the business of Global Custody Services has been lost in recent times because our technology in this area has not been up to the necessary standard.' Girobank went further and claimed that a £2 million fall in profits in 1989 would have been avoided if a new overdraft charging system had been operational on time.

While competitive advantage is not solely a function of the technology, competitive disadvantage can easily result from inadequate IT investment. Understanding the competitive dynamics that underpin the business processes technology supports forms a key element in achieving the correct balance and level of IT investment.

It is the successful combination of all resources – people, finance and technology – and their application through the organization structure, management processes and operational procedures to meet customer requirements that determines competitiveness and, through that, profitability.

Of course, the massive investments in technology have not been entirely wasted. Technology has enabled companies to cope with dramatic increases in volumes over the last fifteen years. It has also played a crucial role in the development of new and sophisticated products and services. However, the promised reductions in operating expenses, improvements in employee productivity and improved service have rarely materialized.

- In the US, often cited as one of the more advanced banking markets, productivity declined by 13% in the ten years to 1987 (Figure 7.1) yet over the same period IT expenditure increased by around 300%.
  Outstanding service is rare. Customers blame poorly trained employees and the increasing use of computers. Employees make excuses to consumers blaming computer errors. Even renowned customer service companies suffer as the following notice seen by the author outside an American Express office in London shows:

- 'Due to a computer failure we will be unable to undertake any foreign exchange transactions until 2pm at the earliest.'

- For three of the four largest UK banks, staffing levels grew faster than assets, adjusted for inflation, during the period 1986-90.

- Since 1986, only one of the eight largest UK retail banks, the Bank of Scotland, has reduced its cost-to-income ratio (see Figure 7.2).

Executives are clearly frustrated at the results of their investments. A survey of IT effectiveness in the UK (A.T.Kearney, 1990) found that only 11% of financial sector companies could be objectively classified as successful users of IT. While a similar survey of CEOs in the US (Lane and Hall, 1987) found that less than half believed their companies received an above average return on their IT investments.

7.3 AUTOMATING INEFFICIENCY

Why have productivity improvements proved so elusive?

Operations managers point to poor systems design, criticizing the technological tools as incomplete, inflexible, impersonal and too complex. While having some validity, the real problem is not that systems design is poor, but that operations and technology are not being coupled together. The approach of applying technology to a business process rather than integrating technology into a process is a common complaint. Three factors contribute to the shortfall in the returns from IT investments:

- Over a period of time, day-to-day operations become outdated and inefficient. Rarely are changes in the market place reflected in changes in daily operating routines.
- IT projects frequently superimpose new systems on inefficient and outmoded operations without taking the opportunity to re-engineer the process first.
- Systems tend to be exclusively complex. Companies often automate processes that could be better handled manually since volumes are low, products are unique, service is specialized, product lifespan is short, or automation is simply too expensive.

Winning companies build automated systems on a foundation of well designed and executed operations. This often means that to achieve sustained improvements, operations must first be re-engineered before automation is attempted.

Successful operating strategies are founded upon the requirements of the market, customers and the competition. The combination of operational drivers and technological capabilities tempered by real-world constraints defines how well a company can deliver its services. The real problem a company faces is its ability to deliver products and services to its customers, not the product or service itself.

Many operational units were never planned, they simply evolved in response to the perceived needs of the business they support. For example, a major international bank's loan approval process had evolved over time into an inefficient multiple review process which resulted in over 70% of all loan applications being sent back for re-work at the sixth review stage. (See Figure 7.3.)

The introduction of automation to support this process is clearly inappropriate without first redesigning the process itself. Unfortunately, all too often inefficiencies in existing processes are automated which simply preserves the problem and often makes it harder to rectify.

Building successful operating strategies begins with converting the requirements of the market place into a series of operating imperatives. For financial institutions, these include customer waiting time, credit application turnaround, cost of service provision, flexibility and customization of the product and service, and error rates. Traditionally, financial institutions have not been good at understanding customer needs; often all that exists is a vague operating mission such as 'good service and low cost'. The result tends to be average service for everybody. This ignores the specific needs of different customer groups which banks are working so hard to identify and target. Service through branches, ATMs or via home banking systems rarely distinguishes between the valued high net worth customer and the high-volume, low-value customer.

The most frequent approach to introducing new technology is to superimpose new systems onto existing operations. Major change is resisted and management tend to replicate current procedures regardless of how inefficient they may be. Sometimes a 'package' that appears to match present operations is customized. This approach dangerously institutionalizes inefficient and ineffective operating procedures, making it difficult to streamline and update operations. Given the tremendous pressure on costs all organizations are experiencing this can seriously damage the realization of the perceived benefits from technology investment.

For example, a major US servicer of mutual funds (unit trusts) invested over $20 million to automate its operations. But the expected 15% improvement in productivity, including a 200-person headcount reduction, upon which the investment was justified, did not materialize. Instead, operating expenses increased and customer service deteriorated. The firm had automated inefficient processes and failed to recognize the distinct requirements of the different customer segments it aimed to serve.

The problem was particularly acute in the fund accounting area. Before automation, most tasks – such as form filling – were completed manually. One accountant was assigned to each fund, and each accountant was utilized 80% of the time. After automation, utilization dropped to 55%, but the same structure maintained. Paperwork was now processed by computer, the accountants had more time but less work to do, although the reduction was not sufficient to reduce the ratio of one accountant to each fund. As a consequence the accountants' jobs became boring, turnover increased and continuity of customer contact broken. The investment in automation had been wasted.

This approach to technology is rather like driving a Ferrari in a traffic jam. The potential for high performance exists, but there are too many limiting factors – restrictive policies, outdated operating procedures, cumbersome organizations and poorly trained employees. However, by analysing operations from the correct perspective, managers can identify major cost and service improvements before investing in automation.

An example of taking a traditional business process and re-engineering using technology to deliver a distinctive service can be found at Direct Line, the telephone-based insurance subsidiary of the Royal Bank of Scotland. Direct Line was established in 1985 with a $20 million investment from the Royal Bank. The business concept was to take the basic process of selling insurance and transform the process to reduce acquisition and retention costs, through the development of a telephone-based selling process supported by carefully targeted media campaigns.

Traditionally, insurance has been sold through brokers who receive commissions of between 10 and 20% on motor insurance both for new business and renewals. Direct Line in effect cut out the middle man. Telephonists take calls and using specially developed computer systems offer instant quotes. The systems also allow the company to exercise much tighter control over risk than those companies who sell though intermediaries. The result is that Direct Line is the UK market leader in direct insurance and its premium income is expected to be around £120 million for 1991 while its costs are significantly below its more traditional competitors. Up to 1991 the Royal Bank had invested £62 million into a business which was estimated to be worth three times that amount.

Direct Line's success has been founded upon the intelligent use of technology to support a re-engineered business process, whereas many competitors simply automated existing processes which offered little competitive advantage.

In order to make such transformations which radically alter the cost structure of a business it is important to understand that operating costs are influenced in different ways (Figure 7.4).

- Inherent costs are driven by market and competitive requirements and embrace the costs of maintaining a viable presence in a market. Generally, changing these costs requires long-term commitments and strategic re-direction. However, the opportunities for cost improvement and market differentiation are large.
- Structural costs are driven by operational performance and organization on a daily basis. Structural change can be achieved by working more intelligently.
- Execution costs are driven by the quality of management. Improvements can be realized through tighter control and harder work.

Structural costs offer the greatest opportunity for cost reduction and for maximizing the benefits of technology investment. Companies can eliminate hand-offs, streamline the workflow, build flexibility into operations, minimize controls, reduce management layers, increase spans of control, eliminate low value-added activities, consolidate similar operations, and retrain employees. All of these actions can substantially improve customer service, raise productivity and reduce operating costs. More importantly, a sound base can be established from which technology investments can be effectively evaluated.

7.4 WHEN NOT TO AUTOMATE

How often have you heard people say 'I need a computer system to ...'. This presupposes that a computer is the right answer. Rather than stating the requirement, the user specifies the solution – a computer. This can turn into an expensive supposition. Many UK and foreign banks invested millions of pounds in technology for newly acquired securities trading businesses (stockbrokers and market makers) in the run-up to deregulation of the UK securities market or 'Big Bang' in 1986. Many of these investments were completely wasted, the post-Big-Bang market was characterized by chronic over-capacity, declining margins and high volatility. The Stock Market crash in October 1987 simply exacerbated these problems. Many respectable names suffered, including Lloyds Bank, Citicorp and National Westminster. A major factor contributing to the problems was the very high and largely fixed costs incurred in setting up 'high-tech' dealing rooms. There simply was not sufficient business available to recoup such investments. Some of the more successful players adopted a much more selective approach to IT investment focused on minimizing the cost of operations at required service levels.

Over-automation has two effects. Firstly, it substitutes variable labour costs with largely fixed systems costs. This makes downsizing in slack periods to reduce expenses extremely difficult. Two other sufferers of the events following Big Bang were the bureau companies that process Stock Exchange business for stockbrokers. NMW and Quotient invested large sums in new computers to automate the processing of equity bargains prior to deregulation in 1986. However, following the market collapse in October 1987, they were left with massive over-capacity and lots of expensive computer hardware (most of it still not paid for) sitting idle. By 1991 both companies had changed dramatically;NMW had returned to profitability by actively reducing its dependence upon Stock Exchange business. This included launching a disaster recovery service as a means of utilizing the spare capacity. Quotient failed to survive as an independent entity and was taken over by ACT in early 1991.

The second impact of over-automation is that there is a point where automating minor products and processes adds substantially to system complexity and cost. In turn this increases the risk of non-delivery or non-performance. Automating such activities adds little value while increasing operating expenses and complexity. Products which are highly complex, generate low volumes or have a potentially short lifespan must generate significant returns if they are too justify a high level of IT investment.

Management should strive to strike a balance which recognizes the impact upon customer service and operating costs of technology investments.

7.5 CONCLUSION

Taking a pragmatic approach to technology investment based upon the realities of business operations can result in 20-25% reductions in operating expenses, service improvements recognizable in the market, reduced error rates and increased operating flexibility. Automation by itself is not a panacea. As manufacturing industry found in the 1980s, a company cannot be competitive without improved levels of productivity and quality. Service industries now face the same challenge. Increased competitive pressure will not allow excessive overheads to survive. New, low-cost competitors will enter the market and margins will be driven down forcing high-cost companies out of the market.

The latent value of technology cannot be tapped unless the operations strategy recognizes the market and competitive requirements. Day-to-day operations must be re-engineered before technology is added. Finally, critical evaluation of the need for technology must be undertaken.

Making technology part of the overall operating strategy has not yet become a reality for most financial institutions. The inability to identify their true customers severely handicaps the decisions on the level and direction of technology investment.

REFERENCES

Hackett, G P (1990) Investments in Technology – The Service Sector Sinkbole? *Sloan Management Review*, USA.

A T Kearney, (1990) *Breaking the Barriers – IT Effectiveness in Great Britain and Ireland*, A T Kearney, London.

Lane, R and Hall, R (1987) Elusive Returns – Managing Information Technology Investments. *Information Technology Viewpoint*, Booz, Allen & Hamilton, USA.

Roach, S (1991) Service under Siege – The Restructuring Imperative. *Harvard Business Review*, USA.

VNU Business Publications (1990) The DP Expenditure Survey 1990, VNU Business Publications, London.

Source : American Productivity and Quality Center, December 1988

Figure 7.1

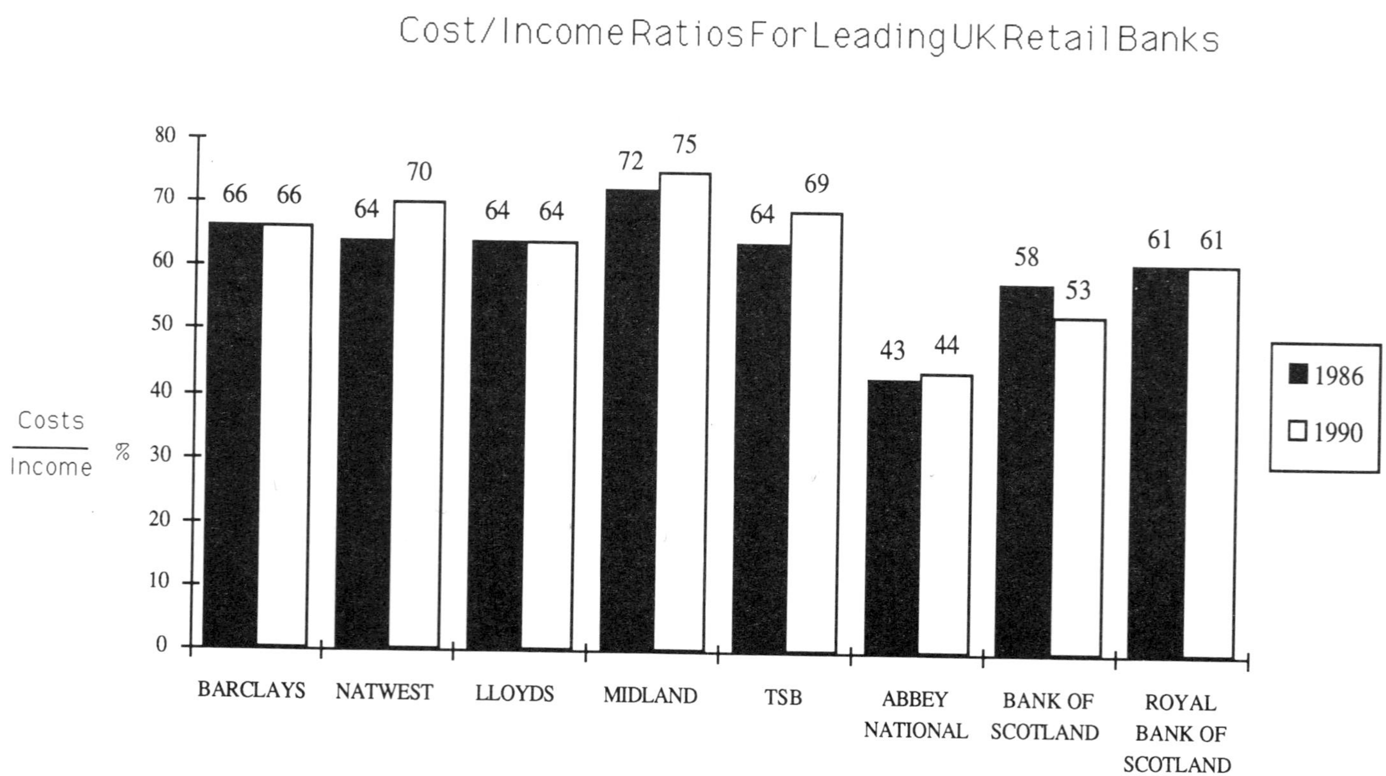

Figure 7.2 Cost/income ratios for leading UK retail banks

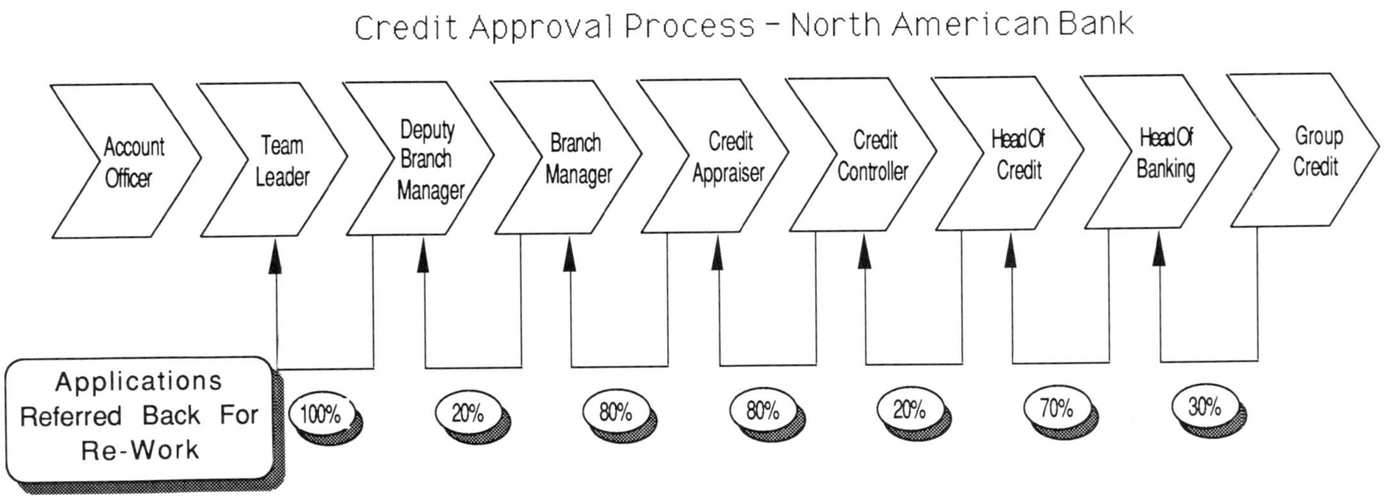

figure 7.3 Credit approval process – North American Bank

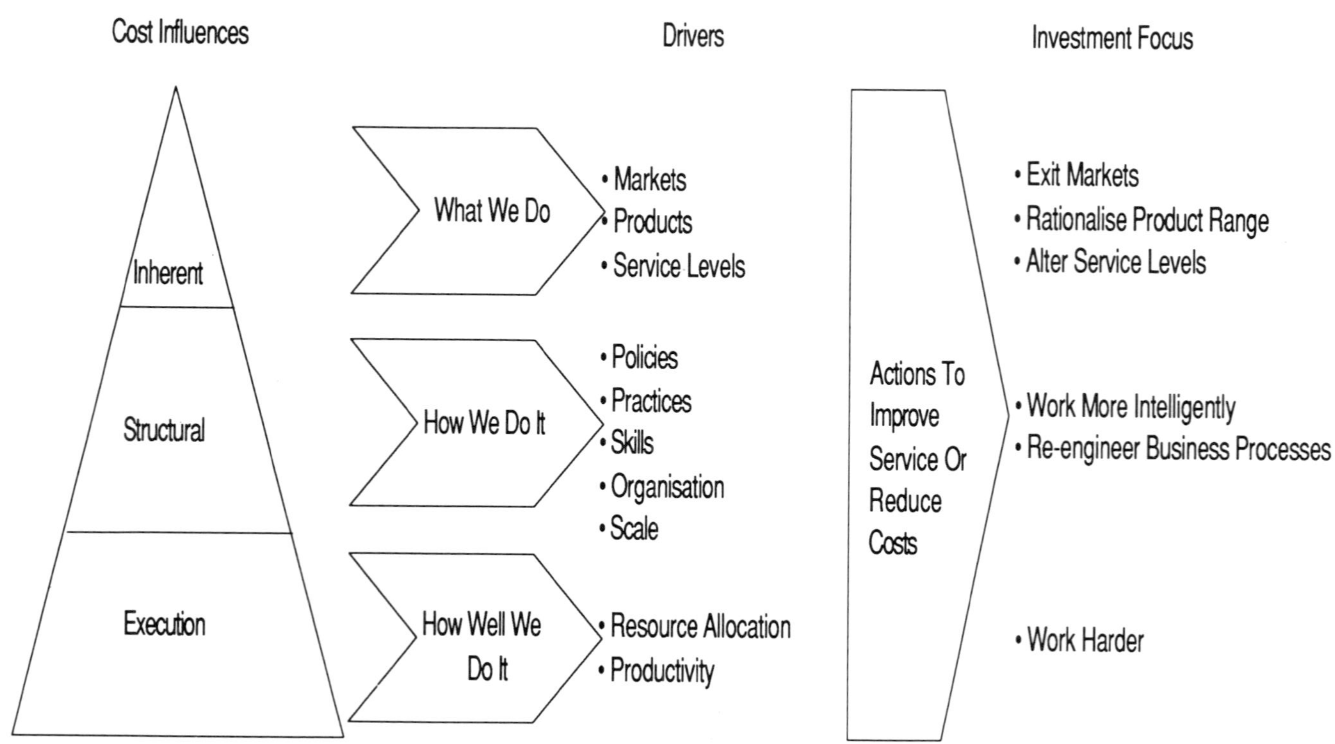
Cost Influences
Drivers
Investment Focus
Inherent
Structural
Execution
What We Do
How We Do It
How Well We Do It
• Markets
• Products
• Service Levels
• Policies
• Practices
• Skills
• Organisation
• Scale
• Resource Allocation
• Productivity
Actions To Improve Service Or Reduce Costs
• Exit Markets
• Rationalise Product Range
• Alter Service Levels
• Work More Intelligently
• Re-engineer Business Processes
• Work Harder

Figure 7.4

8 The culture gap

K. Grindley
Price Waterhouse and the London School of Economics

8.1 INTRODUCTION

In a recent survey of IT directors' problems (Price Waterhouse/*Financial Times*, February – 1990), the one that came out on top showed that the major constraint on further progress was neither technical nor managerial. Nor was it a problem of resources. It was one of understanding.

> 47% OF IT DIRECTORS STATED THEIR MAIN PROBLEM WAS THE CULTURE GAP EXISTING BETWEEN IT AND BUSINESS PROFESSIONALS

The nearest rival problem (integrating IT with imprecise corporate objectives) trailed the so-called culture gap problem by five percentage points. It was a startling admission. But, stated so baldly, it was hard to get a handle on what the culture gap problem really was. It begged a lot of questions. Chief among them was 'What does culture gap really mean?' A further survey was conducted therefore, specifically to probe the cause and effects of the gap, and what were the two cultures that were being separated. This survey provided dramatic confirmation of the problem.

> 56% OF IT DIRECTORS BELIEVE THE CULTURE GAP IS LOSING OR SERIOUSLY DELAYING IT OPPORTUNITIES FOR THEIR COMPANY TO GAIN A COMPETITIVE EDGE

8.2 WHAT IS THE CULTURE GAP?

On a first analysis, the culture gap seems to be one of understanding. And it all seems to be weighted on the side of the technicians; who perceive the way the world is going, who see so clearly what is best for us, and who sigh each day, 'If only the user could understand'. There is an attempt to blame the manufacturers for over-praising their product, as though the rule of *caveat emptor* should in some way be suspended in the case of computer salesmen. And there is some condescending acknowledgement that we technicians, blessed with the truth, are yet to blame – we have failed to explain, we are trying in the wrong ways, and so on. And so on.

To be fair, there are some who do not feel it is such a problem. Some five per-cent of IT directors questioned on the subject expressed this view. They either didn't believe it presented a major difficulty, or stated they'd solved it.

Another interesting group (eight percent) dismissed the problem to some extent, saying that, while their company experienced a culture gap, it was normal that professionals in any field knew more about their subject than the layman. That was why they were there.

It is the consideration of this view, and confronting it with the fact that, after thirty years of applying the new information technology in business, an overwhelming majority of companies, who live happily enough with accountants, lawyers, plumbers and the canteen manager, have been unable to absorb either the computer or the computer professionals into their culture, that suggests there is something more to this gap than just not understanding the IT jargon. A clue to what this might be is suggested by the comment 'Their knowledge threatens mine' made by one user manager. And by the cry of one IT director: 'No one would believe the continual frustration this job entails'.

8.3 CAUSES OF THE PROBLEM

One of the main causes of the culture gap is change. IT cannot be taken in isolation. Each dose involves the recipient in changing their behaviour. By definition, a machine is going to do part of your job, control is going to be exercised in a different way. To this extent, culture gap is a euphemism for threat. The gap exists, because those comfortable with the existing culture do not want it changed.

Changing someone's job, responsibility, prestige: these things are key to IT resistance. Astonishingly, many IT professionals are still surprised that they are not welcomed with open arms; and believe they would be, if only the user understood. It is, however, because he understands only too well, that enthusiastic IT evangelists encounter such wooden hostility.

One of the effects of the culture gap is to encourage resistance to change, and for firms to take their computer medicine in such palatable doses as require little or no new behaviour or thinking on the part of the patient.

> ONE IN FOUR IT DIRECTORS ADMIT THE CULTURE GAP HAS RESULTED IN WRONG OR ILL-CONCEIVED SYSTEMS – ONE IN FIVE SAY IT HAS FORCED THEM TO CONCENTRATE ON CHEAP SOLUTIONS AND COST CUTTING
>
> 89% STATE THEY ARE ENCOURAGED TO AUTOMATE EXISTING SYSTEMS RATHER THAN CONSIDER NEW WAYS OF DOING BUSINESS

The culture gap is more than a lack of IT understanding. It is more than the fact that its application involves resistance: resistance to change and resistance because of a real or perceived threat. One of the main causes is a fundamental difference in attitudes between the users and the IT professionals.

Many feel that, if attitudes differ, it is up to the IT department to adjust, that the business is what is important, and no computer system should be allowed to cause disruptive cultural problems there. Others admit to what is surely to be expected when confronted with change of a fundamental nature. There are two stages of perception, they say. It is one thing to accept that something is theoretically right. It is quite another to give it the green light and go for it in practice. Most of senior management has moved to the first stage and accept the business novelty that IT could introduce. But few are prepared to lead the revolution.

8.4 OWNERSHIP OF INFORMATION

There are certain specific attitude problems which contribute to the culture gap. On the user side (if there is a gap, then we have to admit there are two sides) one of the most important concerns the ownership of information.

A legacy from the traditional way of collecting and storing data (manual recording and filing) is the concept of the personal ownership of information. It is thought of as a possession. If you work for something and acquire it as a result of your own labour, you own it. So it is with information. We feel we own what we know. There is a sense of prestige: 'I know something you don't know'. But knowledge is power and is worth money. To let it go is to relinquish power, to dilute its value. To release control over it is to risk its misuse, its corruption, its loss.

IT challenges this concept. It works on the premise that the corporation owns the information, not the individual or department that collects it. And it makes it available according to corporate permission, and not as a personal favour.

It is extremely difficult to change established attitudes in this area. Departments needing the same information frequently duplicate it, develop it and jealously guard what they have developed. In the early days of computing, when data was first stored in a central database, users would commonly continue to maintain their own duplicate files, and set more store by their own lists than the computer's. This was understandable: they took more care to keep their own lists accurate. They did not trust the computer. Today, computers are more trustworthy. But the attitude dies hard. The departmental attitude to information is held by many to be the biggest barrier to building the IT infrastructures that twenty-first century survival strategies are beginning to demand.

8.5 MANAGEMENT AGAINST TECHNOLOGY

An attitude which greatly contributes to the culture gap is that management are basically against technology when it comes to using it in their own field. Until the advent of the electronic computer, management was about judgement and motivation. Judgement was exercised intuitively, and often brilliantly, based on unformulated experience. Motivation, similarly, relied on personal qualities: of charisma and of persuasion. It is an entirely new concept that management can be partly exercised by a machine, that routine administration can be automated. Attitudes change slowly. And the change process is inhibited in two ways.

Firstly, by fear. Everyone is down on what they're not up on, as one US IT executive put it. What's more natural than that any manager who doesn't understand IT, and this must include ninety percent, should be afraid of it to some extent.

Secondly, by cynicism. By a frank disbelief that IT will work, produce benefits, be up and running on time, be free of serious errors and keep within budgeted costs. The IT department's past performance, unfortunately, does little to dispel this attitude.

8.6 ATTITUDES OF THE IT PROFESSIONALS

Attitude problems are not all in the user departments. The technicians are notorious for their inclination to pursue, some might say indulge, technical objectives at the expense of the business. No one would deny the professional pride a system analyst or programmer takes in performing feats of wizardry on the computer. Nor the pride they take in working with the latest equipment. In this respect they are no different from any other professional. In every other profession it is controlled within practical and economic bounds by the price the client is prepared to pay and his satisfaction with the work done. Most of the IT profession, however, do not practice as professionals in this sense, working under contract for clients. They are employees of the business. There is no contractual control exercised on professional self-indulgence therefore. Many IT staff put the business interests first. But we do well to remember that the business is not their first love. They joined to work on computers, and it would not be surprising if, consciously or subconsciously, they got a kick out of standing them on their heads.

There is a noticeable attitude on the part of IT staff to prefer and to discuss hard rather than soft solutions. By hard, we mean definitive procedures, with no room for discretion. This is because these are the only procedures a computer can carry out, and they are motivated and used to thinking in this way. Management, on the other hand, deal with people, and people do not respond well to detailed prescription. They prefer some latitude. Management also have to contend with moving targets and instinctively shun detailed planning. At the detailed level, plans may quickly become obsolete. Management deal in soft possibilities, not hard certainties.

> 18% OF IT DIRECTORS ARE DENIED THE OPPORTUNITY TO BRAINSTORM IT BUSINESS POTENTIAL WITH TOP MANAGEMENT
>
> 31% SAY BUSINESS PEOPLE HAVE DIFFICULTY UNDERSTANDING AND APPRECIATING THE WORTH OF IT PEOPLE, AND ABSORBING THEM WITHIN THE ORGANIZATION

A FURTHER 30% SAY BUSINESS PEOPLE HAVE DIFFICULTY TRUSTING IT STAFF

8.7 SOLVING THE PROBLEM

Many pin their hopes on education. General education on IT, for users and top management, is universally condemned as a waste of time however. To be effective, it has to be specifically addressed to a corporate need. Disenchanted by general education, many have recourse to the submission of papers to senior managers, again addressing specific topics. This may release a lot of the author's frustration, but, to use the vernacular, appears in most cases to be a cop out. The culture gap cannot begin to be addressed in the popular one-page management summary.

IT directors need to face the fact, however, that papers of any length irritate rather than lubricate user relations.

IT history is littered with bandwagons. Wheels off, lying in the ditch, they are there for all to see and wonder over. The one that is up and rolling at the moment is called the Hybrid Manager. To bridge the culture gap, the theory goes, we need a manager, or preferably all managers, who have experience in both the business and in IT. It must, by definition, be true that when everyone has been brought up in an IT in business culture, there will be no culture gap. According to many IT directors, the bandwagon seems to have rolled obliviously over a couple of red lights. Being actually brought up in a culture is a world away from a retraining course and six months' exposure to the problems. True hybrids, they say, are a generation away. More important, hybrids on their own will not solve the problem. IT benefits mean doing something new. They mean visionaries, creative people. Such people do not grow on trees. Nor can they be forced in a training plus experience greenhouse.

Near the top of the list of solutions is the big stick technique. It is perhaps a quibble to note that the stick does not cure the culture gap. It drives IT into the business by ignoring it. The popular big stick is the CEO. If the top man supports an IT project it is likely to take off. In addition to his authority, the chief executive has, by virtue of his position, two important immunities to the culture gap. He is the only person whose job is not affected by a major IT project. And he is the only person who can truly take a cross-departmental view.

The chief executive, however, is not the only person who can wield the big stick. Any visionary, who is in a position of sufficient authority, can become the necessary instrument of change. As we have seen, most successful cases illustrating business advantage through the imaginative use of IT have their user champion, usually the head of the function which will spearhead the application. Once again, the culture gap is not closed. The visionary is followed, not out of a sense of conviction, but as an act of faith, loyalty and obedience to the leader.

The most popular solution is to keep whittling away at the problem in a very practical way; that is, by constantly providing examples of what IT can achieve. Small examples at first. Low cost, quick to implement. And always directed at a problem recognized by, and currently concerning, a senior manager. 'Show them IT can give them what they want. That's the first step,' said one IT director. 'Then, when they're finally listening, show them it can also transform the business.'

> 55% OF IT DIRECTORS STATE THE BUSINESS POTENTIAL OF IT IS NOT APPRECIATED BY TOP MANAGEMENT – 46% STATE THE BUSINESS IMPLICATIONS OF IT ARE NOT APPRECIATED BY IT STAFF

9 Bridging the culture gap from IT to IS: a practitioner's approach

I. Perring
Mindworks

9.1 INTRODUCTION

A crucial factor in the success of information technology (IT) strategies is the extent to which IT staff can communicate their understanding of the business to its managers. However, there is a 'culture gap' between IT staff and the business which prevents this and which must be bridged before IT people can help the business improve its performance. This gap is recognized in many organizations: one indicator is that comments are heard beginning 'If only the users ...' and 'If only the computer people ...'

This article describes some of the root causes of the culture gap and the responses of DP organizations to the symptoms. It outlines an approach our company has developed and tested in a wide range of public and private sector organizations which has proved to bridge the gap in practice.

9.2 HOW DOES THE CULTURE GAP ARISE?

9.2.1 Ambiguity

Business is full of risk and uncertainty, especially with regard to information. Managers thus run business (according to Herzberg's observations of their behaviour) on a mixture of intuition and reason, often biased heavily towards intuition. An important consequence of this behaviour is that the business strategy of an organization – although 'real' to managers – is rarely expressed in a form which IT staff can make operational. Mission statements are often of symbolic rather than practical value: corporate plans indicate direction but at a level that leaves out specifics.

This attitude can be a frustrating experience for IT professionals, who are trained to build complex engines out of ones and zeros. They look for precision and completeness, where none exists and may never do so. When they ask questions in pursuit of clarity, it may look like criticism to managers who may resent it – especially if the questions are perceptive!

9.2.2 Tools

Who buys a TV on the basis of its circuit diagram? Yet that is exactly what is expected of a manager whose information system specification is presented via data flow diagrams. IT people are brought up in a technical culture focused on data, and their methods are data-driven. They have powerful but complex tools which have little connection to business concepts; they are designed for a different job. IT staff do not have appropriate tools for understanding the business, nor can they communicate their understanding in a way which managers recognize. This is a crucial source of uncertainty in managers' minds, and a prime factor in their lack of commitment to change.

9.2.3 Static Versus Dynamic Views

Data models of the world ignore the time dependency which is a crucial feature of managers' thinking. Managers are often more concerned with getting the sign right immediately when looking at a trend, than in having two decimal places of precision in six weeks' time. Risk and uncertainty are also absent from programs and data structures: they are farmed out to 'change control' processes. The languages that analyst and manager speak are different, and this can lead to mistrust.

9.2.4 The Role of DP Departments

The role of DP organizations also has an influence on the culture gap. Although they are now becoming more focused on their roles – even having business plans of their own – the DP department finds it difficult to shake off the notion that it is a kind of 'universal contractor'. All demands are accepted (delivery is another matter). This leaves IT staff in the role of 'order-takers' rather than playing a questioning and sceptical role to ensure systems have real value.

Instead, DP is rather like a pretentious restaurant with too long a menu. The systems analyst is the waiter who takes the order into the kitchen, and there is a long delay before the food arrives. What happens in the kitchen is secret ... this metaphor may be extended by the imaginative reader.

9.2.5 Management Support

A further factor operates to box IT staff in. Very often, because of 'order backlog', the role of management becomes that of 'production scheduler'. The pressures to respond to user demands mean that managing consists of resource allocation to projects. Support for new and different behaviour is not even considered: 'We've got our hands full here building systems'.

9.2.6 The Double Bind

These different ways of looking at their job cause managers' and analysts' expectations of each other to collide on assignments. Systems analysts can't (don't) question managers sceptically, because their training doesn't orient them that way, and anyway the managers may appear to expect them to take down lists of requirements. The managers, on the other hand, are in a position of not being allowed to be unsure; they can't 'not know'. These expectations create a situation where the systems analyst is asking 'What information do you want?' and thinking 'Why on earth don't they know what they want?' and the manager is saying 'Well I need this and that information' but thinking 'I thought these people were here to help me; don't they understand that I'm not sure what to do?'

Because of this role confusion, IT staff behave like plumbers when they need to be architects, and managers behave as if they had all the answers, when they don't even know all the questions. The risk of misunderstanding is high under these circumstances.

The results of these difficulties are plain enough. There is often only a tenuous connection between business and information systems strategy in many organizations, and few systems in place which effectively support the strategic intent. The technical culture and toolset used by IT staff does not create the needed understanding of the business, and there is recognition of the need for change in only a few companies (Haughton, 1991).

9.3 HOW DP DEPARTMENTS RESPOND

DP organizations have developed a number of responses to the problem of the culture gap; here is a sample.

End-user computing is of course a 'good thing' – but was often forced in by users irate at IT staff's lack of understanding of (or response to) their needs. **Devolution** gets IT people closer to users, who thus gained notional control of a resource. But has it solved the underlying problem of 'understanding the business'? Some DP departments have redefined their role more narrowly: **Carry on coding** is a common denial mechanism: 'If we work hard enough at building systems it will come out all right' – but where?

Facilities management can also be a good idea if you are sure you are not passing the buck, and you really understand users' requirements. Building a **network infrastructure** can be an exciting technical challenge, but such projects are often hard to justify in hard business terms. More often they are a tacit acknowledgement that the DP organization can understand users' needs in only the most general terms.

There are other responses too. **Prototyping** has a real place in the systems building process – at the design stage. Too often, however, it is used as a substitute for analysis. Screens are designed and the user invited to agree to them, without a clear understanding of the implications of acceptance.

All these responses have their place, and can materially help the DP department to contribute. But these are structural remedies: the limiting factor remains the culture gap. In order to ensure effective development and implementation of an information systems strategy, **the role and skills of the staff at the 'customer facing' end of DP organizations must alter materially.**

9.4 HOW TO BRIDGE THE GAP – THE NEW JOB

9.4.1 A Rough Definition

We believe that 'the new job' is a fundamental enlargement of the present systems' analyst role. Staff at the 'front end' of the DP cycle are more properly called 'business analysts', although this title scarcely reflects its whole character. We see them as having three key roles: they must learn about the business, they must manage the learning of others, and they must manage the whole process for useful results to time and budget.

This definition is much more of a communication and management task than the mainly analytic one hitherto assigned to such staff. This is because the role we see for business analysts is much more **support to management, rather than just reporting** to them. If 'the learning organization' is becoming the best model for survival, then it will be vital for managers to make use of the skills of these people.

So, what sort of skills? One response to the culture gap appears to be an IT person with a veneer of MBA on top (Palmer, 1990). While this may bring a much needed breadth to IT people, the risk is that they will acquire another jargon and set of techniques. We believe that they need much more fundamental development.

9.4.2 Not Experts: Just Fast Learners

In the first place, the business of learning is different. In the past, IT staff have been accustomed to building a model of 'what happens now' (an essentially descriptive process) and using this as a basis for change. Many methodologies indeed require a detailed phase, 'describe existing system', which can absorb considerable effort. While this might have been an acceptable way to work when systems were less central to business strategy, it is less obvious now. How, for example, is a 'greenfield' system designed?

With the percolation of information systems into the heart of decision-making areas of the firm, today's IT staff are being asked (sometimes rather indirectly) to help re-think the way in which the business is conducted. Describing what is there now is therefore not much use and 'automating a mess' happens too often with predictable lack of benefits.

IT staff therefore need skills not so much of description and observation, but of imagination and conceptualization, in order to invent new possibilities for the business. While this idea is often given lip service, in practice IT staff are often hemmed in by paper-heavy approaches. These are necessary for generating the enormous detail and consistency for designing and building a computer system, but are not appropriate for the early stages of an assignment.

We believe that the focus when learning should be on model building and testing. What could the organization look like in the future; would that be feasible and solve existing problems? The emphasis must be on robust models of the business, from which the information strategy and systems requirements – amongst other needs – are derived. Descriptive approaches will only show what information systems can be built for the organization now, and thus ignore business risks to IT investment.

Some IT staff can readily conceptualize and communicate; they are rare. We have therefore adapted and enlarged an approach – soft systems methodology – as the core of the learning task (see references). Having trained hundreds of internal support staff in the last six years, we are convinced by the results that the use of this tool radically improves the quality of the thinking on projects. Business analysts are forced into developing a perspective on what the business or its sub-units are trying to achieve, rather than looking at the existing organization. They are thus led to ask penetrating questions of the managers. We find that analysts with these systems thinking skills can provide insights that managers recognize and value.

This belief in the value of systems thinking is echoed elsewhere. A recent book (Senge, 1990) makes a telling case for the conceptual modelling skills that problem solvers – and indeed managers – of the future will need. The author argues that only systems thinking can deliver the understanding needed to solve contemporary management problems.

9.4.3 Communicating, Not Being Clever

'Solving a problem' is often the least of a business analyst's worries. Persuading all those involved to believe in – and commit to – a model of the way forward (as opposed to just signing the specification) is much harder. Successful assignments often require spending as much as 80% of the time and effort available on showing and testing ideas, and listening to others' contributions and criticisms. Communication of this sort requires lots of persistence and openness, and the ability to stop yourself – and others – leaping to instant solutions. Which systems analyst has not been called in to 'get me a computer to solve this problem'?

The ability to work with uncertainty (and to accept that the learning process requires it if all are to learn) is not found everywhere. Keats called this quality negative capability – 'the ability to be in doubt and uncertainty, without any irritable reaching after fact and reason.' Hard decisions must of course emerge, but the business analyst has to learn to suspend judgement as long as necessary, rather than ignoring aspects of the problem that are inconvenient.

9.4.4 Teams make a Difference

Teamwork is more vital than ever for several reasons. In the first place, the business models developed to solve the organization's problems cover all aspects of the work, and not just the information systems. They deal with staffing, skills, redundant or missing activities, structure and organization of the work and so on. A multi-discipline approach is essential to come up with the best overall solution, and a common model of the task is vital.

Change in a more integrated organization is also harder to accomplish. The impact over the whole organization must be considered and introduction must be synchronized carefully. In such situations, business analysts often meet active hostility and fear born of ignorance. At a personal level they need to know they are part of a team, not 'lone rangers'. A team is a more visible unit inside an organization and is a sign of change in itself.

It is therefore important to take a careful look at each individual's role and their needs for support. A better understanding of personal capabilities and areas for development helps others in the team to provide support when needed, while still ensuring results. Our team preparation and support activity is designed to create the trust within the team and momentum for action which overcomes organizational inertia and resolves fears about change.

The combination of these new emphases makes a considerable difference to managers' perceptions of what IT can offer. DP departments have long moaned that they are not taken seriously, but managers' reactions are human enough. They will commit fully to recommendations only if they believe they are worthwhile: analysts will gain legitimate influence only by demonstrating a deep understanding of the manager's business.

9.5 HOW TO DEVELOP THESE SKILLS

Cultures cannot be changed by edict: new behaviours must appear. When they are seen to be useful, the organization legitimates them and a new role is established.

The culture change for IT staff therefore involves an initiative by IT people, and training on its own will not change analysts' behaviour unless the system in which they work is changed. Working with managers of support services, we have developed a programme which offers a mixture of off-site preparation and continuing live project support to business analysts. Offsite preparation allows time not just for planning, but for reflection and team building, as well as identifying and learning about new techniques needed. The live support is organized around projects, as these can provide identifiable results, and the customers can evaluate the benefits of the new method of staff development.

The benefits our customers identify from this way of working are:

- Support on live projects ensures **learning from experience.** Since much of this way of working is different in its practice even if it serves the same objective, staff need to be able to try it out for real if they are to believe it is valuable. Judicious support on 'real' projects is effective in creating conviction about the 'new job' and the worth of the tools.
- **Skills are learned when needed,** not taught and forgotten. Much training investment is wasted by poor synchronization of theory and practice. By

focusing on individual needs for a specific project, skills taught are always relevant, and the ideas put to immediate test.

- Planned staff development creates **career commitment**. Too often, the role of internal consultant is seen as a provisional role. Yet mastering the skills outlined is an excellent preparation for management.
- External support to teams **reduces the fear of mistakes,** and provides some measure of 'objectivity' in the early stages until the independence of the staff is established.
- The approach provides both **business benefits and staff development** in one programme, with prejudice to results.

9.6 WHAT SORT OF PEOPLE?

The new skills needed are often hard to see immediately in the present IT community, but they can be grown. Some individuals will immediately take to the new tasks, because they have the right instincts. Others will have little taste for a world where personal risk-taking is essential, and where coping with uncertainty is an everyday requirement. Assessment and selection of suitable staff is therefore vital: we are presently developing psychometric tests for this purpose.

The new job clearly emphasizes 'people skills', including influencing and 'active listening', and the ability to handle resistance and deal with it constructively. Often the diplomatic side of an assignment is more challenging than the intellectual demands. A lively scepticism about managerial ideas is valuable, together with qualities of imagination and conceptualization.

We find in practice that basic qualities like persistence and an independent judgement prove more valuable than brains. Of course 'firepower' helps, but very clever people may ironically be disadvantaged, if they find it harder than others to recognize the primacy of results over analysis. Abandoning the safety of a technical expertise may also prove difficult for some, and those who rely too much on past experience may find it hard to keep learning to view new problems with fresh eyes.

This may sound like a recipe for a superperson, but there are many of them in disguise in IT organizations, not always in the expected places. One response is to recruit non-specialists from elsewhere in the organization. It is possible to make a strong case that junior management staff can acquire the IT-related analytic skills faster than the other way around. The only flaw in this argument is the low status of IT compared with management jobs: staff may be unwilling to transfer in unless this is a standard route to promotion.

This type of organizational difficulty illustrates the need for a great deal of support from managers. It is a risky business for individuals who have to take personal and career risks. A recent report on training needs (Palmer, 1990) also highlighted the managerial support needed for improved IT staff performance.

9.7 IMPLICATIONS FOR A 'STRATEGIC APPROACH'

It is our belief that IT staff can play an enormously enhanced role in the development of their organizations. However, this role will not be automatically assigned to them: it must be earned. To do this and 'bridge the culture gap', new behaviours are required of them, supported by their own managers who can see the value of the new role. This takes a certain amount of courage and a focused development programme. The notion recently advocated that this gap will be bridged by adding an MBA to IT skills does not hold in practice. Other skills are far more relevant, and they must be developed under fire, not on paper. Once business managers see the benefits, support will be forthcoming for the new role.

In the long term, these changes will materially alter the traditional role of the DP department. Developments of this sort will create a sharper division between the business-oriented and the technically-inclined careers in DP. The benefits that IT staff can offer will be clearer when they hide the technical complexity from managers and show an ability to engage with the uncertainties of business. The Business and Information Systems (not DP) Department of the future must acknowledge and respond to these challenges.

REFERENCES

Haughton, E, (1991) What's in Store for Sainsbury, in *Computer Weekly*, 13 June 1991.

Palmer, C, and Palmer, F, (1990) *From Potential to Reality, Hybrids – A Critical Force in the Application of Information Technology in the 1990s*. British Computer Society, London.

Senge, P, (1990) *The Fifth Discipline*, Doubleday/Currency, New York. ISBN 0-385-26094-6.

There is extensive literature pertaining to soft systems methodology, but very little of it is digestible. For an extended discussion of the intellectual roots of the approach, the reader is referred to :
Checkland, P B, (1976) *Systems Thinking, Systems Practice*, Wiley.

Other books showing a variety of approaches to problems using soft systems ideas include:
Wilson, B, (1984) *Systems: Concepts, Methodologies and Applications*, Wiley.
Checkland, P B, (1991) *Soft Systems in Practice*, Wiley, London.

In addition, the Open University in the UK has published a number of course booklets on soft systems. It forms the subject of several modules in the Technology BA course.

10 Strategy development and delivery: dealing with the IT evaluation question

L. Willcocks
City University Business School

'As far as I am concerned we could write off our IT expenditure over the last five years to the training budget.' (Senior executive, quoted by Earl, 1990)

'We are in the position where a $230 billion industry is being relegated to the status of the photocopier, that is to the status of overhead.' (Glen Peters, Price Waterhouse, 1991)

'... the area of measurement is the biggest single failure of Information systems while it is the single biggest issue in front of our board of directors. I am frustrated by our inability to measure cost and benefit.' (Head of IT: AT&T, quoted in Coleman and Jamieson, 1991)

10.1 INTRODUCTION

It is clear that, on any measure, Information Technology (IT) is big business in private and public sector organizations alike. By 1991, UK company expenditure on IT was exceeding £10 billion per year, equivalent to an average of over 1.2% of annual turnover. Public sector IT spend, excluding Ministry of Defence operational equipment, was over £2 billion per year, or 1% of total public expenditure. The size and continuing growth in IT investments, coupled with a recessionary climate and concerns over cost containment from early 1990, have served to place IT issues above the parapet in most organizations, perhaps irretrievably. Understandably, senior managers need to question the returns from such investments, and whether the IT route has been, and can be, a wise decision.

This is reinforced in those organizations where IT investment has been a high risk, hidden cost process, often producing disappointed expectations. This is a difficult area about which to generalize, but research studies suggest that at least 20% of expenditure is wasted and between 30-40% of IT projects realize no net benefits, however measured (see Willcocks and Lester, 1992 for a review of research). Even the more optimistic 1990 AT Kearney survey contained mixed messages. On the one hand, some 17% of new systems did not bring the advantages expected of them, leaving 83% of projects producing benefits as expected or better. On the other, only 11% of respondent organizations were successful IT users according to the relatively modest objective criteria established by AT Kearney.

The reasons for failure to deliver on IT potential can be complex. Technical, human resource, environmental, organizational and management issues interrelate where explanations are sought. However, major barriers, identified by a range of studies, occur in how the IT investment is evaluated and controlled. For example, Wilson (1991), looking at over 100 companies, found benefit measurement as the overall major barrier to the formulation and implementation of what he defined as Information systems strategy. AT Kearney (1990) found the major constraint on further investment in IT was benefit, followed by cost justification, credibility. These relate back, again, to problems of measurement and evaluation. This is supported by other commentators, who also point to indifferent IT evaluation practice as a major problem area (for example, Hochstrasser and Griffiths, 1991; Strassman, 1990; Willcocks and Lester, 1992).

This chapter focuses on improving IT evaluation practice. It will first highlight common problems encountered in appraising and monitoring the IT contribution to organizational performance. It will then detail approaches that can be utilized in the process of arriving at a strategy for IT-based applications. Research findings on evaluation practice at the critical feasibility stage will then be reviewed, and processes, methods and techniques for better practice developed. The importance of continuing the evaluation across subsequent stages and across the lifetime of IT-based systems will emerge as fundamental, but neglected. Above all, with IT development and usage – and evaluation practice itself – yet to be imbedded in the routine texture of how most organizations are managed, this chapter will stress the need for evaluation to be set up as a learning process – to build up experience and reduce risk on future IT investments.

10.2 EVALUATION: EMERGING PROBLEMS

It is useful to be clear what is meant by evaluation in the context of IT and organizations. Taking a management perspective, evaluation is about establishing by quantitative and/or qualitative means the worth of IT to the organization. Evaluation brings into play notions of costs, benefits, risk and value. It also implies an organizational process by which these factors are assessed, whether formally or informally.

There are major problems in evaluation. Many organizations find themselves in a Catch-22 situation. For competitive reasons they cannot afford not to invest in IT, but economically they cannot find sufficient justification, and evaluation practice cannot provide enough underpinning, for making the investment. One thing all informed commentators agree on: there are no reliable measures for assessing the impact of IT. At the same time, as will emerge below, there are a number of common problem areas that can be addressed. Some of these are indicated in Figure 10.1.

10.2.1 Inappropriate Measures

It is now widely accepted that certain measures do not assist the process of establishing how IT adds net value to an organization. Strassman (1990) establishes convincingly that size of IT spend bears no relationship to subsequent IT effectiveness. Relatedly, IT expenditure as a percentage of turnover, then compared to an industry average, or what a competitor is spending, will do little to focus investment on where IT adds value to the organization. Internal systems efficiency measures do not relate performance to added value for the organization. The more appropriate measures relate IT spend not to revenue but to profitability. However, even here the more traditional measures of profit, for example return on assets, return on sales, tend to penalize IT investments, particularly where the payoffs are likely to be long-term. Keen (1991) suggests that tracking IT progress over time is most meaningful in relation to organizational revenue or profit per employee. This is because IT rarely reduces cost; rather its main value more often is changing the cost structure of the organization so that it can increase sales or output without increasing personnel.

The IT impact may also be traced by establishing non-financial measures around key business processes where IT is now being heavily used, for example ratio of seats occupied to seats available in an airline. Given the unreliability of single measures it may be wise to use several. Butler Cox (1990) suggest that IT expenditure can be usefully controlled and evaluated if measured against revenue, IT spend per employee, business volume (measured non-financially), and key business process measures. Another area that can be usefully evaluated is levels of customer/user satisfaction with what is delivered.

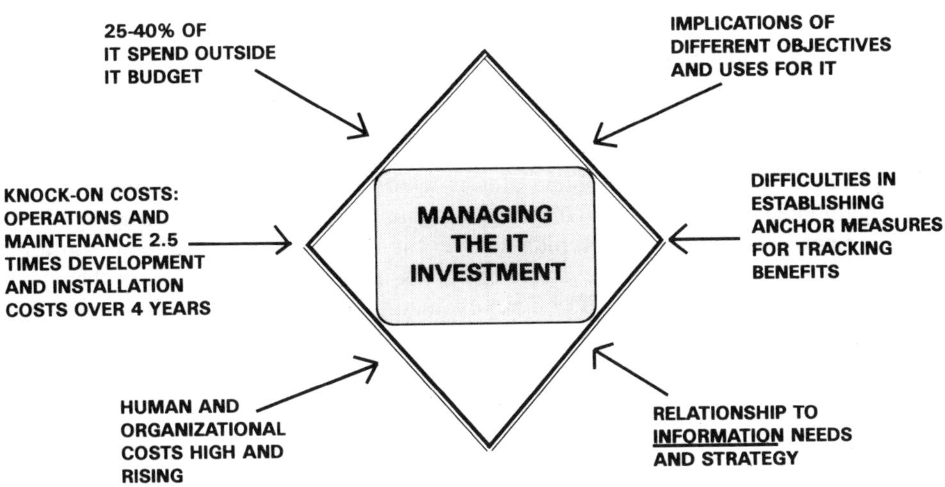

Figure 10.1. Evaluation of IT investments: emerging issues

10.2.2 Budgeting Practice Conceals Full Costs

Costs can be understated where size of IT budget – present and predicted – is used to evaluate an IT investment proposal. Recent studies show that up to 40% of relevant costs can be outside the traditional IT budget. In one large manufacturing company studied by the author, user department IT and training costs were in fact 29% of total costs but hidden in departmental, often non-IT related budgets. Clearly, the IT budget as a control mechanism may need to be reformulated to reflect full costs. IT costs are no longer equatable with the budget of the IT department.

10.2.3 Understating Human and Organizational Costs

As hardware and equipment costs get driven down, IT-related human and organizational costs are rising. Strassman (1990) estimated these to be as much again over the lifetime of a system. Hochstrasser (1990) suggests they can be as much as three to four times as high as hardware/equipment costs. Invariably, however, these costs are rarely fully budgeted for in IT investment proposals, and may partially explain the phenomenon of cost-creep that occurs over the course of most IT projects. In a retrospective analysis of an insurance company database application, the author and project manager analysed human and organizational costs three years after development began. These included such items as training, management and staff time, extra staff, staff turnover, losses in productivity and organizational restructuring during changeover. These were over two times equipment costs, and only 20% were included in the original feasibility assessment.

10.2.4 Understating Knock-on Costs

There may be political reasons for understating costs, the main one being to gain support for, and acceptance of the project from senior managers. Furthermore, in a recessionary climate, a concern for cost-justification, quick returns and, indeed, applying IT for cost reduction purposes would seem to be paramount, as the Price Waterhouse 1991/2 Review shows. This again can pressure proponents of IT into understating costs. A major problem area is where knock-on costs are understated. Thus maintenance costs may well be one to four times as much again as systems development costs, and are not avoidable over the lifetime of a system. An additional problem is incurred here. Development costs incur maintenance costs that then feed into the future IT budget. If you are evaluating IT by size of spend, the picture will be one of rising investment. However, this will conceal that most of the expenditure will be on existing systems; it will not be focused on future systems possibly critical to the organization's competitiveness or health.

10.2.5 Overstating Costs

Few projects come in within time and under budget. However, in two projects researched by the author, it was clear that the project managers overstated costs at the feasibility stage with the express purpose of making sure they could deliver systems within time and budget. In one case a £500,000 home help organizer system was delivered to a social services department within three years. In another, a CAD/CAM system was brought into a small manufacturing company within the £2.1 million budget, though two months outside deadline. In each case the project manager revealed political astuteness and gained a reputation for effectiveness.

10.2.6 Neglecting 'Intangible' Benefits

There is a whole raft of such benefits, some quite critical to operation and future competitiveness and direction, that are regularly omitted from feasibility proposals, often on the grounds that they cannot be financially quantified, are not cost justifiable, not certain and/or cannot produce obvious short-term paybacks.

To some extent this caution is understandable. Thus at Trustee Savings Bank the Banking Division contains some 1,600 branches. A very large six-year strategic network redesign project is under way to automate branch administration and sales support systems. According to its director, a rigorous business case had to demonstrate early payback; therefore the first two years focused on automation of administrative tasks. In fact subsequent phases produced major intangible benefits excluded from the original business case, notably increased office space worth £15 million, reduction in headcount, and redesigned branch layout to give 75% of the space to customers and new revenue-generating opportunities.

Nevertheless, failure to assess intangible benefits may well check potentially profitable proposals. Some, possibly the major, potential benefits from IT are not measurable using traditional financially-based evaluation techniques. These include: improved customer service, development of systems architecture, higher job satisfaction, higher product quality, improved internal/external communications and management information, gaining competitive advantage, cost avoidance, avoiding competitive disadvantage, improved supplier relationships. Techniques for their evaluation will be discussed below.

Another problem on assessing intangible benefits is where evaluation procedures lead to understating costs. A corollary is to be lazy on searching for benefits to match against those costs. Thus bad practice reinforces itself, and can lead to pursuing very limited objectives relative to what IT could do for the organization.

10.2.7 Not Fully Investigating Risk

There are two major areas of risk that are frequently downplayed in evaluating IT proposals. The first is the cost to the organization where implementation may be less than smooth, and where additional implementation time begins to add very large cost burdens. Thus in the £2 billion Department of Social Security operational strategy much of the speed in implementation between 1987-92 can be explained in terms of the otherwise inhibiting costs of delay. The risk of disruption to the organization and to customers, indeed loss of customers, may also not be fully assessed.

The second area involves the risk exposure of the organization in terms of security and what happens when, for example, a complex network management system is no longer functioning. A networked organization like a bank or an airline and its booking system needs very high reliability and back-up systems. When systems are not working, neither is the business. Managing such risk can incur substantial costs, and only some of the risk can be offset through insurance.

10.2.8 Failure to Devote Evaluation Time and Effort to a Major Capital Asset

Many organizations have a number of limitations in their IT evaluation practice. These will be detailed below. This remains surprising in the light of the substantial investment IT now represents in most organizations. Keen (1991) is useful here in suggesting the need to create an IT balance sheet. Senior management rarely know how much capital is tied up in IT resources. In one bank he investigated management were aware of the $200 million annual IT expenditure, and the $120 million value of centrally managed computers. However, when personal computers, departmental telecommunications, small items, and the cost of creating the software and data currently in use were added together, the bank possessed an IT asset worth $2 billion. Keen's point is a good one. Failure to appreciate the size of this investment leads to IT being undermanaged, a lack of serious attention given to IT investment evaluation and control, and also a lack of concern for discovering ways of utilizing this IT asset base to its full potential.

10.2.9 Failure to Take into Account Time-scale of Likely Benefits

The search for quick payoffs from IT is understandable. However, even fairly straightforward office systems automation, for example bringing in word processors, can have delayed cost savings. As a matter of experience the full impact of process innovation – aimed at efficiency and cost savings, that is doing existing things better – can take over two years to materialize, and would still to be difficult to isolate on traditional financial statements like cash flow and profit and loss statements.

As Keen (1991) suggests, we are still learning about the likely time-frame for assessing the impact of IT investments. In fact he suggests that infrastructure investments – for example those in telecommunications networks, shared database management resources, network management utilities – may be long-term, critical but difficult to evaluate. They need to be evaluated separately and funded by top or corporate divisional management as a long-range capital investment justified by corporate policy requirements.

The issue of time-scale of benefits is illustrated by the case of a US manufacturing company (Willcocks, 1989). Here, one casualty of erosion of market share was the IT budget. The plan to migrate existing applications to a common manufacturing, engineering and purchasing database was deferred. However, sales people were to get laptop computers because competitor salesforces were seen to make good use of these for rapid order entry. The problem rested in the evaluation approach adopted. Traditional cost-benefit analysis proved the need for a freeze on IT spending. Only when the long-term 1987-92 implications of IT spending on core activities were taken into account, did it emerge that without such expenditure the very survival of the firm was jeopardized. As Strassman (1990) establishes, there is no real way of knowing what IT can do for the business, and the risks of not using, as compared with using IT, always have to be significant factors in the subsequent investment appraisal. In the case in question the real way to evaluate IT plans was to establish the value-added by comparing the business plan with changes to IT costs over five years against the business plan without changes to IT costs.

As will emerge, this discussion of common problems is by no means exhaustive of the problems faced. Two more are signalled in Figure 10.1: those of failure to match techniques to type of IT projects, and the failure to relate IT needs to the information needs of the organization. Both these will be dealt with in more detail below. The latter relates to the broader issue of strategic alignment and in the next section.

10.3 STRATEGY AND STRATEGIC INFORMATION SYSTEMS

The organizational investment climate has a key bearing on how investment is organized and conducted, and what priorities are assigned to different IT investment proposals. According to Butler Cox (1990) the investment climate is affected by: the financial health and market position of the organization; industry sector pressures; the organizational business strategy and direction; and the management and decision-making culture. As an example of the second, 1989-90 research by Datasolve shows IT investment priorities in the retail sector focusing mainly on achieving more timely information, in financial services around better quality service to customers, and in manufacturing on more complete information for decision-making. As to decision-making culture, senior management attitude to risk can range from conservative to innovative, their decision-making styles from directive to consensus-driven. As one example conservative consensus-driven management would tend to take a relatively slow, incremental approach, with large-scale IT investments being unlikely. The third factor will be focused on here, that is creating a strategic climate in which IT investments can be related to organizational direction. Shaping the context in which IT evaluation is conducted is a necessary prelude to then applying appropriate evaluation techniques and approaches from those detailed later in this chapter.

Other contributors to this book have offered extensive discussion on formulating Information Technology/Systems strategy and the nature and importance of 'strategic Information systems'. They have also provided a number of relevant frameworks for IT/IT strategy analysis. Here we will focus on a few valuable pointers and approaches that work in practice to enable IT investment decisions that add value to the organization.

Firstly, to clarify the definitional minefield. Information Technology is taken to refer to the hardware, software and communications technologies – essentially equipment – and attendant techniques. Information Systems (IS) is a wider concept referring to how designed information flows attempt to meet the information needs of the organization. IS may be more, or less, IT-based. The process of managing the information needs of the organization is often referred to as Information Management (IM). IS strategy slightly amends the Earl (1988) definition: it is a long-term directional plan which decides what to do with IT and information. It is business/organizational led, demand-oriented and mainly concerned with exploiting IT either to support business strategies or create new strategic options. A strategic Information system is taken to be one on which the organization's survival, growth and future direction are critically dependent. A number of issues need to be addressed, and several frameworks can be adopted so as to establish a strategic climate for selecting appropriate IT investments, and establishing anchor measures and processes for subsequent on-going evaluation. These are addressed below.

10.3.1 Alignment

A fundamental starting-point is the need for alignment of business/organizational needs, what is done with IT, and plans for the human resources, organizational structures and processes. The highly publicized Landmark Study tends to conflate these into alignment of business, organization and IT strategies (Walton, 1989). A simpler approach is to suggest that the word 'strategy' should be used only when these different plans are aligned. There is much evidence to suggest that such alignment rarely exists. Thus in a study of 86 companies Ernst and Young (1990) found only two aligned. In detailed research Willcocks (1991a) has shown the lack of alignment to be a common problem in public sector informatization.

The case of an advertising agency researched by the author is instructive. In the mid-1980s this installed accounting and market forecasting systems at a cost of nearly £100,000. There was no real evaluation of the worth of the IT to the business. It was installed largely because one director had seen similar systems running at a competitor's premises. Its existing systems had been perfectly adequate and the market forecasting system ended up being used just to impress clients. At the same time as the system was being installed the agency sacked over 36 staff and asked its managers not to spend more than £200 a week on expenses. The company was taken over in 1986. Clearly there had been no integrated plan on the business, human resource, organizational and IT fronts. This passed on into its IT evaluation practice. In the end the IT amplifier effect may well have operated. IT was not used to address the core, or indeed any of the needs, of the business. A bad management was made correspondingly worse by the application of IT (Willcocks and Mason, 1992).

One result of such lack of alignment is that IT evaluation practice tends to become separated from business needs and plans on the one hand, and from organizational realities that can influence IT implementation and subsequent effectiveness on the other. Both need to be included in IT evaluation, and indeed are in the more comprehensive evaluation methods, notably the information economics approach (see below).

Another critical alignment is that between what is done with IT and how that fits with the information needs of the organization. Most management attention has tended to fall on the 'technology' rather than the 'information' element in what is called IT. Hochstrasser and Griffiths (1991) found in their sample no single company with a fully developed and comprehensive strategy on information. Yet it would seem to be difficult to perform a meaningful evaluation of IT investment without some corporate control framework establishing information requirements in relationship to business/organizational goals and purpose, prioritization of information needs, and, for example, how cross-corporate information flows need to be managed. An information strategy directs IT investment, and establishes policies and priorities against which investment can be assessed. It may also help to establish that some information needs can be met without the IT vehicle.

10.3.2 IT Strategic Grid

The McFarlan and McKenney grid is a much-travelled, but useful framework for focusing management attention on the IT evaluation question: where does and will IT give us added value? A variant is shown in Figure 10.2.

Used by the author with a group of senior managers in a pharmaceutical company, it was found that too much investment had been allowed on turnaround projects. In a period of downturn in business it was recognized that the investment in the previous three years should have been in strategic systems. It was resolved to tighten and refocus IT evaluation practice. In a highly decentralized multinational mainly in the printing/publishing industry, it was found that most of the twenty businesses were investing in factory and support systems. In a recessionary climate competitors were not forcing the issue on other types of system, the company was not strong on IT know-how, and it was decided that the risk-averse policy on IT evaluation, with strong emphasis on cost justification, should continue.

SYSTEMS APPLICATIONS MATRIX

STRATEGIC	TURNAROUND or HIGH POTENTIAL
* applications critical to sustaining future business strategy	* applications that may be important in achieving future success
* applications on which the organisation currently depends for success	* applications that are valuable but not critical to success
FACTORY or KEY OPERATIONAL	SUPPORT

Figure 10.2. Strategic grid: an analytical framework

The strategic grid is useful for classifying systems then demonstrating, through discussion, where IT investment has been made and where it should be applied. It can help to demonstrate that IT investments are not being made into core systems, or into business growth or competitiveness. It can also help to indicate that there is room for IT investment in more speculative ventures, given the spread of investment risk across different systems. It may also provoke management into spending more, or less, on IT. One frequent outcome is a demand to reassess which evaluation techniques are more appropriate to different types of system.

10.3.3 Value Chain

Porter and Millar (1985) have also been useful in establishing the need for value-chain analysis. This looks at where value is generated inside the organization, but also in its external relationships, for example with suppliers and customers. Thus the primary activities of a typical manufacturing company may be: inbound logistics, operations, outbound logistics, marketing and sales, and service. Support activities will be: firm infrastructure, human resource management, technology development and procurement. The question here is what can be done to add value within and across these activities? As every value activity has both a physical and an information-processing component, it is clear that the opportunities for value-added IT investment may well be considerable. Value-chain analysis helps to focus attention on where these will be.

10.3.4 IT Investment Mapping

Another method of relating IT investment to organizational/business needs has been developed by Peters (1988). The basic dimensions of the map are shown in Figure 10.3, and were arrived at after reviewing the main investment concerns arising on over 50 IT projects.

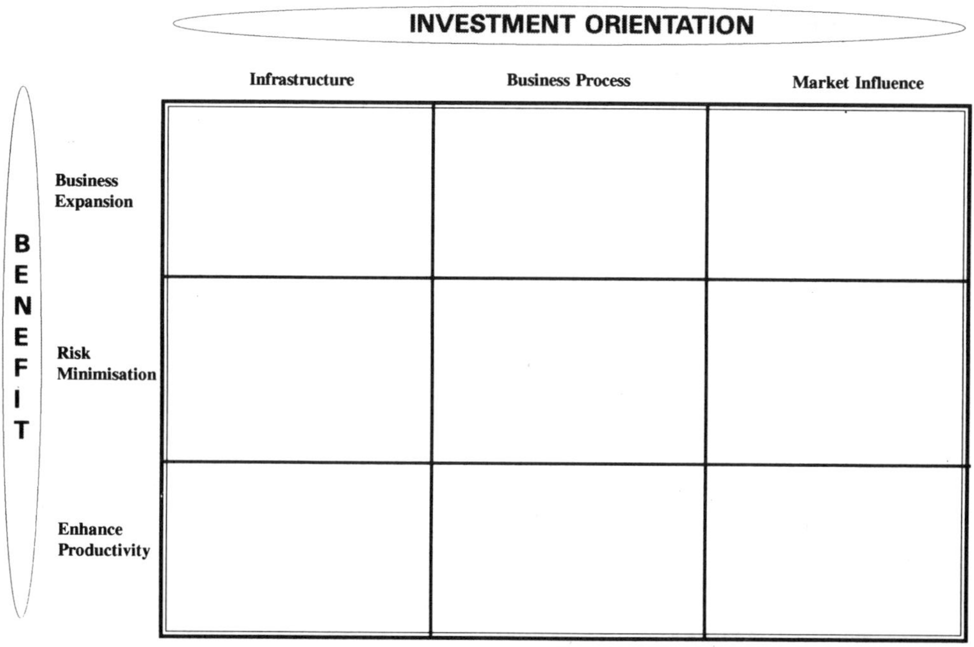

Figure 10.3. Mapping IT investments

The benefits to the organization appeared as one of the most frequent attributes of the IT investment. Thus one dimension of the map is benefits ranging from the more tangible arising from productivity-enhancing applications to the less tangible from business expansion applications. Peters also found that the orientation of the investment toward the business was also frequently used in evaluation. He classifies these as infrastructure, e.g telecommunications, software/hardware environment; business operations, e.g. finance and accounts, purchasing, processing orders; and market influencing, e.g.increasing repeat sales, improving distribution channels. Figure 10.4 shows the map being used in a hypothetical example to compare current and planned business strategy in terms of investment orientation and benefits required, against current and planned IT investment strategy.

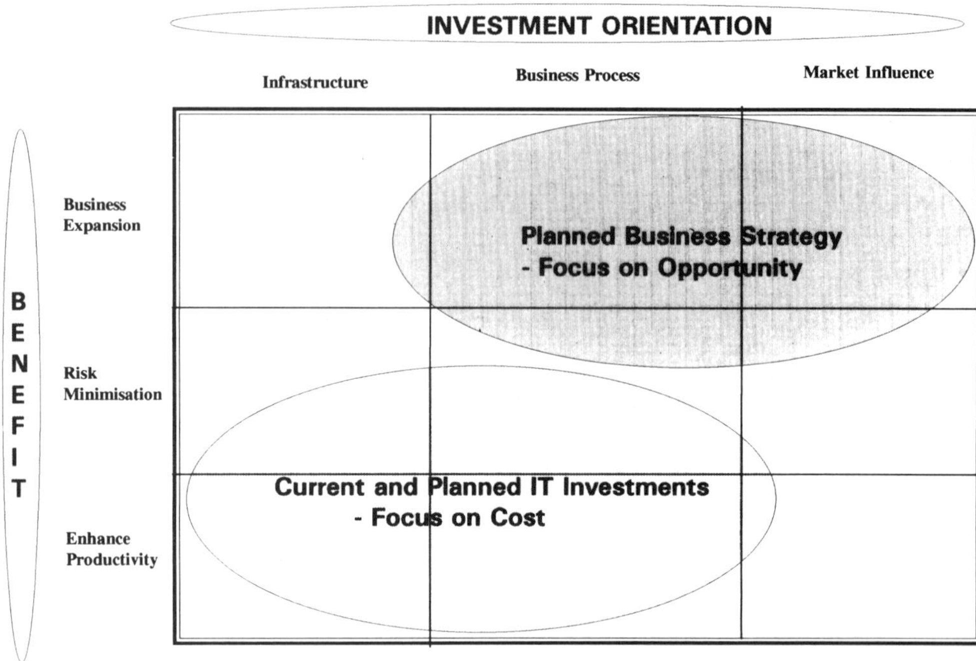

Figure 10.4. Comparing IT investment with business strategy

Mapping can reveal gaps and overlaps in these two areas and help senior management to get them more closely aligned. As a further example: 'a company with a clearly defined, product-differentiated strategy of innovation would do well to reconsider IT investments which appear to show undue bias towards a price-differentiated strategy of cost reduction and enhancing productivity.'

10.3.5 Multiple Methodology

Finally, Earl (1988) wisely opts for a multiple methodology approach to IS strategy formulation. This again helps us in the aim of relating IT investment more closely with the strategic aims and direction of the organization and its key needs. One element here is a top-down approach. Thus a Critical Success Factors (CSF s) analysis might be used to establish key business objectives, decompose these into critical success factors, then establish the IS needs that will drive these CSFs. A bottom-up evaluation would start with an evaluation of current systems. This may reveal gaps in the coverage by systems, for example in the marketing function or in terms of degree of integration of systems across functions. Evaluation may also find gaps in the technical quality of systems and in their business value. This permits decisions on renewing, removing, maintaining or enhancing current systems. The final plank of Earl's multiple methodology is 'inside-out innovation'. The purpose here is to 'identify opportunities afforded by IT which may yield competitive advantage or create new strategic options'. The purpose of the whole threefold methodology is, through an internal and external analysis of needs and opportunities, to relate the development of IS applications to business/organizational need and strategy.

10.4 EVALUATING FEASIBILITY: FINDINGS

The right 'strategic climate' is a vital prerequisite for evaluating IT projects at their feasibility stage. How this can be developed was discussed in the previous section. Here, we find out how organizations go about IT feasibility evaluation and what pointers for improved practice can be gained from the accumulated evidence. The picture is not an encouraging one. Organizations have found it increasingly difficult to justify the costs surrounding the purchase, development and use of IT (Hochstrasser and Griffiths, 1991; PA Consulting Group, 1990; Price Waterhouse, 1989). The value of IT/IS investments are more often justified by faith alone, or perhaps what adds up to the same thing, by understating costs and using mainly notional figures for benefit realization (Peat Marwick, 1989). A whole string of second-order costs are often missed out of the evaluation (Hochstrasser and Griffiths, 1991; National Audit Office, 1987, 1989). Hochstrasser and Griffiths found only 16% of their sample relying on rigorous methods to calculate the benefits of investment in IT. Over a quarter of managers did not know (presumably because it was not measured) whether or not IT was producing better or worse returns than other investments. In a survey of 90 managers, Vowler (1990) found 66% admitted their organizations were poor at measuring the IT contribution to the business. All this is put into sober perspective when set against the AT Kearney (1990) finding that successful users are twice as likely to set formal targets for return on investment, and to measure the performance of new IT systems against them, than unsuccessful users.

Willcocks and Lester (1991) looked at 50 organizations drawn from a cross-section of private and public sector manufacturing and services. We found all organizations completing evaluation at the feasibility stage, though there was a fall-off in the extent to which evaluation was carried out at later stages. This means that considerable weight falls on getting the feasibility evaluation right. Some 14% were 'very satisfied' (the results from the evaluation reach a high standard), and 72% 'satisfied' (the organization can use the results with a degree of satisfaction and reliability though improvements would be welcomed) with the evaluation methods and process. However, these perceptions need to be qualified by the fact that only 8% of organizations measured the impact of the evaluation; that is, could tell us whether the IT investment subsequently achieved a higher or lower return than other non-IT investments. Additionally there emerged a range of inadequacies in evaluation practice at the feasibility stage of projects. The most common are shown in Figure 10.5.

Organization revealed a variety of practice on evaluation at the feasibility stage of projects. Their experience suggests the need for flexible, regularly reviewed approaches to evaluating intended IT investments. This arises from each organization having its own IS objectives and strategies, which themselves may change over time. Most organizations surveyed used cost/benefit at the core of their evaluation, often of a traditional type. However, it does not follow that this is the most appropriate, or a sufficient, way to evaluate IT projects.

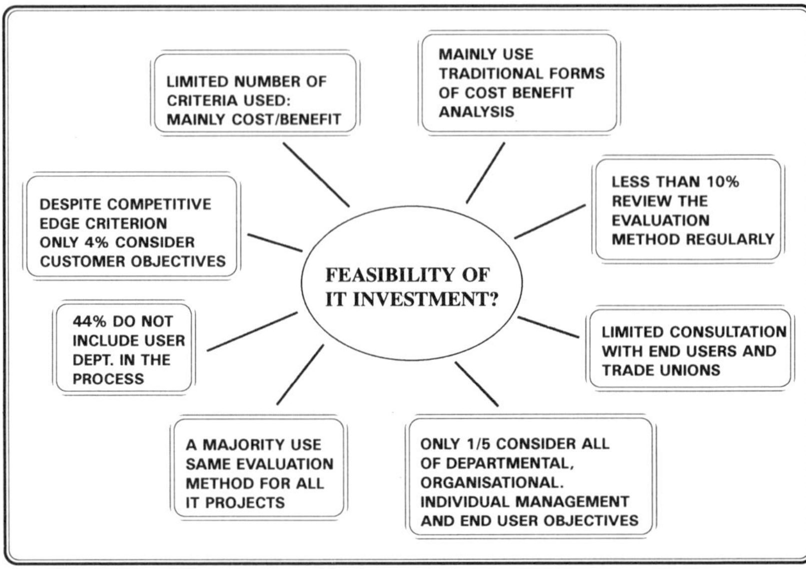

Figure 10.5. IT investments: evaluation at the feasibility stage

The literature shows that the cost/benefit analysis used by organizations is outdated and fails to assess the real worth of IT. Cane (1987) found that organizations had not changed their analysis techniques even though their systems were becoming more sophisticated. Goodwin (1984) shows that if quality is not assessed, projects which could give a better product or competitive advantage are likely to be passed over. The case for enhanced cost/benefit analysis is regularly made. Malitoris (1990) is typical in suggesting that measurement techniques must match the task. Where efficiency and effectiveness objectives are pursued with IT, these are more easily measured using financial appraisal methods, but the rigour applied will vary with the likely size of perceived net benefit. Where inputs and benefits are increasingly intangible but sizeable, as is common when pursuing innovation and competitiveness objectives, then the information economics approach of Parker, Benson and Trainor (1988) becomes more appropriate. These approaches will receive attention in the next section.

However, our sample evidence and interviews indicate that few organizations adopt these techniques, or a planned, contingency approach in practice. Senior managers increasingly talk of, and are urged toward, the strategic use of IT. This means doing new things, gaining a competitive edge, and becoming more effective, rather than using IT merely to automate routine operations, do existing things better, and perhaps reduce the headcount. However, only 16% of organizations use over four criteria on which to base their evaluation; 62% use cost/benefit as their predominant criterion in the evaluation process. The survey evidence here suggests that organization may be missing IS opportunities, but also taking on large risks, through utilizing narrow evaluation approaches that do not clarify and assess less tangible inputs and benefits. There is also little evidence of a concern for assessing risk in any formal manner. However, the need to see and evaluate risks and 'soft' hidden costs would seem to be essential, given the history of IT investment as a 'high risk, hidden cost' process.

Further findings indicate room for improved practice. A sizeable minority of organizations (44%) do not include the user department in the evaluation process at the feasibility stage. This cuts off a vital source of information and critique on the degree to which an IT proposal is organizationally feasible and will deliver on user requirements. Only a small minority of organizations accept IT proposals from a wide variety of groups and individuals. In this respect most ignore the third element in Earl's multiple methodology (see above). Despite the large literature emphasizing consultation with the workforce as a source of ideas, know-how and as part of the process of reducing resistance to change, only 36% of organizations consult users about evaluation at the feasibility stage, while only 18% consult unions. While the majority of organizations (80%) evaluate IT investments against organizational objectives, only 22% act strategically in considering objectives from the bottom to the top, that is evaluating the value of IT projects against all of organization, departmental individual management, and end-user objectives. This again could have consequences for the effectiveness and usability of the resulting systems, and the levels of resistance experienced. In one case cited by Hochstrasser and Griffiths (1991) IT professionals installed an integrated OA system with over one hundred functions. Later evaluation found users accessing only up to twelve of these. Clearly earlier evaluation embracing user needs would have stemmed the cost of this overfunctionality. Finally, most organizations endorsed the need to assess the competitive edge implied by an IT project. However, somewhat inconsistently, only 4% considered customer objectives in the evaluation process at the feasibility stage. This finding is interesting in relationship to our analysis that the majority of IT investment in the respondent organizations were directed at achieving internal efficiencies. It may well be, as the Hochstrasser and Griffiths (1991) survey evidence also suggests, that the nature of the evaluation techniques, but also from our own study the evaluation process adopted, had influential roles to play in this outcome.

It is useful at this stage to consider the more traditional and widely used techniques for feasibility evaluation. We encountered many of these in the respondent organizations. Here, a variety of methodologies were used, with 46% using their own methodologies, which, incidentally, seemed no more likely to produce better results than more standardized approaches. A common element, however, could be characterized as cost-benefit assessment described in monetary terms, allied with managerial judgement. The more traditional methods of relating benefits to the costs of obtaining them are discussed by Coleman and Jamieson (1991); Earl (1988); and Parker et al. (1988). They include:

Return on Investment (ROI)
This is the ratio of the average annual net income of the project divided by internal investment in the project. Widely used as a 'hurdle rate' against which the merits of different projects are assessed. Dangers occur where the method is not allied to discounting cash flow; for example, failure to account for variations in timing and risk.

Discounted Cash Flow/Internal Rate of Return
The most widely used in our sample. This establishes the discount rate at which the present value of cash receipts equals the present value of cash expenditures. Coleman and Jamieson (1991) note that it finds favour because of its relative simplicity but fails to take account of the relative scale of projects and the time loading mentioned in the Net Present Value method.

Net Present Value (NPV) and Profitability Index (PI)
Both are discounting techniques taking cash flows back to their value at the commencement of the project. Much depends on the discount rate adopted. If used alone, normally the project with the highest NPV will be adopted. PI is less used for IT projects. PI involves dividing estimated cash flows by the initial capital investment, but, as discussed above, IT projects rarely incur most costs at their beginning.

Payback Period
A method frequently used in respondent organizations because it determines the amount of time required for the cumulative cash inflow to equal the initial investment. Managers find attractive the question: how long will the project take to pay for itself? However, Parker et al. (1988) note technical deficiencies with this method.

Present Worth
This assumes that the finding acquired to support a cost-justified project is borrowed or acquired through the sale of stock. Simple ROI calculations are extended by discounting future cash flow on the basis of the cost of acquiring funds.

There are more sophisticated methods for developing a cost-benefit analysis. These include probability of attainment, decision models, break-even analysis, structural models and the hedonic wage model (Sassone, 1988). A number of composite methods have also been developed. All methods need to be used with some care.

(a) In themselves they largely exclude the significant problem of risk. Coleman and Jamieson (1991) convincingly make the case for more widespread use of risk analysis, based round formal techniques like measures of variance, sensitivity analysis and simulation/modelling techniques.

(b) Based on monetary value they can exclude costs and benefits that may be difficult to quantify but could be critical to the evaluation. For example, some of the best returns may well be from IT projects that deliver competitive advantage, improved customer service, higher product quality, innovation, more timely information. One manufacturing company installed a flexible manufacturing system costing $18 million. The project's return would only be 10% per annum, even taking into account significant labour savings over a 20-year period. The project would be appraised as unprofitable against typical hurdle rates of 15% expectations of payback within five years. However, it offered significant productivity and performance benefits, as well as flexibility. Kaplan (1986) makes the point that the major benefits from computer-integrated manufacturing – such as quality, flexibility, responsiveness, functional integration – fall very much in the intangible class.

(c) Arising from (a) and (b) it is clear that discount rates may be difficult to arrive at for IT projects. Also hurdle rates set for non-IT capital investment may need to be lowered for IT with the capability of impacting on competitive advantage, creating new businesses or that represents significant innovation with unclear payoffs. This applies especially to application projects like CIM, electronic mail networks, and to infrastructure investment. These will tend to have a longer useful life than non-IT projects and deserve different treatment in feasibility evaluation. Unfortunately ROI-type measures can create minimum hurdle rates that shield managers from understanding the differences between IT projects, and between IT and non-IT projects.

(d) In his case study work Norton (1986) usefully concludes that, in respect of IT, CBA and ROI approaches are microeconomic, encouraging low-risk investments with small returns; are the result of a manufacturing economy that treats labour as an expense; and the analysis tends to be static and short term.

10.5 LINKING STRATEGY AND FEASIBILITY TECHNIQUES

Much work has been done to break free from the limitations of the more traditional forms of capital investment appraisal detailed in the previous section. The major concerns seem to be to relate evaluation techniques to the type of IT project, and to develop techniques that relate the IT investment to business/organization value. A further development is in more sophisticated ways of including risk assessment in the evaluation procedures for IT investment. A method of evaluation needs to be reliable, that is consistent in its measurement over time, able to discriminate between good and indifferent investments, able to measure what it purports to measure, and be administratively/organizationally feasible in its application.

10.5.1 Return on Management and SESAME

Strassman (1990) has done much iconoclastic work in the attempt to modernize IT investment evaluation. He concludes that:

> Many methods for giving advice about computers have one thing in common. They serve as a vehicle to facilitate proposals for additional funding ... the current techniques ultimately reflect their origins in a technology push from the experts, vendors, consultants, instead of a 'strategy' pull from the profit centre managers.

He has produced the very interesting concept of return on management (ROM). This receives a detailed description and critical assessment elsewhere (see Willcocks and Lester, 1992). ROM is a measure of performance based on the added value to an organization provided by management. Strassman's assumption here is that in the modern organization, information costs are the costs of managing the enterprise. If ROM is calculated before then after IT is applied to an organization then the IT contribution to the business, so difficult to isolate using more traditional measures, can be assessed. ROM is calculated in several stages. Firstly, using the organization's financial results, the total value-added is established. This is the difference between net revenues and payments to external suppliers. The contribution of capital is then separated from that of labour. Operating costs are then deducted from labour value-added to leave management value-added. ROM is management value-added divided by the costs of management. There are some problems with how this figure is arrived at, and whether it really represents what IT has contributed to business performance. For example, there are difficulties in distinguishing between operational and management information. Perhaps ROM is merely a measure in some cases, and a fairly indirect one, of how effectively management information is used. A more serious criticism lies with the usability of the approach and its attractiveness to practising managers. This may be reflected in its lack of use, at least in the UK, as identified in different surveys (Butler Cox, 1990; Coleman and Jamieson, 1991; Willcocks and Lester, 1991).

IBM have developed SESAME to provide a more flexible approach to cost/benefit analysis. This method has the merit of basing much of the assessment on user opinion. A limitation is that it seeks to compare the cost/benefits of an IT system with those of performing the tasks manually. This may be a cumbersome, and less than meaningful comparison to make in many already computerized operations. However, the IT projects to which it has been applied reveal generally good results (Lincoln and Shorrock, 1990).

10.5.2 Matching Objectives, Projects and Techniques

A major way forward on IT evaluation is to match techniques to objectives and types of projects. A starting-point is to allow business strategy and purpose to define the category of IT investment. Butler Cox (1990) suggest five main purposes:

(1) surviving and functioning as a business;
(2) improving business performance by cost reduction/increasing sales;
(3) achieving a competitive leap;

(4) enabling the benefits of other IT investments to be realized;
(5) being prepared to compete effectively in the future.

The matching IT investments can then be categorized, respectively, as:

(1) Mandatory investments, for example accounting systems to permit reporting within the organization; regulatory requirements demanding VAT recording systems; competitive pressure making a system obligatory, e.g. EPOS amongst large retail outlets.

(2) Investments to improve performance, for example Allied Dunbar and several UK insurance companies have introduced laptop computers for sales people, partly with the aim of increasing sales.

(3) Competitive edge investments, for example SABRE at American Airlines and Merrill Lynch's Cash Management Account system in the mid-1980s.

(4) Infrastructure investments. These are important to make because they give organizations several more degrees of freedom maneouvrability in the future.

(5) Research investments. In our sample we found a bank and three companies in the computer industry waiving normal capital investment criteria on some IT projects, citing their research and learning value. The amounts were small and referred to CASE tools in one case, and expert systems in the others.

Hochstrasser (1990) provides additional detail when suggesting that different business purposes will produce a classification of eight types of project. These are infrastructure (as above); cost replacement (e.g. automating manual activities); economy of scale (e.g. EDI allows increased volume of data); economy of scope (e.g. a relational database performing an extended range of tasks); customer support; quality support; information sharing and manipulation (e.g. DSS and MIS); and new technology (e.g. smart cards and home banking have been late 1980s innovations in some organizations). There seems to be no shortage of such classifications now available (for a review see Willcocks, 1990). One of the more simple but useful is the sixfold classification shown in Figure 10.6.

Once assessed against, and accepted as aligned with required business purpose, a specific IT investment can be classified, then fitted on to the cost-benefit map (Figure 10.6 is meant to be suggestive only). This will assist in identifying where the evaluation emphasis should fall. For example, an 'efficiency' project could be adequately assessed utilizing traditional financial investment appraisal approaches; a different emphasis will be required in the method chosen to assess a 'competitive edge' project. Figure 10.7 is one view (with no great claims of accuracy) of the possible spread of appropriateness of some of the evaluation methods now available.

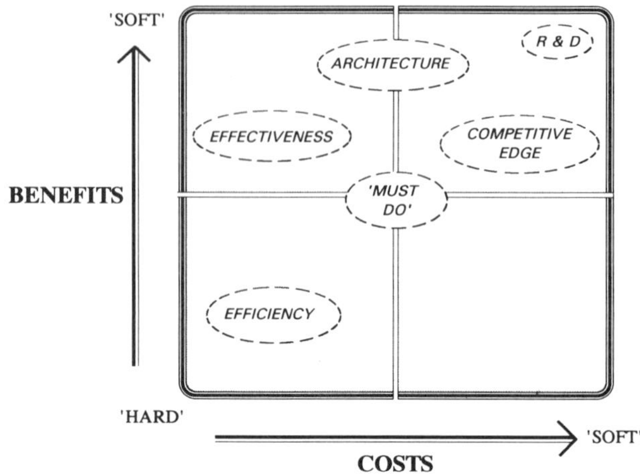

Figure 10.6. A classification of types of IT project

Another, complementary-way of looking at evaluation methods is suggested by Silk (1990). For him, quantifying the benefits of IT/IS is the core problem in justifying IT investment. At the root of the evaluation methods available he finds seven types of benefit justification. In fact the first type involves little formal justification at all – that is, in the case of a 'must-do' project. An example is a clothing manufacturer required by British Home Stores to adopt Electronic Data Interchange as a condition of business. But should such investments be made at minimum cost with no benefit assessment? An assessment may be useful to see if additional benefits can be gained from higher investment.

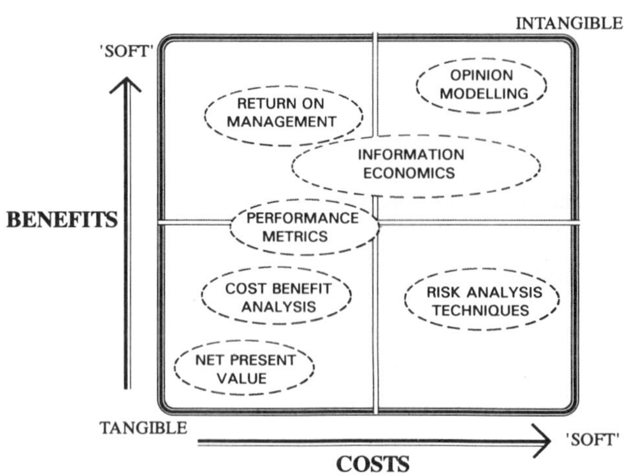

Figure 10.7. IT evaluation techniques: discovering appropriateness

Thereafter the modes of justification range from soft and subjective to hard and more objective depending upon the generic benefit expected, that is competitive edge, effectiveness or efficiency. As an act-of-faith justification, Silk cites setting up a customer-operated information service in a food supermarket. Benefits might include better company image, higher turnover, need for new products identified, better understanding of customers. The decision might be based merely on senior management judgement or 'hunch'. A logic justification would sharpen the business case by arguing how and why these benefits would materialize. A direction justification would specify observable measures, e.g. more purchases, more shoppers. A size justification would give a quantitative estimate of these changes. A value justification would weigh the relative merits of different benefits – e.g., are more shoppers desirable even if each buys less. A money justification would seek to express such benefits in terms of profit and/or revenue. Of course, in the case cited it might not be possible to apply all these justifications in an informed and useful manner. The point is to apply a mode of justification where it can contribute to sharpening the business case for a particular IT investment.

10.5.3 From Cost-benefit to Value

A particularly ambitious attempt to deal with many of the problems in IT evaluation – both at the level of methodology and of process – is represented in the information economics approach (Parker, Benson and Trainor, 1988). They build on the critique of traditional approaches. Costs have been taken from the IT department who often use chargeback systems, or taken from departmental costings. Benefits are seen differently according to the department carrying out the calculation. Monetary gains may, or may not be, easy to evaluate, but matters like staff satisfaction, competitive advantage are not. One way round this, of course, is to leave them out. At worst traditional modes of analysis ignore IT as an organizational asset, and all that entails. Another problem occurs. Too frequently a Gresham law applies: technology management problems drive out business perspective and awareness. Furthermore, justification processes often fail to take account, or are unable to quantify new risks associated with IT. Information economics emphasizes the necessity of dealing with these problems on the way to defining the value of information to an organization.

Parker et al. look beyond benefit to value. Benefit is a 'discrete economic effect'. Value is seen as a broader concept based on the effect IT investment has on the business performance of the enterprise. How value is arrived at is shown in Figure 10.8. The first stage is building on traditional cost-benefit analysis with four highly relevant techniques to establish an enhanced return-on-investment calculation. These are:

(a) Value linking. This assesses IT costs which create additional benefits to other departments through ripple, knock-on effects.

(b) Value acceleration. This assesses additional benefits in the form of reduced timescales for operations.

(c) Value restructuring. Techniques are here used to measure the benefit of restructuring a department, jobs or personnel usage as a result of introducing IT. This technique is particularly helpful where the relationship to performance is obscure or not established. R&D, legal and personnel are examples of departments where this may be usefully applied.

(d) Innovation valuation. This considers the value of gaining and sustaining a competitive advantage, whilst calculating the risks or cost of being a pioneer and of the project failing.

Information economics then enhances the cost-benefit analysis still further through business domain and technology domain assessments. Thus on the benefits/value side, Parker et al.'s valuable suggestions may be summarized as expansion to include six classes (see Figure 10.8).

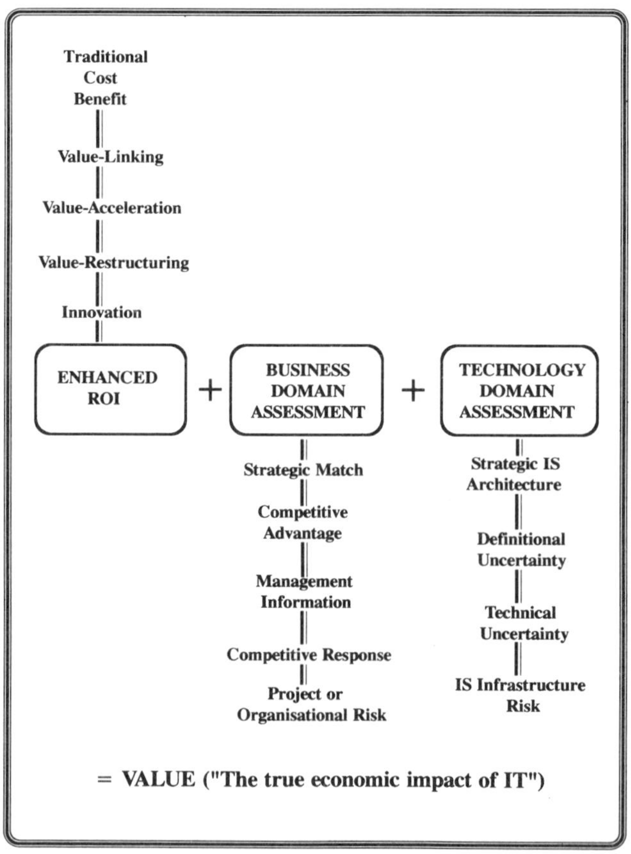

Figure 10.8. The information economics approach

These involve the enhanced view of ROI established above; strategic match, that is assessing the degree to which the proposed project corresponds to established corporate goals; competitive advantage, that is assessing the degree to which the proposed project provides an advantage in the market place; management information – assessing the contribution toward management need for information on core activities; competitive response – assessing the degree of corporate risk associated with not undertaking the project; and strategic IS architecture – measuring the degree to which the proposed project fits into the overall information systems direction. As an example of what happens when such factors and business domain assessment are neglected in the evaluation, Parker et al. point to the case of a large US truck-leasing company. Here they found that on a 'hard' ROI analysis IT projects on preventative maintenance, route scheduling and despatching went top of the list. When a business domain assessment was carried out by line managers, customer/sales profile system was evaluated as having the largest potential effect on business performance. An important infrastructure project – a Database 2 conversion/installation – also scored highly where previously it was scored bottom of eight project options. Clearly the evaluation technique and process can have a significant business impact where economic resources are finite and prioritization and drop decisions become inevitable.

Except for strategic IS architecture, all the above form part of the business domain assessment. When the cost/risk side of traditional analyses is expanded, the Business Domain is also required to assess organizational risk, that is looking at how equipped the organization is to implement the project in terms of personnel, skills and experience. A technology domain assessment will then embrace three additional classes of risk and uncertainty. IS infrastructure risk measures the degree to which the entire IS organization needs, and is prepared to support, the project. Definitional uncertainty assesses the degree to which the requirements and/or specifications on the project are known. Incidentally, research into more than 130 UK organizations shows this to be a primary barrier to the effective delivery of IT (Willcocks, 1991b). Also assessed are the complexity of the area and the probability of non-routine changes. Technical uncertainty evaluates a project's dependence on new or untried technologies.

Parker et al. have provided an impressive array of concepts and techniques for assessing the business value of proposed IT invesments. Their concern for fitting IT evaluation into a corporate planning process, and for bringing both business managers and IS professionals into the assessment process is also very welcome. Some of the critics of information economics suggest that it may be over-mechanistic if applied to all projects; it can be time-consuming, may lack credibility with senior management, particularly given the subjective basis of much of the scoring. The latter problem is also inherent in the process of arriving at the weighting of the importance to assign to the different factors before scoring begins. Additionally there are statistical problems with the suggested scoring methods. For example a scoring range of 1-5 may do little to differentiate between the ROI of two different projects. Moreover, even if a project scores nil on one risk, e.g. organizational risk, and in practice this risk may sink the project, the overall assessment by information economics may cancel out the impact of this score and show the IT investment to be a reasonable one. Clearly much depends on careful interpretation of the results, and much of the value for decision-makers and stakeholders may well come from the raised awareness of issues from undergoing the process of evaluation rather than from its statistical outcome. Another problem area may lie in the truncated assessment of organizational risk. Here, for example, there is no explicit assessment of the likelihood of a project to engender resistance to change because of, say, its job reduction or work-restructuring implications. This may be compounded by the focus on bringing user managers, but one suspects not lower-level users, into the assessment process.

Much of the criticism, however, ignores how adaptable the basic information economics framework can be to particular organizational circumstances and needs. Certainly this has been a finding in trials in organizations as varied as British Airports Authority, a Central Government department, and a major food retailer. In the latter case, a 1991 study at City University Business School investigated a three-phase branch stock management system. Some of the findings are instructive. Managers suggested including the measurement of risk associated with interfacing systems and the difficulties in gaining user acceptance of the project. In practice few of the managers could calculate the enhanced ROI because of the large amount of data required and, in a large organization, its spread across different locations. Some felt the evaluation was time-dependent; different results could be expected at different times. The assessment of risk needed to be expanded to include not only technical and project risk but also the risk/impact of failure to an organization of its size. In its highly competitive industry any unfavourable venture can have serious knock-on impacts and most firms tend to be risk-conscious, even risk-averse. Such findings tend to reinforce the view that information economics provides one of the more comprehensive approaches to assessing the potential value to the organization of its IT investments, but that it needs to be tailored, developed, in some cases extended, to meet evaluation needs in different organizations. Even so, information economics remains a major contribution to advancing modern evaluation practice.

10.6 CODA: FROM DEVELOPMENT TO ROUTINE OPERATIONS

This chapter has focused primarily on the front-end of evaluation practice, and how it can be improved. However, we know too little about IT, how it can be managed, its impacts, and the evaluation techniques at our disposal are too undeveloped for evaluation to be conceived as anything other than a learning process. In our own research on evaluation beyond the feasibility stage of projects, we have found evaluation variously carried on through four main additional stages. Respondent organizations supported the notion of the evaluation learning cycle, with evaluation at each stage feeding into the next to establish a learning spiral across time - useful for controlling a specific project, but also for building organizational know-how on IT and its management (see Figure 10.9). The full research findings are detailed elsewhere (see Willcocks and Lester, 1992). However, some of the limitations in evaluation techniques and process discovered are worth commenting on here.

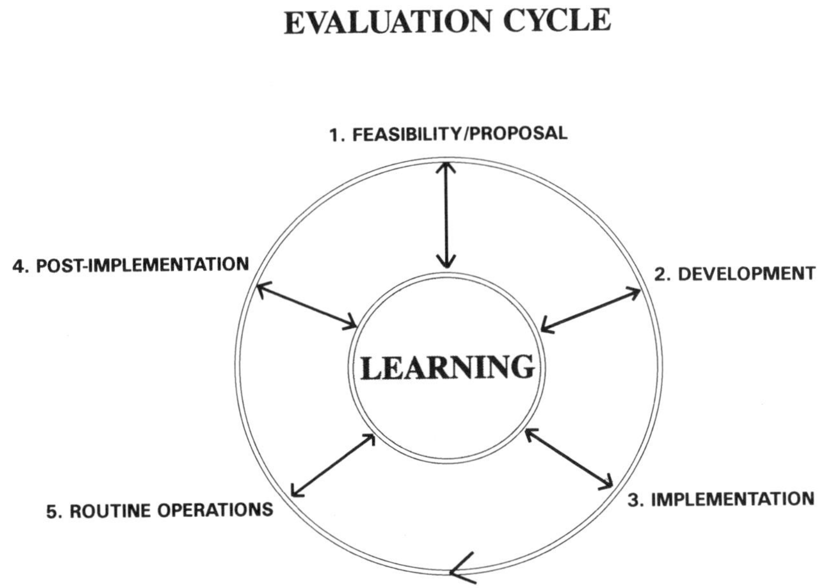

Figure 10.9. IT evaluation as a learning process

We found only weak linkage between evaluations carried out at different stages. As one example 80% of organizations had experienced abandoning projects at the development stage due to negative evaluation The major reasons given were changing organizational or user needs and/or 'gone over budget'. When we reassembled the data, abandonment clearly related to underplaying these objectives at the feasibility stage. Furthermore, all organizations abandoning projects because 'over budget' depended heavily on cost-benefit in their earlier feasibility evaluation, thus probably understating development and second-order costs. We found only weak evidence of organizations applying their development stage evaluation, and indeed their experiences at subsequent stages, to improving feasibility evaluation techniques and processes.

Key stakeholders were often excluded from the evaluation process. For example, only 9% of organizations included the user departments/users in development evaluation. At the implementation stage 31% do not include user departments, 52% exclude the IT department, and only 6% consult trade unions. There seemed to be a marked fall-off in attention given to, and the results of, evaluation across later stages. Thus 20% do not carry out evaluation at the post-implementation stage, some claiming there was little point in doing so. Of the 56% who learn from their mistakes at this stage, 25% do so from 'informal evaluation'. At the routine operations stage, only 20% use in their evaluation criteria all of systems capability, systems availability, organizational needs and departmental needs.

These, together with our detailed findings, suggest a number of guidelines on how evaluation practice can be improved beyond the feasibility stage. At a minimum these include linking evaluation across stages and time. This enables 'islands of evaluation' to become integrated and mutually informative, while building into the overall evaluation process possibilities for continuous improvement. Many organizations can usefully reconsider the degree to which key stakeholders are participants in evaluation at all stages. The relative neglect given to assessing the actual against the posited impact of IT, and the fall-off in interest in evaluation at later stages, mean that the effectiveness of feasibility evaluation becomes difficult to assess and difficult to improve. The concept of learning would seem central to evaluation practice but tends to be applied in a fragmented way. Moreover, the increasing clamour for adequate evaluation techniques is necessary, but may reveal a 'quick-fix' orientation to the problem. Moreover, it can shift attention from what may be a more difficult, but in the long term more value-added area, which is getting the process right.

10.7 CONCLUSION

The high expenditure on IT, growing usage that goes to the core of organizational functioning, together with disappointed expectations about its impact have all served to raise the profile of how IT investment can be evaluated. From the arguments and evidence in this chapter it is not only an under-developed, but also an under-managed area which organizations can increasingly ill-afford to neglect. There are well-established traps that can now be avoided. Organizations need to shape the context in which effective evaluation practice can be conducted. Traditional techniques cannot be relied upon in themselves to assess the types of technologies and how they are increasingly being applied in organizational settings. A range of modern techniques can be tailored and applied. However, techniques can only complement, not substitute for developing evaluation as a process, and the deeper organizational learning about IT that entails. Past evaluation practice has been geared to asking questions about the price of IT. Increasingly it produces less than useful answers. The future challenge is to move to the problem of value of IT to the organization, and build techniques and processes that can go some way to answering the resulting questions.

REFERENCES

Butler Cox Foundation (1990) *Getting Value from Information Technology*. Research Report 75, June. Butler Cox: London.

Cane, A (1987) Cost Monitoring Omitted in Plans for Technology. *Financial Times*, 30 November.

Coleman, T and Jamieson, M (1991) Information Systems: Evaluating Intangible Benefits at the Feasibility Stage of Project Appraisal. Unpublished MBA thesis, City

University Business School: London.

Earl, M (1988) *Management Strategies for Information Technology*. Prentice-Hall: London.

Earl, M (1990) Education: The Foundation for Effective Strategies. IT and the New Manager Conference, *Computer Weekly/Business Intelligence*, London, June.

Ernst and Young (1990) *Strategic Alignment Report*: UK Survey. Ernst and Young: London.

Goodwin, C (1984) How OA can Justify Itself. *Computing*, 4 October, p. 6.

Hochstrasser, B (1990) Evaluating IT Investments – Matching Techniques to Projects. *Journal of Information Technology*, Vol. 5, No. 4, pp. 215-221.

Hochstrasser, B and Griffiths, C (1991) *Controlling IT Investments: Strategy and Management*. Chapman and Hall: London.

Kaplan, R (1986) Must CIM be Justified by Faith Alone? *Harvard Business Review*, March-April, pp. 87-95.

Kearney, A T (1990) *Breaking the Barriers: IT Effectiveness in Great Britain and Ireland*. A T Kearney/CIMA: London.

Keen, P (1991) *Shaping the Future: Business Design through Information Technology*. Harvard Business School Press: Boston.

Lincoln, T and Shorrock, D (1990) Cost Justifying Current Use of Information Technology. In Lincoln, T (ed), *Managing Information Systems for Profit*. Wiley and Sons: Chichester.

Malitoris, J (1990) IT Measurement: Delivering the Goods. Paper at the Technology and People Conference, London, 15 June.

National Audit Office (1987) *Inland Revenue: Control of Major Developments in Use of IT*. HMSO: London.

National Audit Office (1989) *Department of Social Security: Operational Strategy*. January session 1988-89, HC-111. HMSO: London.

Norton, D (1986) A Case Study: Hercules Incorporated. *Stage by Stage*, Vol. 6, No. 5, pp. 11-17.

PA Consulting Group (1990) *The Impact of the Current Climate on IT – The Survey*

Report. PA Consulting Group: London.

Parker, M M, Benson, R J, and Trainor, H E (1988 *Information Economics*. Prentice-Hall: London.

Peat Marwick (1989) *IT Survey among CEOs*. Peat Marwick: London.

Peters, G (1988) Evaluating Your Computer Investment Strategy. *Journal of Information Technology*, Vol. 3, No. 3, pp. 178-188.

Porter, M E and Millar, V E (1985) How Information Gives You Competitive Advantage. *Harvard Business Review*. Vol. 63, No. 4, July-August, pp. 149-160.

Price Waterhouse (1989) *Information Technology Review 1989/90*. Price Waterhouse: London.

Sassone (1988) A Survey of Cost Benefit Methodologies for Information Systems. *Project Appraisal*, Vol. 3, No. 2, pp. 73-84.

Silk, D (1990) Managing IS Benefits for the 1990s. *Journal of Information Technology*, Vol. 5, No. 4, pp. 185-193.

Strassman, P (1990) *The Business Value of Computers*. The Information Economics Press: New Canaan.

Vowler, J (1990) The Theory – and the Reality. *Computer Weekly*, November 15, p. 18.

Walton, R (1989) *Up and Running: Integrating Information Technology and the Organization*. Harvard Business School Press: Boston.

Willcocks, L (1989) Measuring the Value of IT Investments. *Journal of Information Technology*, Vol. 4, No. 4, pp. 239-242.

Willcocks, L (ed.) (1990) Theme Issue: The Evaluation of Information Systems Investments. *Journal of Information Technology*, Vol. 5, No. 4.

Willcocks, L (1991a) Informatization in Public Administration and Services in the United Kingdom: Toward a Management Era? *Informatization and the Public Sector*, Vol. 1, No. 3, pp. 1-23.

Willcocks, L (1991b) Information Technology and Human Resource Issues in the 1990s: Integration through Culture. Paper at the Fifth Annual Conference of the British Academy of Management, University of Bath, 22-24 September.

Willcocks, L and Lester, S (1991) Information Systems Investments: Evaluation at the Feasibility Stage of Projects. *Technovation*, Autumn.

Willcocks, L and Lester, S (1992) *Of Capital Importance: Evaluation of IS Investments.* Chapman and Hall: London.

Willcocks, L and Mason, D (1992) *Computerising Work: People, Systems Design and Workplace Relations.* Blackwell Scientific: Oxford.

Wilson, T (1991) Overcoming the Barriers to the Implementation of Information System Strategies. *Journal of Information Technology*, Vol. 6, No. 1, pp. 39-44.

11 Making provision for IT impacts

V. Symons
Leicester City Council

11.1 INTRODUCTION

The impacts of information systems (IS) are profound and wide-ranging. Organizational impacts often provide a crucial motivation for the introduction of information technology, and may be critical to the effectiveness of implementation. Yet despite their importance, less attention has been given to the measurement of the human and organizational impacts of IT than to their technical and economic consequences.

This paper comments on problems in measuring organizational impacts, and discusses the link between IT impacts and IT strategy. It is suggested that analysis of IT impacts should concentrate on four areas: organizational context, stakeholders, informal information systems and the management of change. These impacts should be considered explicitly in strategy formation.

11.2 IT IMPACT ASSESSMENT

There has been a steady transition in the application and impacts of information technology over the past two decades. The original emphasis on cost-cutting and reduction in staff numbers shifted to increasing the capabilities of organizational information processing, and from there to the use of IT to support business strategy. IT has been used to great advantage to differentiate existing products and services and to introduce new ones. In addition it can alter the balance of power between an organization and its customers and suppliers. This change may take a number of forms: establishing entry barriers, limiting access to distribution channels, raising switching costs, setting up inter-organization and inter-sectoral links and cooperation. American Hospital Supplies and American Airlines in the US, and Thomson Tour Operations in the UK, were pioneers in building electronic links to their customers, and became well-known for their success in shutting out the competition[1].

The potential gains from such applications are enormous, but so too are the risks, and if the impacts are not carefully thought through they can backfire. One major European car manufacturer set up a viewdata network enabling its dealers to locate a vehicle to a customer's exact specifications when they did not have it in stock. A thorough economic appraisal of the system seemed to demonstrate that it

---

1. *Financial Times,* 24 November 1989.

would be cost-effective, assisting dealers' sales efforts and giving more efficient management of the manufacturer's inventories. Unfortunately the analysis did not anticipate the principal economic impact of the system, which was that dealers cut their own stocks at the maker's expense – in some cases to no more than the demonstration vehicles[2].

The impacts of information systems within organizations are profound and wide-ranging. Organizational impacts often play an important role in support of business strategy, and may provide the chief motivation for the introduction of new technology. They may also be critical in user acceptance of the new systems. Changed routines, procedures and information flows may result in shifts in the distribution of power and control. IT can be used to increase management's span of control. It may enable centralization or decentralization. Specialized resources and suppliers give rise to new forms of dependency. Jobs may be de-skilled or upgraded, lost or gained; the quality of working life may be radically altered. These impacts hinge on human judgements and choices.

The introduction of IT may change the structure of the organization. It is likely to have a large impact on the roles, responsibilities and influence of the individual managers and departments. The successful adoption of IT allows systems managers to increase their responsibility and influence, and may also enable user managers to increase their status and power.

There is no doubt that the potential of IT is enormous; but the reality has consistently turned out to be less glamorous (and less frightening) than the theory and the media hype. Many organizations experience substantial difficulty in linking IT strategy to business strategy, and the problems in implementing IT are legion. A survey by the Confederation of British Industry and PA Consulting Group concluded that UK companies are unsophisticated in their use of IT, receive poor value from their investment in computer systems, and have senior executives only weakly committed to IT[3]. Surveys of this type are common. But such studies are rather superficial and do not probe the complexities of cause and effect. The reasons for these problems in strategy and implementation can be traced, the author believes, to a lack of understanding of the impacts of IT in organizations, and of the mechanisms by which it can be assimilated smoothly. This is due in large part, it will be argued, to an excessive emphasis on the formal and technical aspects of information processing.

Computer-based information systems encompass only part of the total information processing that takes place in an organization. The complete information processing system consists of 'public' and 'private' systems. Public is used in the sense of being known to relevant persons in the organization and available to all who have authority to access the information. Private systems are kept by individuals, and may supplement or duplicate the public systems. There are within the public and private systems both 'formal' and 'informal' information systems. Formal systems

---

2. *Management Today*, September 1982.

3. *Financial Times*, 6 June 1989.

are manifested by documents and other records, usually indicating compliance with prespecified rules and procedures. Informal information systems may process information that is essential to the functioning of the organization, but without formal records of that process (Davis and Olson, 1984). Hopwood (1983) makes an additional distinction between official and unofficial and routine and non-routine modes of information processing.

These categories are overlapping. Private systems (e.g. manual record cards) may be officially sanctioned, or unofficial and discouraged. The unofficial, non-routine category comprises many of the informal information systems (such as 'the grapevine') on which employees depend. Most computer-based information systems (CBIS) constitute part of the formal information processing system. They are usually public, though the individually developed systems of end-user computing may prove an exception. Other CBIS applications, electronic mail for example, impinge on the informal public system.

Davis and Olson (1984) suggest that the effect of a comprehensive CBIS is to reduce the need for private formal information systems and probably also both public and private informal systems. However, many studies of the way organizations work stress the significance of informal information channels. Mintzberg (1972) argued that the concept of the total management information system (MIS) was a myth. There is in fact a continuing debate over how much organizational information processing should or can be formalized and handled effectively by technology (see for example Kiesler, 1986).

Davis and Olson define an information system as 'an integrated, user-machine system for providing information to support operations, management, and decision-making functions in an organization. The system utilizes computer hardware and software; manual procedures; models for analysis, planning, control and decision making; and a database.' This definition is useful in its juxtaposition of user and machine, but does not otherwise capture the richness of organizational information processing. The formal/informal and public/private distinctions are, we believe, worth making explicit.

In what follows the term IS will be used in favour of the less ambiguous CBIS, in order not to exclude from consideration the manual and informal information flows around the technology which may be linked inextricably with its functioning and impacts. By information system, then, we wish to signify a computer system embedded in an organization. With such a view of information systems, it can be seen that analysis of IT impacts must include a consideration of the impacts on both formal and informal information processing within the organization.

11.3 IMPACT ASSESSMENT

Measurement of IT impacts can prove extremely difficult. The traditional appraisal methods which worked reasonably well when IT was used mainly to reduce costs are no longer adequate, but remain the ones most commonly used. Western financial management techniques lay heavy emphasis on cost audit and return on investment, the result of which is to discourage innovation by favouring a short payback period. Developments in evaluation methods have not kept pace with the shift in use of information systems which has over time widened the scope of their effects.

IT impact assessment is generally aimed at the identification and quantification of costs and benefits. But the current use of IS in support of business strategy has consequences which are both complex and difficult to measure. The implications of a new system often extend outside the context for which it was initially introduced (Hopwood, 1983). Increasingly it is the case that the benefits of IT are strategic or qualitative – improved level of customer service for instance, or high-tech company image. Costs spread over a long timescale for project development are often hard to pin down. Some, like expenses for training and recruitment of skilled staff, are reasonably clear but it is less obvious how to allocate them fairly. There may also be insidious impacts such as a decline in job satisfaction. Quantifications of IT impacts are thus uncertain and subjective. In addition, it is often extremely difficult to separate such impacts out from other organizational change associated with or enabled by the introduction of IT.

As well as this consideration of organizational context, it is necessary to plan in advance for the process of change which is needed to bring about a new and desired situation. Change includes not only technical aspects such as new hardware, software and systems but also new work roles and responsibilities for individuals and groups and, equally important, new attitudes with respect to such issues as the value of their work to themselves and to the organization. In planning for the process of change, three key questions need to be asked. The first of these concerns who is going to manage change, the second is how they are going to do it and the third is what is needed in terms of resources (Walsham, 1991).

Walsham notes that the actual management of the change process cannot be determined in advance, since the management of people and resources for IS development (in line with day-to-day management in general) is a craft skill in which elements such as chance and opportunism are as important as design and planning. Nevertheless, a consideration of the process of change is both feasible and desirable at the strategy development stage, even though it will not provide a complete blueprint for change.

11.4 ANALYSING IT IMPACTS

We have discussed the view that IS include informal (human) as well as formal (machine) information processing. They are thus not purely technical systems, but also social systems. Conceptualizing an IS as a computer system embedded in an organization, it is a complex social object separable only analytically from the organizational context within which it is situated. Elements that should be taken into consideration in analysing IT impacts are context (including history and infrastructure), stakeholder perspectives, informal procedures and information flows, and the management of change. These are considered in turn.

11.4.1 Context

Organizational context is important because the ease with which IS are implemented hangs on the extent to which they are congruent with the environment into which they are placed. The environment includes organizational goals, culture and politics. Effective IT strategy also necessitates a historical understanding, as computer projects evolve over time and at any particular point present a series of constraints and opportunities shaped by the previous history of IT development within the organization (Kling, 1987). Infrastructural needs for new IS include physical, financial and human resources, and the capability of access to these as required.

11.4.2 Stakeholders

Analysis of the human resources that support IS brings social and political interaction to centre stage, and with it the importance of stakeholder perspectives. Stakeholders may be individuals (one actor as a stakeholder), groups (multiple actors as a stakeholder) or larger collectivities (e.g. an organization). Conflicts of interest often emerge within as well as between stakeholder groups.

Lyytinen and Hirschheim (1987) comment that the concept of stakeholder cannot easily be distinguished from notions of agency (i.e. potential for action) and power (i.e. capability to employ various resources to secure stakeholders' sectional interests). Stakeholder groups often organize themselves to increase their influence. Values, which frequently have cultural and ideological components, surface in the interaction of such groups and are used to rationalize and justify action.

Stakeholder perspectives relate to notions of agency and structure in the instrumental/institutional aspects of IS. An IS is best described as a tool or instrument for stakeholders who can shape it to serve their interests and discard it easily when it is ineffective or too costly. In contrast, an institution refers to some social arrangement that persists, even when it is not working well for some of its participants. IS are intrinsically neither just tools nor just institutions. They can be tools for stakeholders with power over their shape and use, while appearing as institutions for those who are limited in their capacities to negotiate the conditions of IS use (Kling, 1987). Analysis of multiple stakeholder perspectives is crucial: the larger and more complex the IS, the greater the number of stakeholders and the wider the range of differing, sometimes conflicting, perspectives. A failure to understand the views of various interest groups leads almost inevitably to unanticipated resistance in implementation and, consequently, negative impacts.

11.4.3 Informal Information Systems

The informal procedures and information flows around an IS are often integral to the work done using it. They are reliant on the complex network of social relationships within an organization. Kling and Scacchi (1982) suggest 'lines of work' and 'going concerns' as more apt expressions than formal job descriptions and official tasks for describing the organizational activity into which computing developments are grafted. Active consideration should be given to the ways in which new IS will influence the diversity of official and unofficial information flows (Hopwood, 1983). Informal patterns should be identified, together with their organizational roles and consequences, but this analysis should not be used as a starting-point to formalize them. They are valuable to the organization and individual because they are informal; the system should allow their continued existence (Wynne, 1983).

The implication is that IS strategists should concern themselves with designing the work, not just the tool. Howard (1987) suggests that this means also to 'intimately shape new social structures for organizational life and to contribute to new forms of identity at work'. Instead of designing merely for task routines, those involved in the design of IT should also aim to design for the contexts of those routines (Blackler, 1990). IT strategy development must recognize uncertainties in immediate user requirements and in future business needs, and give priority to providing sufficient flexibility in the system to adapt to changes.

Users, however inexperienced, are not idiots; nor are they 'irrational'. Understanding IT impacts means taking seriously the perspectives of individual stakeholders and interest groups. It also means examining the mechanisms for representation of different interests, the institutional means by which divergent opinions can be discussed, and the ability of different groups to have access to relevant information about the options available (Hopwood, 1983).

11.4.4 Management of Change

The advantages and disadvantages of a particular IT strategy are not distributed equally within any organization. It is vital to understand the direction and size of redistributive effects produced, and how various IS stakeholders organize their action around these effects (Lyytinen and Hirschheim, 1987). Avoiding all redistributive effects is likely to lead to a conservative development strategy – using IT simply to automate existing organizational procedures, not as a vehicle for organizational change.

> 'This can be counter-productive in the long run and can negatively affect the viability of the organization and interests of all stakeholders. If redistributive effects are too radical, on the other hand, IS change can deeply disrupt the organizational situation. In such a case, it is important that any IS development initiative has strong political support from key stakeholder groups, and evidence of gains for each group.'
> (Lyytinen and Hirschheim, 1987)

IS will be implemented easily to the extent that they exhibit congruence with the organizational context (e.g. in terms of corporate objectives, company culture, and distribution of power and control). Where organizational change is required the IS should be incongruent with its environment in one or more respects, but well matched in others if implementation is not to be too problematic.

Arguably, the most fundamental issues in the management of change are commitment and incrementalism. As Samuel Johnson remarked, 'Change is not made without inconvenience, even from worse to better.' The sources of resistance to change can rarely be ascribed to pure bloody-mindedness. More often they are fear/anxiety of the unknown, fear of loss of status or power, fear of destroying what is known to work, or local knowledge which is superior to that of those planning the change.

The vital importance of senior management championship of the project is well documented in the management literature. The commitment of less senior participants, which is equally crucial, is dependent partially on their understanding of the proposed change and their interest in its potential benefits – aspects that can be addressed by education and training programmes and participation in IS development. Where sources of resistance are fundamentally structured (e.g. opposition to the use of IS for managerial surveillance), however, process-based strategies such as user participation and training are largely ineffective in overcoming them.

The importance of high-quality training cannot be over-emphasized. There is mounting evidence that the most important training needs for companies implementing IS are not even specifically related to IS; rather they are dependent on good communication and consultation processes, and on the provision of adequate time for both trainers and trainees to undertake the learning process involved. Communication can be regarded as the key to the management of change.

Another difficulty in measuring IT impacts is that what appears as a benefit or opportunity in one part of the organization may be viewed very differently in another. For instance, increased access to information at headquarters may be highly beneficial for the board while divisional managers see it as an erosion of their power base. Individuals, groups and functions may well have divergent (sometimes conflicting) perspectives on the same IS, according to their views and their role within the organization. A failure to understand alternative viewpoints can lead to unanticipated resistance and hence operational problems. It is therefore crucial that the impacts of IT on different stakeholder groups are addressed in advance, as part of the process of strategy formation.

11.5 IT IMPACTS AND IT STRATEGY

Authors such as Mintzberg (1987) show that strategy development is not formal, objective, or even necessarily 'rational'. Rather, it is a complex, incremental process which emerges from the activities of organizational decision-making and is bound up with organizational culture and politics. 'Formation' is a better description than 'formulation' for the process of strategy development.

Strategy development does not take place in a vacuum isolated from the business. If strategy is to be effective it must produce plans which not only address business needs, but which provide a foundation for their successful implementation within the organization. Strategies for improved use of IT cannot be separated from the tactics of implementing the improvements. As Mintzberg (1987) points out, 'The notion that strategy is something that should happen way up there, far removed from the details of running an organization on a daily basis, is one of the great fallacies of conventional strategic management. And it explains a good many of the most dramatic failures in business and public today.'

Making the link between IT strategy and implementation means forming policies for the application of IT in support of business objectives which also take into account the constraints and opportunities of the organizational context. Harris (1990) emphasizes the crucial importance of the implementation process as the most likely area of failure or success in the management of IT. Since implementation is key, planning for how to achieve effective implementation should form a central part of the strategy. This means analysing and providing for impacts as part of the IT strategy.

Planning for the implementation process requires an understanding of the organizational impacts of IT as well as its technical effects. Organizational structure, culture and politics are increasingly being recognized as important factors in the management of technical change. For instance, Rockart and Scott Morton (1984) conceptualize technology impact in terms of the interactions between corporate strategy, information technology, organization structure and culture, management processes, and individuals and their roles. Explicit consideration of these elements is essential to effective implementation and, hence, to effective strategy.

11.6 CONCLUSIONS

It is important for an organization's senior management to understand the changes associated with IT and the effects they may have in the future. One way of achieving this is to carry out a review of a long-term systems plan, looking specifically at organizational issues. This review can be carried out by considering the areas of impact described above. Such a review could be initiated by senior general management or by the personnel department. Failing that, the systems director should prepare his or her own analysis of the situation and seek opportunities to ensure that its findings are understood at the highest level in the organization.

It is also important for the systems director to think through the possible effects of new systems, particularly on the jobs of departmental managers. This should be done before the allocation of specific responsibilities for user involvement in system development activities. Systems directors should use their influence to ensure that user managers' whose roles might change as a result of new systems, are not in a position to block or delay the implementation of the systems (Butler Cox Foundation, 1987).

IS strategy development requires a strong partnership between business and technical people. If possible, the skills of business management and IT management will be combined in one person. The development of business/IT generalists necessitates well thought-out education, training and career development schemes. It will also involve a well thought-out committee and reporting structure, high level management and involvement, and good participation and communication. The importance of these should not be underestimated, since there is currently a gap in culture and language between business and IT specialists which inhibits communication and understanding. This gap must be bridged if IT strategy is to be linked effectively with business strategy.

The main point arising from this paper is the need to give better consideration to the human and organizational impacts of IT at the strategy formation stage. This would normally involve additional work when compared to IT strategy which concentrates mainly on technical and economic aspects. In addition, the conclusions from such work would often point to anticipated difficulties in the implementation process implying the need for more resources or a longer time scale. Walsham (1991) notes that in some cases approval for an IS project would not be given if the full magnitude of the difficulties were spelt out. However, those managing an IS project surely need to have a realistic view of the difficulties of introducing new technology if serious problems (such as those described in Symons (1990)) are to be avoided.

In summary, it has been argued that IT impacts have been neglected from IT strategy formation, with dysfunctional results. IT strategy development should include an explicit analysis of human and organizational impacts, concentrating on the areas of organizational context, history and infrastructure, stakeholders and their perspectives, informal procedures and information flows, and the management of the change process.

REFERENCES

Blackler F. (1990) Formative Contexts and Organizational Futures, in Reed M. and Hughes M. (eds), *Rethinking Organization: New Directions in Organization Theory and Analysis*, Sage.

Butler Cox Foundation (1987) *The Impact of Information Technology on Corporate Organisation Structure*, Research Report 56.

Davis G.B. and Olson M.H. (1984) *Management Information Systems: Conceptual Foundations, Structure and Development*, 2nd edn., McGraw-Hill: Singapore.

Harris M. (1990) Developing a Business-led IT Strategy: Report on the Computer Weekly Management Programme, 28 November 1989, London, *Journal of Information Technology* 5, 49-50.

Hopwood A.G. (1983) Evaluating the Real Benefits, in Otway H.J. and Peltu M. (eds), *New Office Technology: Human and Organisational Aspects*, Pinter: London.

Howard R. (1987) Systems Design and Social Responsibility: The Political Implications of Computer-supported Cooperative Work, Office: *Technology and People* 3 (2), 175-187.

Kiesler S. (1986) Thinking Ahead: The Hidden Messages in Computer Networks, *Harvard Business Review* 64 (1), 46-60.

Kling R. (1987) Defining the Boundaries of Computing across Complex Organizations, in Boland R. and Hirschheim R. (eds), *Critical Issues in Information Systems Research*, Wiley: Chichester.

Kling R. and Scacchi W. (1982) The Web of Computing: Computer Technology as Social Organization, *Advances in Computers* 21, 1-90.

Lyytinen K. and Hirschheim R. (1987) Information Systems Failures – A Survey and Classification of the Empirical Literature, *Oxford Surveys in Information Technology* 4, 257-309.

Mintzberg H. (1972) The Myths of MIS, *California Management Review* 15 (1), 92-97.

Mintzberg H. (1987) Crafting Strategy, *Harvard Business Review* 65 (4), 66-75.

Rockart J.F. and Scott Morton M.S. (1984) Implications of Changes in Information Technology for Corporate Strategy, *Interfaces* 14 (1), 84-95.

Symons V.J. (1990) Evaluation of Information Systems: IS Development in the Processing Company, *Journal of Information Technology* 5.

Walsham G. (1991) Problèmes d'implémentation dans l'évaluation des systèmes d'information, *Technologies de l'Information et Société* 3 (2), 69-85.

Wynne B. (1983) The Changing Roles of Managers, in Otway H.J. and Peltu M. (eds), *New Office Technology: Human and Organisational Aspects*, Pinter: London.

12 The management of change: guidelines for the successful implementation of Information Systems

F. Land
London Business School

12.1 INTRODUCTION

Despite the many well-known success stories pointing to uses of Information Technology that have transformed organizations and which have played a major part in delivering strategic benefits to the organization (Clemons and Weber, 1990; Clemons, 1991), there is considerable evidence that the implementation of Information Systems can be hazardous. Research such as that of Strassmann (1985), Farbey, Land and Targett (1990) suggests that users fail to achieve the anticipated benefits and that too many new systems are met with scepticism and rejection. Critics, including Lester Thurow, Principal of the Sloan School at MIT (Thurow, 1987), have challenged the industry to provide compelling evidence that the sought after transformations have taken place.

There are many reasons for this sense of under-achievement. These range from problems with the technology – the technology, despite the phenomenal increase in performance, may not always deliver the expected performance – to problems stemming from the inability of management to take advantage of the capabilities the technology does provide. Strassmann (1985) has convincingly demonstrated that a key success factor is management ability and understanding.

One very important factor determining the success or failure of an Information Systems project is how the process of implementation is managed. Whilst a great deal of effort has gone into devising standard ways of designing and developing Information Systems from requirements analysis through to the delivery of the system to the user, the process of systems implementation has been somewhat neglected. Many standard methodologies use the word implementation in the description of the system's life-cycle, but mean no more than the system's testing and hand-over (Finkelstein, 1990; Kumar, 1990). Turner (1987), in defining the activities necessary to bring a new Information System into operation, states 'The implementation stage, of course, produces running code.' Given the importance for the ultimate success of the system of having a good implementation process the lack of research effort in this area has to be regretted.

In recent years much attention has been paid to defining ways of helping organizations create IT strategies (Bakos and Treacy, 1986; Wiseman, 1988; Ives and Learmouth, 1988; Porter and Millar, 1985; Earl, 1989). Most of this work focuses on ensuring a linkage between the strategic business plans and the IT or IS strategy, and of creating an appropriate IT architecture which enables the IT strategy to be realized (Nolan and Mulryan, 1987; Nolan, Norton & Co., 1988). Ciborra (1991) notes that in general these approaches are based on a top-down rationalistic analysis and suggests the limitations of that form of analysis. He firmly espouses a more intuitive, experimental approach in which end-users play a larger role and which permits serendipity to play a major part in achieving success. However, few of these approaches explicitly refer to the problems of implementing the strategy (Galliers, 1991; Galliers and Sutherland, 1991). In practice many apparently excellent IS plans have not been successfully transferred to the workplace.

This paper argues that planning for implementation – planning the management of the change process – is an essential component of the strategic plan. In the first place it is important because the failure of strategic plans can threaten an organization's competitive position. But failure also has a long-lasting effect on managements. Previous failures can make managements question the potential of IT as an agent for strategic change.

This paper is based on a research project carried out as part of the Alvey programme (Alvey, 1986) between 1986 and 1988, which attempted to identify some of the organizational and management-related factors which can help or hinder the successful implementation of an Information System. The outcome of the research enabled the researchers to suggest a series of guidelines for the effective implementation of Information Systems.

12.2 SUMMARY OF RESEARCH FINDINGS

The outcome of the Alvey project is fully reported in a series of documents and papers (Land, Le Quesne and Wijegunaratne, 1989; Land, Le Quesne and Wijegunaratne, 1991; Le Quesne, 1988). The research study looked at how a number of organizations set about implementing new Information Systems. The Information Systems being studied were Integrated Project Support Environments (IPSEs) being introduced into commercial Information Systems development departments. Although the research focused on a system designed to be used by Information Systems professionals, the researchers were looking for factors which would equally apply to systems designed for any other group of users.

The research identified six groups of factors as playing an important role in determining the successful adoption by a user group of the new system. Successful in this sense means that the new system is accepted in the workplace as the way of doing the tasks that the system has been designed to carry out, or, in the case of decision support systems, that the systems are invoked as a support tool on a regular basis. The other meaning of success – that the system delivers the anticipated benefits in terms of more effective working and adequate return on the capital employed was not tested as the time for the study did not permit performance to be measured.

The six groups of factors identified by the research were:

12.2.1 Motivation for Introducing the New System

Motivation is related to the objectives for introducing the new system, and the perceptions of stakeholders of what objectives the system has been introduced for.

The study found that failure to clarify objectives and failure to share in the validity of the objectives reduced the motivation of stakeholders to work with the system.

12.2.2 Commitment to the System

Commitment measures the strength of belief in the new system and the extent to which ways are found to solve problems and overcome obstacles.

The research corroborated the notion that commitment is related to leadership and championship and failure to provide these can reduce commitment to the new system. High motivation tends to lead to high commitment but is rarely sufficient.

12.2.3 Organizational Culture

Organizational culture is concerned with the style of management, the relationships within the organization and the extent to which the organization has an 'enterprise' culture.

The research found that an important feature of successful implementation is a sharing of values by stakeholders. Shared values could be achieved both in an authoritarian and participative culture.

12.2.4 The Management of the Implementation Process

The management of the implementation process is concerned both with the planning of the implementation activities – training, pilot running etc. – and with the management style – authoritarian, bureaucratic or participative.

The study revealed that it was more important for stakeholders to understand the implementation process and to be clear about their own role in it than the actual style. However, it was important that the style fitted in with the organizational culture.

12.2.5 The 'Distance' between the Existing System and the Replacement System

The distance between the existing system and the new system is a notional measure of the extent of the change. The greater the distance, the less does the new system resemble the old system, and hence its user or operator has to invest time and effort in becoming adept in its use.

The research found that to traverse the distance, the user had to have strong motivation and a perceived positive payback from making the change. At the same time, the greater the distance the greater the dispersion of outcomes in individual use, partly because individual learning curves differ.

12.2.6 The Technology Itself

Although the research attempted to identify behavioural and organisational factors it became clear that features of the technology also played an important role in determining the success or failure of the new system. The most important technology related factors were:

(i) The extent to which the new system delivered the expected functionality.

(ii) The actual performance of the system in terms of factors, such as response time, response time predictability, security, help facilities etc.

(iii) The way skills in using the system could be acquired. A system which provided for incremental learning seemed to be favoured over systems which deliver large blocks of functionality, but require considerable learning and practice before the necessary skills are acquired.

A finding from earlier research (Land, Detjejaruwat and Smith, 1983) was that users tend to focus on problems with the technology to indicate their disaffection of the system, when the underlying reason may be very different – perhaps that they find the system has reduced the autonomy they had in organizing their work schedule under the old system. Thus the same response time may be regarded as perfectly satisfactory by one group of users, but as unacceptable by a similar group. The former may have a high regard for the new system, the latter for reasons which have nothing to do with the technology itself, wish to reject the new systems. Users often find it easier to articulate a complaint about the technology – poor response time – than about the underlying reasons for discontent.

12.3 DISCUSSION

The research produced few surprises. Some earlier work received corroboration. Indeed many of the factors had been identified in previous studies. But previous studies had tended to be fragmented. 'Most studies focus on small pieces of the MIS implementation puzzle, without considering larger issues' (Kwon and Zmud, 1987). None of the six factors identified by the study operate independently. Commitment is related to motivation, and to the style of implementation process chosen – degree of participation, for example. But the style of participation is itself not independent of the culture prevalent in the organization. The interactions between the factors are complex and there is no clearly defined set of cause-and-effect relationships.

Kling's (1987) notion of a web model provides the best way of approaching the issues.

The only real surprise was that none of the managements of the organizations studied had taken the factors into account in planning the implementation of their systems, and none of the standard development methodologies pay serious attention to the problem of technology transfer from design and construction to user.

What was possible was to construct some managerial guidelines which should help managers plan the implementation process for Information Systems and avoid failures stemming from poor implementation strategies. Many elements of the guidelines pick up ideas which has been suggested in the literature of related topics, such as that of the management of innovation (Humphrey, 1987). However, most of the guidelines contain advice not commonly used in the implementation of Information Systems.

12.4 THE GUIDELINES

The guidelines suggest the pre-conditions for change and the range of tools and techniques which may be employed to achieve the necessary conditions.

12.4.1 Ensure Organizational Climate is Right

For effective transfer of technology into the workplace it is essential that those who will be affected by the change share values and visions (Land, Detjejaruwat and Smith, 1983). The greater the extent of the change the more important it is that values and visions are shared. Transformations, much talked about in discussions on competitive strategy, are difficult to achieve when people do not share the values of the advocates of change. The notion of organizational invalidity (Newman and Noble, 1991) captures the problems of implementing systems where the fit between the system and the organizational 'scene' is missing.

Without shared values and visions change is hazardous, and it may be necessary to scale down the level of ambition of the change programme.

On the other hand there are a number of approaches which can help to achieve the required pre-conditions. These include:

(a) Establish mechanisms for collaboration within the organization. One such mechanism which has had success in many organizations is the quality circle (Deming, 1982; Price, 1986; Schonberger, 1983) or variants of the quality circle.

(b) Spread ownership of the problem and its solution by the use of participative methods in planning, requirements elicitation, design and implementation (Knight, 1989; Land, 1987; Mumford and Henshall, 1983). As far as is practical, involve all stakeholders in having a say in what the new system should do.

Design teams for Intranet

(c) Include quality of working life and job satisfaction as specific design objectives for the new system.

(d) Ensure that the workforce at all levels is provided with a high level of training and education. Experience suggests that a well trained workforce is more likely to share the values of the organization, provided that organization is not anti-social, than an ill-educated workforce.

(e) Identify sources of alienation and friction and try to eliminate them. Sometimes alienation and friction are the result of poor communications resulting from a tight policy based on information dissemination 'on the need to know' principle.

(f) Be prepared to share in the payoff from the new system with the work force. A policy based on equity rather than market forces can sometimes transform a hazardous situation.

12.4.2 Ensure that all Stakeholders Understand

One of the greatest problems in the management of change is the problem of uncertainty. The introduction of new systems is hampered by uncertainty. A typical reaction to the uncertainty engendered by change is anxiety accompanied by actions to resist the change and attempt to maintain or restore the status quo. In general the greater the distance between the desired change and the status quo the greater the possibility of uncertainty arising.

Hence the need to establish mechanisms which help all stakeholders to understand:

(a) The motivation for change.

(b) What payoffs can be expected from the change, even if these are negative for the stakeholder in question.

(c) The process of change, including the role the stakeholder is expected to play in the change process.

(d) The role others in or out of the organization will be playing.

(e) The nature of the new tasks the stakeholder will be expected to carry out, any new skills required, the training to be undergone, and the new relationships that will be required.

(f) Who has authority and who will be responsible for managing the change.

Mechanisms which can help to spread understanding include:

(i) Establish a help and counselling service for the duration of the change. Make this freely available to stakeholders who have problems related to the change.

(ii) Arrange group meetings attended by members of the design team as well as stakeholders, to disseminate mission statements, define expected payoffs and can clarify issues raised by stakeholders.

(iii) Provide training to stakeholders at the right time.

(iv) Positively seek to identify gaps in understanding through questionnaires and surveys.

12.4.3 Set up Organization to Manage Change

There is no single ideal organizational structure for managing the change process. Different organizational forms are appropriate for different organizational cultures. But even though the organizational forms may vary, the functions performed are similar. Some of the desired conditions include:

(a) Establish communication channels throughout the organization which enable stakeholders at any level to communicate their concern and knowledge. Much so-called resistance to change arises from the non-availability of communication channels. A stakeholder may 'know' that a feature of the new system is dysfunctional. If there is no channel readily available to communicate that knowledge, the stakeholder may be forced to signal the problem through resistance to the change. But because of the absence of a communication mechanism that signal will be misinterpreted by those in authority as mere bloody-mindedness.

(b) Ensure that champions are identified and legitimized. In the absence of legitimization the champion may be regarded as a faction leader and thereby not get the widespread support required.

(c) Set up a project team with a project leader with well-defined and well-disseminated responsibilities. Many problems occur because lines of command are not clear, and responsibilities muddled. Note responsibilities and lines of command may be assigned top-down in an organization with a command structure, or defined bottom-up in an organization with a more democratic, participative culture.

(e) Set up a project command structure. A frequently successful structure consists of a project steering committee with senior representatives from all stakeholder groups. The steering group defines terms of reference for a design group which is responsible for the detailed specification of requirements and design and implementation of the new system. An important function for the steering committee is to act as umpire for situations in which the design group cannot agree, and to act as court of appeal where stakeholders outside the design group have problems with the work of the design group.

The design group may be user-led or led by the Information Systems department. In recent years the principle of user-led design teams have received much advocacy. Perhaps the most important point is that the design team should represent as many stakeholder groups as possible and that power should be distributed equally between the various groups.

12.4.4 Identify Obstacles to Change

Most systems development methodologies include techniques of scouting for business opportunities and perhaps getting competitive advantage. A good example is the Critical Success Factor technique developed by Rockhart (1979). But it is equally important to identify constraints which may hold back the implementation of the project.

A semi-formal technique of constraints analysis was developed by IBM (Lincoln, 1980). Stakeholders are assembled together for a period of two days. Using brainstorming and delphi techniques they identify obstacles to implementation and attempt to rank these in order of importance. They then review the obstacles and define ways of overcoming them. Sometimes an obstacle is so overwhelming that it threatens the project as first conceived. If no way of overcoming the obstacle can be found it may be necessary to rethink the primary mission of the project and perhaps reduce the level of ambition.

A variation of the IBM method groups obstacles under five headings:

(i) Financial constraints. Here the issues may revolve around the resourcing of the project and in particular the availability of reserves should the project run into trouble. Other issues may arise out of changes in the economic climate or the possibility of mergers and take-overs.

(ii) Technical constraints. May there be unexpected problems with the technology? Do we have the skills to handle that technology? Will the chosen hardware and software vendors continue to be in the market? What constraints on future action may any technological choice impose on us in the future? That question is of particular importance in the choice of the technical infrastructure. Questions of compatibility may be important.

(iii) Organizational constraints. Important concerns may be the ability of the organization to absorb all the changes required by the new system at this time. Perhaps the project needs to be phased in more gradually. Where systems cross organizational boundaries or require new organizational structure these issues may turn out to be critical to the success of the project.

iv) Social constraints. These are mainly concerned with the attitude of the workforce at all levels to the changes. Problems may arise from the position taken up by the trade unions to the changes. Often social issues dominate the implementation process, but are not recognized as important until the damage is done.

One of the most widely quoted problems (Keen, 1981) is resistance to change. Resistance to change is often regarded as a luddite tendency which inhibits progress. In practice resistance to change is more likely to be a call for help from individuals or groups who are not satisfied that the changes to which they are reacting are as useful as its advocates claim, or they are not satisfied that the change process has taken sufficient account of their problems. Frequently those who resist have superior knowledge about the effects of the new system than the designers, but have no channel available to communicate their problems to those in authority. Hence the first step in coping with resistance to change and opening the lines of communications is to listen to the signals.

Another often disregarded obstacle to change related to the resistance problem is the presence of an anti-champion; that is an individual strong enough to gather a following who for whatever reason opposes the change. When the anti-champion is more influential than the champion, the implementation process is unlikely to succeed. Hence it is important in the constraints analysis to identify potential anti-champions.

(v) Legal constraints. Does the new system infringe any existing rules or law, or are there new regulations in the pipeline which need to be taken into account now?

12.4.5 Determine Implementation Strategy

An implementation strategy has to be part of the initial plan for the new system (Humphrey, 1987). Decisions have to be taken:

(a) The degree and level of participation and involvement, and the choice of participants.

(b) Where is the project leadership role going to come from – from users, from the IT department, or from some independent non-involved individual.

(c) The kind of project management to be adopted and the responsibilities of the project manager.

(d) The extent to which implementation is to be staged or phased.

(e) The incentives and rewards to be given to those who cooperate with the implementation of the system or the sanctions which may be visited for non-compliance.

(f) The extent and timing of training and education programmes.

(g) The extent to which experimental techniques such as prototyping are going to be used.

(h) The provision of help and counselling facilities.

12.5 CONCLUSION

This paper has attempted to set out some practical guidelines based on research into the success of the implementation process. Many of the guidelines can be regarded as mere common sense. Nevertheless they bring together a range of ideas which between them should help to facilitate the management of change. Perhaps the most important message is that to succeed in transforming an organization through the strategic use of Information Systems it is essential that the preconditions for successful transfer are present and that planning the management of the change process must be part of the strategic plan.

REFERENCES

Alvey, (1986) Alvey Programme, Annual Report, IEE Publishing, London.

Bakos, J Y, and Treacy, M E, (1986) Information Technology and Corporate Strategy: A Research Perspective, *MIS Quarterly*, pp 107-119, June.

Ciborra, C, (1991) From Thinking to Tinkering: The Grassroots of Strategic Information Systems. Paper to be read at ICIS Conference, New York, December.

Clemons, E K, (1991) Evaluation of Strategic Investments in Information Technology, *Communications of the ACM*, 34 (1), pp 23-36, January.

Clemons, E K, and Weber, B W, (1990) Strategic Information Technology Investments: Guidelines for Decision Making, *Proceedings, 23rd International Conference on Systems Sciences*, pp 147-156, January.

Deming, W E, (1982) *Out of the Crisis*, pp 136-138, Cambridge University Press, Cambridge, England.

Earl, M J, (1989) *Management Strategies for Information Technology*, Prentice-Hall International, Hemel Hempstead, England.

Farbey, B, Land, F, and Targett, D, (1990) *Benefits from IT Projects: Possibilities, Expectations and Realisations*, London Business School Working Paper, June.

Finkelstein, C, (1990) *An Introduction to Information Engineering*, Addison-Wesley, Sydney, Australia.

Galliers, R D, (1991) Strategic Information Systems Planning: Myths, Reality, and Guidelines for Successful Implementation, *European Journal of Information Systems*, 1 (1), pp 55-64, January.

Galliers, R D, and Sutherland, A R, (1991) Information Systems Management and Strategy Formulation: The 'Stages of Growth Model' Revisited, *Journal of Information Systems*, 1 (2), pp 89-114, April.

Humphrey, W S, (1987) *Managing for Innovation: Leading Technical People*, Prentice-Hall, New Jersey.

Ives, B, and Learmouth, G P, (1988) The Information Systems as a Competitive Weapon, *Communications of the ACM*, 27 (12), pp 1193-1201, December.

Keen, P G W, (1981) Information Systems and Organisational Change, *Communications of the ACM*, 24 (1), pp 24-32, January.

Kling, R, (1987) Defining the Boundaries of Computing across Complex Organizations, in *Critical Issues in Information Systems Research*, (R J Boland and R A Hirschheim, eds), pp 307-362, Wiley Series in Information Systems, Wiley, Chichester.

Knight, K, ed. (1989) *Participation in Systems Development*, G&P Publishing Inc, Columbia, Maryland.

Kumar, K, (1990) Post Implementation Evaluation of Computer-based IS: Current Practice, *Communications of the ACM*, 33 (2), pp 203-212, February.

Kwong, T H, and Zmud, R W, (1987) Unifying the Fragmented Models of Information Systems Implementation, in *Critical Issues in Information Systems Research*, (R J Boland and R A Hirschheim, eds), pp 227-251, Wiley Series in Information Systems, Wiley, Chichester.

Land, F, (1987) Social Aspects of Information Systems, in *Management Information Systems: The Technology Challenge*, (N Piercy, ed) Croom Helm, London.

Land, F, Detjejaruwat, N, and Smith, C, (1983) Factors Affecting Social Control: The Reasons and Values, *Systems, Objectives, Solutions*, Part 1 in 3 (3), pp 155-164, August; Part 2 in 3 (4), pp 207-226, November.

Land, F, Le Quesne, P, and Wijegunaratne, I (1989) Effective Systems: Overcoming the Obstacles, *Journal of Information Technology*, 4 (2), pp 81-91, June.

Land, F, Le Quesne, P, and Wijegunaratne, I (1991) Implementing Systems Standards at a Merchant Bank: The Case of an IPSE at MBank, in *Cases in IT: People and Organisations* (K Legge, C Clegg, N Kemp, eds) NCC/ Blackwell, Oxford.

Le Quesne, P, (1988) Individual and Organisational Factors and the Design of IPSEs, *British Computer Journal*, 31 (5), pp 391-397, October.

Lincoln, T J, (1980) *Information Systems Constraints: A Strategic Information Processing '80*, (S Lavington, ed) North-Holland.

Mumford, E, and Henshall, D, (1983) *Designing Participatively*, Manchester Business School, Manchester.

Newman, M, and Noble, F, (1991) Integrated Systems, Autonomous Departments: Organisational Invalidity and Systems Change in a University, *Journal of Management Studies*, forthcoming.

Nolan, R L, and Mulryan, D W, (1987) Undertaking an Architecture Program, *Stage by Stage*, 7 (2), pp 1-10, March-April.

Nolan, Norton & Co, (1988) Implementing Transformation, *Proceedings 1988 European Research Symposium*, Bournemouth, October.

Porter, M E, and Millar, V E, (1985) How Information Systems Give You Competitive Advantage, *Harvard Business Review*, 68 (4), pp 149-160, July-August.

Price, F, (1986) *Right First Time: Using Quality Control for Profit*, Wildwood House.

Rockhart, J, (1979) Chief Executives define their own Information Needs, *Harvard Business Review*, 57 (2), pp 81-93, March/April.

Schonberger, R J, (1983) Work Improvement Programmes: Quality Circles Compared with Traditional Western Approaches, *International Journal of Operations and Production Management*, 3 (2), pp 18-32, March.

Strassmann, P, (1985) *Information Payoff: The Transformation of Work in the Electronic Age*, The Free Press, New York.

Thurow, L, (1987) *Economic Paradigms and Slow American Productivity Growth*, MIT, Cambridge, Mass.

Turner, J A, (1987) Understanding the Elements of Systems Design, in *Critical Issues in Information Systems Research* (R J Boland and R A Hirschheim, eds), pp 97-111, Wiley Series in Information Systems, Wiley, Chichester.

Wiseman, C, (1988) Strategic Information Systems, Irwin, Homewood, Illinois.

13 Top management and IT

A. Brown
City University Business School

13.1 INTRODUCTION

For an organization to master the use of IT, it is essential that top management take responsibility for how it is to be utilized. Most organizations that wish to survive will eventually have to attain such mastery.

This paper considers the changing role of top management in the development of IT strategy. Over the last few years we have seen a swelling chorus of calls for top management to take responsibility for IT strategy. This, not surprisingly, has been paralleled by demands for top management to acquire some IT education. This paper explores why we are hearing these demands now and why they can be expected to increase in urgency. A review of approaches to top management IT education shows that programmes have been concentrating on IT awareness and the significance of IT within managers' own organizations, at its current state of IT development. This paper explores the future role of top management and the implications for IT education programmes.

13.2 TOP MANAGEMENT INVOLVEMENT IN IT STRATEGY CREATION

One framework proposed by Chris Yapp and K. Hugh Macdonald in Part Five of this book and reviewed in the introduction, describes the changing situation of organizations as they increase their investment in or commitment to IT. The starting-point for most companies is the localized use of IT within isolated functions (level 1). At this stage the use of IT is largely unrelated to the overall business strategy of the organization and the aims are cost reduction and efficiency increases. IT applications are independent of the strategic context and can be implemented with moderate success by IT professionals together with the local management concerned. In attempting to move towards a more integrated use of IT resources, the situation in which companies then find themselves begins to change in a radical way. They seek to gain added value from utilizing existing and new IT facilities on behalf of the corporation as a whole. Data collected by one department for its own purposes, could be valuable to other parts of the corporation and needs to be made generally accessible. In an information-rich environment all parts of the organization can interact with each other in far more effective ways. It is at this stage that IT strategy becomes an integral part of the strategy of the whole business. Formulating this strategy is a complex problem involving many if not all parts of the organization and hence the corporate head office. New systems suggested by such strategies usually mean far-reaching changes to current work practices. The implementation of such systems is not a trivial exercise. It is at this point that top management can no longer avoid getting involved with the way IT is used in their organization.

It seems clear that many organizations have reached this point.

A number of indicators support this view. Various surveys in the last two years have established that top management support is thought to be crucial if major new IT projects are to be successful (e.g. AT Kearney, 1990). Three contributors to Part Two, David Norman, David Axson and John Swift identify lack of top management support for or understanding of IT as a key factor in the current poor return on IT investment. All the contributions to this section bear out the current concern with issues that surface when IT becomes a corporate issue. Many companies have a large investment in IT, but located in a series of separate applications. They are only now beginning the struggle to find a corporate stance.

Southwestern Ohio Steel provides a good example of what happens when a company moves towards this position (Rockart and Crescenzi, 1984). A major review of the company's information systems capability was turned over to a consulting firm which had been used by Ohio Steel in the past. The resulting proposals were expensive and management felt that the tie between the systems proposed and the business needs were unclear. The company rejected these proposals and set out to find ways of enabling its top management to plan for new system development. The Dairy Crest case, reported by John Freestone in Chapter 6 of this book, came to a similar conclusion. The IT application was an innovative one. Data communications were to be used to keep all three parties to the business, Dairy Crest the franchises and the catering customers, fully informed of all transactions. It was crucial to the future viability of the business that this be operated economically. Consultants were hired to take sole responsibility for the design and implementation of the system. Their first proposals were expensive and did not meet the needs or objectives of the business. In an interview with the author, the project manager took the view that these proposals embodied little understanding of the requirements of the proposed business. It was at this stage that he decided that he could no longer abrogate responsibility for the IT part of the project, although he himself knew little on the subject at the time. He proceeded to take charge, bringing in IT expertise as necessary and largely teaching himself the knowledge of IT that he needed. The results are described in the case.

13.3 TOP MANAGEMENT'S FUTURE INVOLVEMENT WILL INTENSIFY

A successful transition to the integrated use of IT is merely the beginning. Many more innovative uses of IT for competitive advantage then become possible. Potential choices of strategic direction multiply.

However, this can usually only be achieved through major changes to the business and a commitment to long-term investment. Two recent research programmes into the use of IT stress the potential to be gained from combining appropriate IT applications with basic redesign of business processes (Scott Morton, 1991; Butler Cox, 1991). But to gain this advantage a major reorganization of the company will be necessary.

The matter is urgent. The original isolated examples of using IT to gain competitive edge, such as at Thompson Holidays, are beginning to be joined by others. Companies in various industries are making the investment and going through the pain of reorganization (Hammer, 1990; Hammer and Mangurian, 1987; Scott Morton, 1991). The magnitude of the benefits that they experience means that they are going to dominate their markets. Companies that have mastered IT will accelerate away from the competition. The long-term nature of the investment means that it is too late to react when your competitor unveils a radical new IT-enabled strategy. Hence the consequences of action or inaction now will affect the organization for years to come.

Only top management can initiate such projects. There will be major choices of direction to be made. Investment will be high. There will be extensive disruption to operations. The consequences will be radical. Payoff will be comparatively slow. Time horizons could be long.

13.4 TOP MANAGEMENT KNOWLEDGE OF AND ATTITUDES TO IT

It seems likely that many senior managers will as yet know too little about IT in general or more particularly about how it could affect their business. Most will have gained their business experience at middle management level prior to the recent explosion of end-user applications. They could well have reached senior management levels without personal exposure to IT. Since many organizations are still in the level 1 stage of isolated IT applications, it is inevitable that many senior managers will have progressed upward without having to consider the use of IT in their own functional departments. In any case their attitudes will have been formed in the period when it was usual and acceptable to leave project proposals to the IT department.

The available evidence certainly supports this view. The latest Price Waterhouse Information Technology Review (1991) quotes the results of its survey of IT directors' views on 'the culture gap' (between IT professionals and the rest of the company). IT directors consider that 'the IT potential for improving business performance is not appreciated by top management'. The article cites imprecise corporate objectives for IT as the second most serious problem for these executives, and goes on to interpret this as top management's lack of understanding (of IT). Many other writers have reported on the neglect of management education generally in IT, so it seems safe to assume that a significant proportion of senior management are likely to have a less than adequate understanding of the subject when IT strategy is brought up for discussion as part of the business strategy (Earl, 1989) (IT and the New Manager, 1990; conference). In the case example at Dairy Crest, the manager in charge of the project told the author that he had no knowledge of IT prior to the inception of the project. Neither did any of his staff.

Resistance to and fear of IT on the part of many managers has been variously reported (Holtham, IT and the New Manager, 1990; conference). At the City University Business School until the last few years our experience has always been that a small number of MBA students every year would resist learning to use a keyboard, and clearly felt that IT would be of little relevance to their future work. We no longer find this attitude. Fear can be attributed to ignorance, resistance can be attributed to the lack of understanding of the potential importance of IT. But Kit Grindley, in Chapter 8 of this book, also makes a powerful case for fear of the inevitable changes that IT brings to people's (and managers') working lives. Exposure to successful IT applications and education and training programmes can help to increase knowledge and understanding of IT. However, to the extent that IT brings painful change, resistance and fear can be expected to continue. To make continuing change not only acceptable but sought after, organizations will need to restructure themselves so as to incorporate change as a way of institutional life.

The mutual suspicion of IT professionals and management referred to by a number of writers (Price Waterhouse 1991), (Kit Grindley, John Swift and Iain Perring in this book), seems in part due to mutual ignorance, in part due to mutually unrealistic expectations, but also in part due to the profound differences in the way in which the two groups work and in the nature of the work that they do. It is clearly desirable that this suspicion is mitigated to some extent if both groups are to sit down together to shape an IT strategy.

Senior managers, because they have less chance to be exposed to IT as part of their routine activities, may need to make a greater effort to obtain a balanced assessment of the role of IT in their organization. Exactly what they need to know will vary from organization to organization and it is yet far from clear what should be included in any education programme. Their time is scarce. How much of it needs to be devoted to this issue? The design of any top management IT education programmes will not be simple.

13.5 CURRENT APPROACHES TO TOP MANAGEMENT EDUCATION IN IT

The one aspect on which there appears to be general agreement is that any top management IT education must form part of a general organization-wide IT programme for management. Michael Earl (Earl, 1989) suggests that companies need to see senior management IT education as part of their total approach to building their capability in IT and its management. This is clearly the case for those organizations making the transition to the integrated use of IT. At this point IT becomes a significant factor in most aspects of the business and hence potentially important to management at all levels. Top management involvement and hence education only become urgent when this point is reached. It is entirely consistent then that top management IT education programmes are needed when maximum results will be yielded from a company-wide management IT education programme.

Michael Earl reports that such programmes are still rare and those that do exist offer little satisfaction to the participants or their company. Organizations found problems in getting top management's commitment to their own education (and to that of the rest of the company) and did not consider it easy to design courses on IT of relevance to their company's needs. The conference (IT and the New Manager, 1990) supported this finding.

The challenge then is to design a package that fits the time that top management can allocate, that offers useful knowledge which is considered relevant to the company's situation in a user-friendly way. Such a package should intermesh with and complement a range of other courses designed for the rest of the company staff and take account explicitly of the need for some form of continuous learning for the foreseeable future. The two cases described next illustrate the two most common starting positions. British Airways is currently in the middle of a long-term programme of executive education in IT aimed at raising the overall level of understanding of IT company-wide. The company reached a position in 1987, when IT was so pervasive that the need for a high level of management competence in its use was accepted at board level. Southwestern Ohio Steel arrived at the need to educate senior executives in the possibilities of IT, during 1984, when presented with costly and inappropriate proposals for new information systems from their consultants.

13.5.1 British Airways

British Airways launched a new management IT education programme called Catalyst during 1987. The situation at that time was highly pertinent. This was a company with over 20 years' experience of using computers. It had a world-wide network and used a wide range of both technologies and applications throughout the various functions. Many applications were and are at the leading edge. British Airways was moving from purely localized exploitation of IT. Privatization occurred in February 1987, putting pressure on the company to think and behave in a more business-orientated way. At the same time it had the example of American Airlines SABRE computerized reservation system to make clear the potential of IT for competitive advantage.

The programme was initiated by the IT director at BA and is described in some detail in an article by Janet Windeatt and Isobel Knox (Windeatt and Knox,1991). It aimed to revolutionize attitudes to IT in both the IT department and on the part of management. The principal objectives of phase 1 were to get senior management to 'buy in', 'to educate managers in the rest of the business about the changing role of IT' and to build a business-focused IT department. A key assumption was that this was not an objective that could be achieved in a short time. For the management part of the programme there were four components, of which two were aimed specifically at senior management. The programme has now (in 1991) been running for four years during which time it has reached over 75% of all management. Planning for phase 2, aimed at enabling managers to exploit the existing investment in IT to the full, started in early 1991.

The clear aim of the senior management modules was to get their attention and establish the importance of IT throughout the company. All courses were voluntary and hence had to be interestingly presented and seen to be relevant. The format and standard of presentation was therefore extremely important. A bimonthly management briefing timed for late afternoon and early evening proved very effective. Each session was structured around one theme with speakers discussing the business implications of Information Technology. A BA director opened, presenting the airline perspective of the theme. The main speaker was external. The session finished with coffee leaving some time for informal discussion by participants. These sessions were sometimes preceded by a lunch for the speaker together with BA managers or alternatively followed by a dinner for the speaker. Attendance at all briefings has been high – around 250 on average. Their success is attributed to the high quality of all the speakers, the subjects chosen, the format and the presence of a director. The chance for informal discussion was also thought to be as valuable as the formal proceedings. At a later stage, a three-day residential course on IT as a strategic tool, was introduced exclusively for senior managers. Here time is spent reviewing the experience of other companies in using IT as well as in discussion on the potential for BA. The briefings are continuing at present and offer a useful method for dealing with the need for some form of continuous education.

From internal surveys, the size of attendance and individual feedback, BA feel that the programme has been a considerable success. In an interview with the author, Janet Windeatt gave the following key reasons for success:

- The ownership of the education programme by the IT director.
- The total backing of both the CEO and the IT director for the education initiative, and more importantly their support for it in terms of their time.
- The high quality of the external speakers.
- The intensive use of marketing techniques, such as branding, in order to sell the programme to every employee of BA

The approach taken by BA appears to be broadly in line with that advocated by Michael Earl (Earl, 1989) based on his experience of designing management education courses for large organizations at the Oxford Institute of Information Management. Windeatt and Knox's description, however, makes clear the size and scale of such programmes. The BA programme draws a more precise distinction between education for the general understanding of IT and its changing role at BA (phase 1) and courses aimed at identifying more business-specific applications (phase 2). It clearly meets one of Earl's main expectations that a substantial part of any programme will be organization-specific – dependent both on how IT can help the organization in its individual requirements and on the current all-round knowledge of IT within it.

For some educators the teaching of PC skills is seen as a way of reducing fear of computers (Holtham, IT and the New Manager, 1990; conference). It is also a way of starting to understand how computers work and hence the benefits and limitations of IT. However, it is time consuming. Neither BA nor Earl consider the teaching of such skills to senior managers as more than an optional extra, only really justified when significant improvements to individual managerial productivity can be achieved.

13.5.2 Southwestern Ohio Steel

This case forms a contrast to BA (Rockart and Crescenzi, 1984) and is of some interest as it represents in an extreme form the way in which many external consultants first get involved in top management IT education. The company was not initially interested in IT education for its executives. It was concerned about company strategy with respect to one fairly specific issue, namely the design and installation of new information systems which would provide more support for management. At the time it was using computer systems to perform only routine accounting functions. This was a company at level 1 (localized use of IT) wishing to make a move to a more sophisticated use of information systems. Dissatisfied with the proposals put forward by their usual consulting firm, Southwestern Ohio came to the conclusion that their top management had to be much more involved in the process of information system design. This was accomplished with the help of the authors, Rockart and Crescenzi, who acted as consultants and educators. Through a series of workshops and individual interviews the authors enabled the management team to identify what information was important to running the business (the critical success factors), link potential information systems to these needs and establish priorities between them. The consultants clearly carried out much of the analysis, but in a way that put management in charge at every step. In the process the management obtained some knowledge of IT in the areas relevant to the problem facing them.

The case describes a situation where conditions focus top management attention on IT and provide an excellent opportunity to start IT education. Consultants are frequently asked in under exactly similar circumstances. The top management team starts to become uneasy with the cost and purpose of IT investments past and future, and turn to consultants to help them gain a greater understanding of the situation. The consultants can then offer a similar type of approach which, unlike BA, gears education from the start to the specific issues and problems facing the organization at the time (Lockett, 1992).

Such approaches are likely to be of limited value unless followed up with a company-wide education scheme and some commitment to continuing education. Most consultants can be expected to emphasize this point.

13.5.3 The Problem of the Culture Gap

The assumption that education will help to close the culture gap is not unreasonable. Of the three contributors to this book (John Swift, Kit Grindley and Iain Perring) who address the issue of culture gap directly, only John Swift looks at it from the senior management view. His proposal for workshops, at which both groups air the problems that they each see in their own jobs, is an interesting one. For senior management to gain some understanding of the sorts of problems that preoccupy IT departments is an extremely important step. However, Kit Grindley's analysis suggests that this will not overcome a lifetime's experience of different working cultures. Our own experience of the last two years at City University Business School of teaching an MBA in Information Technology Management aimed at producing 'hybrid' managers (Leeming, 1991) bears this out. Those students that arrive with a technical background seldom leave (after one year) with much change to their attitudes. How fast or thoroughly senior management can appreciate and take account of IT professionals' problems and attitudes remains to be seen.

13.6 ROLE OF TOP MANAGEMENT

What role will top management be called on to play in the future? If we understand this we can start to design an education programme that meets their needs. Butler Cox in their latest research programme ask the highly pertinent question, 'To what extent should top management be involved?' (in achieving business alignment for IT). The results of this initiative will be of great interest.

The earlier sections on top management involvement with IT give some pointers as to what can be expected in the future. As organizations reach for integration and are aware of so doing, it is only top management that can take responsibility for aligning IT with the organization's business strategy. It is they who must decide where to introduce IT and establish priorities for competing projects.

Corporate utilization of IT begins to affect jobs, organizational structure, internal and external relations and corporate culture. A number of choices of direction occur. In particular, attitudes to human resource issues are diverging between the traditional Taylorist view that the role of the workforce is to carry out exactly instructions issued by management, and the opposing approach that the workforce has a great deal to contribute to the design and execution of production (Scott Morton, 1991). Making the choices, assessing the scale of the impact and managing the changes can only be their responsibility.

Managing change is a traditional management skill but assessing the impact of IT has not been. Ensuring that the organization works towards a common goal is a traditional responsibility. IT both complicates and aids this job. Networks can enormously improve intra-organization communications, but to make use of them the company will have to change the way it works (Hammer and Mangurian, 1987).

Planning for the future is top management's traditional responsibility. IT could add a new dimension, a greater complexity, a longer time horizon, to such planning. For the importance of being able to look ahead to the longer term in a coherent way cannot be overestimated. Numerous writers have established the potential for long-term payoff in IT investment (Leslie Willcocks in this book; Keen, 1988). Moreover the stakes are reputedly getting higher. Lack of an ability to plan for six to seven years ahead may lead to the organization's eventual demise.

Creative leaps for new business ventures can come from all parts of the organization. It is top management's responsibility to assess new proposals and decide whether to back them or not. Some of these new proposals will depend on IT.

13.7 CONSTITUENTS OF A TOP MANAGEMENT EDUCATION PROGRAMME IN IT

The foregoing suggests that senior management will be affected in a number of ways. This section will concentrate on those relating to their role in the creation of IT strategy. The assumption is made that this role has been accepted by the management in question. Other issues relating to their responsibility for making the chosen strategy work will not be addressed directly here.

Four themes emerge. Some are not as yet well understood and hence will be difficult to incorporate into education programmes. Nonetheless this suggests that there are at least four elements to a programme:

- Discussion of the basic concepts of using IT.

- Information on potential, business-based IT applications for an organization and ways to achieve alignment with business strategy at a particular point in time.

- Ways to understand the impact that IT developments could have on an organization and ways to assess its ability to absorb this.

- Ways to assess an organization's current level in the use of IT and ways to think about what the longer term might look like.

The first element deals with the essential differences that IT brings to working life. It deals with both the capabilities and limitations of IT. For the inexperienced user, for the non-specialist in IT, for the manager who has little personal experience of IT applications, understanding the differences are as important as being able to use a specific application. There is a core of these basic concepts that can be understood without becoming particularly expert in IT. Some are uniquely pertinent to IT strategy. Seven are explored in the next section. Current senior management IT courses introduce these issues, usually within the context of the IT applications being considered for the organization at the time. They therefore run the danger of excluding those that are not directly relevant to current applications.

The second element deals directly with the situation as the company now sees it. Many existing courses concentrate on this issue in the sense that they review current potential applications by case study and other means and attempt to analyse the alignment problem. How to achieve alignment with business strategy is an area that is still not fully understood. Various approaches are discussed by contributors to Part Four and extended by K. Hugh Macdonald in Part Five. Perhaps just as significantly there is no comprehensive framework for identifying which applications suit a particular business. Michael Hammer and Glenn Mangurian propose such a framework for communications – intensive information systems only (Hammer and Mangurian, 1987). As they comment 'Without this framework the growing collection of well-known information technology cases simply represent folklore that won't help managers identify their own opportunities for exploiting this technology'. Such a comment applies equally well across the whole range of IT applications.

The third element deals with the impact of IT strategies on the organization. This is an issue that has been given less attention, but various studies suggest that it is an increasingly important issue as organizations become more sophisticated in their use of IT (Scott Morton, 1991). IT is becoming associated with major organizational change. Such changes require top management leadership. Veronica Symons in this section of the book, suggests one way of analysing this issue.

The fourth element would help top management to view the company in comparison with practice elsewhere and hence to consider its position within a longer time horizon. Top management need to be able to see where they stand in order to see where they may have to go. Three papers in Part Five (by Chris Yapp, K. Hugh Macdonald and David Norman) offer ways of starting to assess an organization's current position in the use of IT and a method of structuring the debate about future directions. However, the need for a framework to analyse which IT applications may be of value to the individual organization is just as urgent for long-term planning as for the immediate situation.

13.8 USING IT – SOME BASIC CONCEPTS

13.8.1 IT should be Viewed as a Tool, not a Solution

IT enables organizations to operate in ways that would be difficult if not impossible without it. IT is a tool that can be used to support business activity. But the choice of where to apply it, to which business activity, to what business strategy remains to be made on commercial grounds. IT has the potential to increase efficiency, but will offer no insights on the direction that such efficiency should take. IT offers new products, more information on company operations but no light on where this is of value to the organization. IT can support a variety of ways of organizing and operating a company (Rockart and Short, 1989), but cannot answer the question of which is best. Business practices that impede company operations lie unrecognized and relatively insignificant until the application of IT allows such practices to flourish at many times the rate. Telephone, fax, email are all devices for improving unstructured informal communications. But where ill-thought-out unnecessary messages are being passed around an organization, improving these facilities may simply lead to an increase of traffic and less productive work. The use to which IT is put is one of those questions that only management can answer.

13.8.2 IT Professionals and Managers find it Difficult to Communicate

To create an effective IT strategy the knowledge and understanding of both IT professionals and senior management are extremely important. Both groups need to be able to cooperate and understand the type of contribution that each can make to the debate. However, there is mounting evidence that the two groups do not communicate well with each other. It is certainly the perception of the IT community that there is a language barrier between them and management (Price Waterhouse, 1991).

Nor is this simply a matter of 'jargon'. The two groups work very differently, as Kit Grindley and Iain Perring have discussed elsewhere. For a manager to understand an IT professional he or she will probably have to spend some time in coming to terms with what is involved in system development just as a manager in the construction industry would have to have some understanding of the logistics of building. There is no reason to expect IT professionals to understand how the business operates or more to the point how it could operate. They are experts at making computers work, they are not necessarily experts at deciding what the computers should do. They are experts at handling precision and expect to find it in the world about them. They or their computers handle ambiguity or uncertainty with difficulty. Perhaps it is equally significant that they can find managers frustrating to deal with. Managers find it difficult to describe their world in terms that can be used by IT professionals. Managers are used to trying out new ideas to see if they work, with the understanding that they can throw away the idea if it does not. This is an expensive attitude when it comes to IT. Each group looks for answers to questions that the other would not ask. Pertinent questions are left unasked by either group. Iain Perring suggests ways for IT professionals to bridge this gap. Management will also have to find ways to do the same.

13.8.3 Automation is Difficult to Achieve and has Profound Consequences

The change from manual working to automation is profound, whether in clerical, administrative or manufacturing operations. It will have an impact on the way people work and less obviously on the organizational structure. Veronica Symons has discussed this in more detail in this book. Manual systems are immensely flexible, operated by that most accommodating of animals – man. In contrast, an automated system is inflexible. To automate an existing manual system you need to know not only how the system is supposed to work but also all the actions that each and every human operator takes to rectify the deviations and plug the gaps that appear. To automate completely means catering for every eventuality before going live. This means obtaining information on all possible combinations of outcomes. It appears that many companies cannot describe their activities in this detail or at the level of abstraction necessary to translate easily into an automated system. So that designing the first system can be far more time-consuming than was ever originally estimated. Almost invariably there are many rectifications required after the system goes live. These, which are cheap to institute with live operators, are very expensive, sometimes impossible with an automated system. It is unproductive to blame systems design for lack of clarity about business process.

Automation is expensive and becomes progressively more so with systems that have many exceptions. Payroll was an early example of automation which proved to be far more expensive than anticipated because of the many minor variations to basic rates of pay. Automation may reduce staffing (it will certainly make demands for differently trained staff) but the equipment and software will require maintenance.

Maintenance costs tend to increase over time, not least because of accumulating small changes to what the business needs. Even small changes can have complex ramifications in an automated system.

Automation in general means greater inflexibility. Any change in the way in which the organization runs itself will precipitate demands for changes to existing systems. An organization intent on changing from an hierarchic structure with strong central control to one with maximum devolution of responsibility to myriad small operating units, would find its centralized large-scale computerized accounting systems irrelevant. It would then be necessary to develop accounting capability at the operating unit level. The centre would need to retain responsibility for consolidation. This is happening now (late 1991) to Berkshire County Council. As Paul Raimond has discussed in Chapter 5 new strategic moves may render an existing system irrelevant.

When first considering automation of a manually-run system, it is worth trying to outline how this move fits into the organization's longer-term future. Because of the probable scale of the investment in terms of money, design time and retraining of staff, subsequent change will be slow. Any decision taken at that point will curtail future options. So choices made at the start are not just a means of solving an immediate problem but an expression of how the company will operate for a long time to come. The banks have large-scale systems that no longer do what is wanted but will take time to change. David Axson and Gregory Hackett, in this book, discuss this matter in greater detail, giving some of the drawbacks of automating existing practices. They urge companies to consider changing business procedure before computerizing.

13.8.4 Getting the Maximum Value out of IT Investment means Major Change

Once past localized exploitation of IT, any organization wishing to make best use of IT will have start thinking in terms of major change.

Successful use of IT from this stage on will depend as much on the skills and understanding of all staff as on the professional IT group. Training becomes of major and continuing importance.

It is likely that fundamental improvements can be made in business operations. Business process redesign is but one example (Hammer, 1990). This will carry with it the need to reorganize the organizational structure, change the nature of many jobs including management and alter cultural norms. Nor will it be valuable to think in terms of one massive reorganization. Environmental turbulence and technology developments now being forecast will conspire to reward organizations that can handle continuous change.

13.8.5 IT will Change the Manager's Job

IT is changing the nature and scope of many managers' jobs, and it is not easy to initiate changes that change your own job.

Middle management is being affected in several ways. Part of their traditional functions of communications coordination and control are being taken on by computer systems. Automation is taking over clerical jobs and reducing the need for clerical workers. This in turn reduces the need for supervisors and hence managers. Sophisticated executive information systems are beginning to appear, providing the sort of information to senior management that middle management previously provided. Downsizing and 'flattening' are gathering pace. The effect on those managers that remain, middle and senior, is or will be to increase their span of control and range of responsibilities. Corporate information systems provide up-to-date knowledge of the company's performance. To handle this, managers will need to take on more of an analyst role. The need will be for sophisticated management.

Future developments can be expected to change the manager's job further, according to such commentators as Applegate, Cash and Mills (1988). They foresee a 'cluster organization' in which groups of people will work together to solve problems and then disband. Management will be a part-time job with leadership rotating. There will be few overseeing jobs and most employees will take on a management role for short periods.

13.8.6 Management of IT for the Whole Organization is a Complex Affair

As organizations move towards the integrated use of IT, the management of IT on behalf of the whole organization involves more than running the DP department. It becomes a top management responsibility.

There are management responsibilities throughout the organization. Equipment becomes physically distributed with control passing in some cases to the users. Basic questions of how IT resources are to be organized arise. Should they be centralized or decentralized? Should some form of federal structure be adopted? How do you choose to support equipment at physically dispersed sites, especially if software support is required?

Other questions become urgent. Who should be responsible for user IT training and who for the IT professionals training? What responsibility should the users be allowed or urged to take? When new systems re-arrange organizational relationships, who should be made responsible for implementing them? Where should the responsibility lie for assessing the company's vulnerability to breakdown, and ensuring that reasonable levels of reliability are maintained?

The problem for many organizations is that IT has spread fast, leaving some of these managerial responsibilities undefined. It is often unclear as to who, if anyone, is responsible for important functions.

13.8.7 Reliable Systems involve Business as well as Technical Decisions

Reliability is a key issue for organizations that become dependent on IT. Marco Kapp, writing in this book, suggests that this is currently one of those issues to which many organizations are devoting too little attention. The core question is how much is it worth spending to achieve greater reliability? It is not, after all, ever possible to achieve 100% reliability. A subsidiary but important practical question is how much reliability in one area is matched by reliability in others. A highly secure system in one department is of little overall use, if it is continually brought to a halt by breakdown in a system in another part of the organization. Since the target degree of reliability must therefore be a business decision, it is not clear who should be responsible for the whole corporation.

13.9 CONCLUSION

Senior managers need to take a far more active role in the development and implementation of IT strategy. Since many of them know little about the subject, senior management IT education is becoming an urgent requirement. Only top management are in a position to ensure the alignment of IT with the corporation's business now and in the longer term, and to initiate and manage the major changes that this is about to bring. Hence they need to know not only what IT can achieve for their business but also how it will impact and change it. Education courses should therefore include more than the appropriate knowledge of relevant IT applications.

REFERENCES

Applegate L, Cash J Jr and Mills D Q (1988) Information Technology and Tomorrow's Manager, *Harvard Business Review*, November-December 1988, vol. 66, no 6.

A T Kearney (1990) *Breaking the Barriers, IT Effectiveness in Great Britain and Ireland*, CIMA

Butler Cox (1991) *The Role of IT in Transforming the Business*, no. 79

Earl M J (1989) *Management Strategies for Information Technologies,* Business Information Technology Series, Prentice-Hall

Hammer M (1990) Reengineering Work: Don't Automate, Obliterate, *Harvard Business Review*, no. 4

Hammer M and Mangurian G (1987) The Changing Value of Communications Technology, *Sloan Management Review*, 65, Winter

IT and the New Manager: designing an IT education programme for executives. Conference organized by *Computer Weekly* and *Business Intelligence* 1990, reported in the *Journal of Information Technology*, June 1990

Keen P (1988) *Competing in Time*, Ballinger Publishing Co.

Leeming A (1991) Management Development for the 90s, *The Computer Bulletin*

Lockett M (1992) From Awareness to Action – The Role of IT Executive Education, *Computer Services Association Yearbook*

Price Waterhouse, *Information Technology Review* 1991/92

Rockart J and Crescenzi A D (1984) Engaging Top Management in Information Technology, *Sloan Business Review*, MIT, vol. 24, no. 4

Rockart J and Short J (1989) IT in the 1990s: managing organizational interdependence, *Sloan Management Review*; 30

Scott Morton M (1991) *The Corporation of the 1990s*, Oxford University Press

Windeatt J and Knox I (1991) Catalyst: a programme for change within British Airways, *Journal of Information Technology*, vol. 6

Part Four

Organizing to Create an IT Strategy

14 Investigating and interpreting business strategy

P. Griffiths
DCE Information Management Consultancy

14.1 INTRODUCTION

An IS/IT strategy can only be of significant value to a business if it is closely coupled to the business strategy.

In most cases this means that each IS/IT investment stemming from the process is defined as an integral part of a business initiative. Examples of a business initiative could include the opening up of a new market or distribution channel, a product development venture, or perhaps a cross-functional project to improve productivity or to provide usable management information.

Increasingly IS/IT is required to provide a flexible infrastructure, capable of responding swiftly to changes dictated by external pressures. As an outcome of planning, the role and competitive stance of IS/IT in the business should be determined. The components of IT supply should be adjusted to fit this role, and meet the prioritized demands of the business. These supply components include the management of the applications portfolio; the processing and communicating architectures; the corporate information environment; methods and standards employed; and the organizational structure.

However, the first essential is to obtain a deep understanding of the business strategy, and of the environment in which it operates, so that opportunities to make significant contributions are identified.

This insight into the current and future needs of the business can then be used in a number of ways:

- Business needs and opportunities are interpreted into information-related requirements for processing, communication and access. This leads to the identification of the required databases and the applications portfolio.
- Priorities associated with business demands feed the development of IS/IT priorities.
- Current IS/IT provisions are examined to assess their coverage of the key elements of the business, their contribution to satisfying existing needs, and their appropriateness for the future.
- The role of IS/IT, its stance and supply characteristics are all determined.

14.2 OBTAINING THE BUSINESS UNDERSTANDING

There are several difficulties that can bedevil attempts to obtain business understanding. Sometimes there is no apparent business strategy, or it may not be written down, or very difficult to extract. Alternatively, the good starting basis of a documented strategy may offer widely differing benefits.

It can come as a thick document containing detailed functional budgets and short-term targets, or at the other end of the spectrum, as a few pages of visionary views about the direction the industry is moving in, and where the company must place itself in order to attain or retain its competitive success. The latter version generally provides a more useful starting-point than the former. It is probable that through a process of discussion with the senior executive body, together with analysis and some further investigation, the basic mission of the organization, its projected image and its high-level business objectives can be identified and confirmed.

The most frequent omission from this type of high-level business strategy statement is the absence of information about the new initiatives that the business needs to introduce to meet its objectives. This would not be so important in a relatively stable business where objectives for, say, incremental growth, improvements in productivity and cost containment drive the business, and change is similarly incremental. However, most businesses today seem to sit in an intensely competitive and fast changing environment, where very tough objectives have to be set, and radical changes introduced to achieve them.

In this case a very close working relationship must be established between the business executives and IS/IT planners, in which the true nature of the business needs are investigated, and the necessary initiatives defined and described, at least at a high level. The impact these will have on the business can then be determined, and business responses formulated. IS/IT responses are then determined as an inherent part of the business responses.

Whilst this poses a hazard for the swift derivation of an IS/IT plan, it can also be a major opportunity, if the right people with the right mix of skills are available, and the right attitudes prevail. This is because, in articulating the initiatives for the business, and the changes needed in business activities, culture, management and organization, it is possible to ensure that the full potential for using IS/IT as a core resource is fully exploited.

Another common difficulty occurs when the strategy is poorly communicated throughout the business. It may not seriously jeopardize the ability of the planning team to build up an understanding of the business needs, and a high-level picture of the initiatives. However, if middle managers, who will be key to the detailed planning and successful implementation of new initiatives, are not fully aware of the strategy, it is difficult for the team to recognize possible pitfalls, and the practicalities involved. Further, if these managers are aware of forthcoming change, they are unlikely to be able to assess the true impact of changing needs on the existing situation, in both business and IS/IT terms. As this is the starting-point for migration planning, it is clearly a problem to be overcome. Its resolution may force a delay in IS/IT planning, until all the business managers are satisfactorily briefed.

Some other obstacles may have to be surmounted. One of these is the avoidance of hidden agendas, not just from the IS/IT arena, but from anywhere in the business. It is necessary to impress on all concerned, that the effort and cost associated with planning are substantial and decisions taken about long-term and substantial investments are significant. They can be damaged, even invalidated, and are certain to be sub-optimized if important factors are kept hidden.

It may be necessary to work hard to dislodge any preconceived views about the appropriate role of IS/IT in the business. In many organizations it is seen entirely as a means of providing efficiency in automating core processes. Much work in marketing a new potential image and role may then be necessary to enable IS/IT to be treated as a core business resource.

At first it may be difficult to convince senior management to start off the planning process, since there always seem to be imminent uncertainties such as are caused by new product development, reorganization, new management appointments, squeezed margins or heavy campaigns from competitors. It is well worthwhile arguing for undertaking the plan ahead of or during such turbulent times, as the proper application of IS/IT can provide unexpected and previously unconsidered benefits.

14.3 THE PLANNING PROCESS

The process for obtaining the necessary understanding varies from business to business but has some common elements. In all cases, it is important to understand the structure of the industry, its maturity, the key players, level of competition and the factors determining success or failure.

It is then possible to investigate the position of the business in relation to the external industrial environment, and to gain awareness of the products and services in its portfolio. It is quite possible that the IS/IT support is not well balanced in relation to the portfolio. For example, it may not support the identification, acquisition and exploitation of new and growing markets.

Further investigation of the competitive arena may indicate opportunities to support the business thrusts that build up barriers against rival businesses or new entrants into the field, or that improve the balance of power with buyers or suppliers. It is also quite likely that, in investigating these areas, it will become evident that too little consideration has been given to business responses to external stimuli, or to perceived business imperatives. If these can be formulated at this time, then the IS/IT element can be built into the overall response.

The internal strategic framework, comprising the mission, objectives, goals, initiatives, critical success factors, strengths, weaknesses, activities and inherent information is assessed in the light of the stimuli acting upon it. (See Figure 14.1.).

By a systematic analysis of the external pressures and their implications for the business, the most appropriate business responses may be identified. It is then necessary to assess how much these will change the business, and what IS/IT can do to make the greatest contribution. This may be a mixture of:

- Upgrading the existing portfolio.
- Developing a set of new systems and databases.
- Investigating future options which may have a worthwhile role to play.

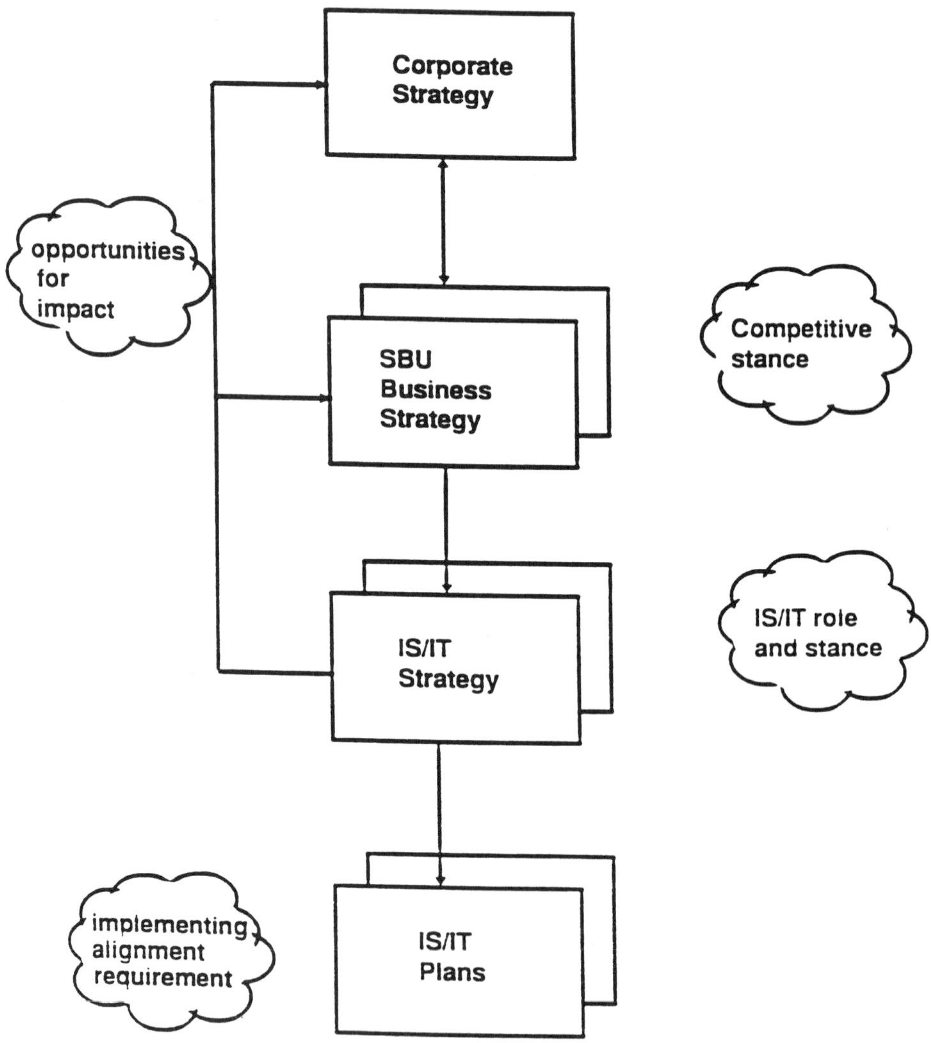

Figure 14.1. Objectives of IS/IT strategy planning

This evolving portfolio represents the IS/IT demand for the business.

Completion of the planning process for the first time does not mark the end of the story. The management and maintenance of the strategy, in line with the business's own evolving strategy, is ultimately rather more important. It requires continuous monitoring of external and internal environments so that changes to the business and IS/IT strategies can be anticipated. (See Figure 14.2.). As a result, the portfolio and its associated priorities may need to be changed.

This very brief description of the process of understanding the business need can only hope to give a flavour of the reality. The process cannot be prescribed in advance and always poses various challenges.

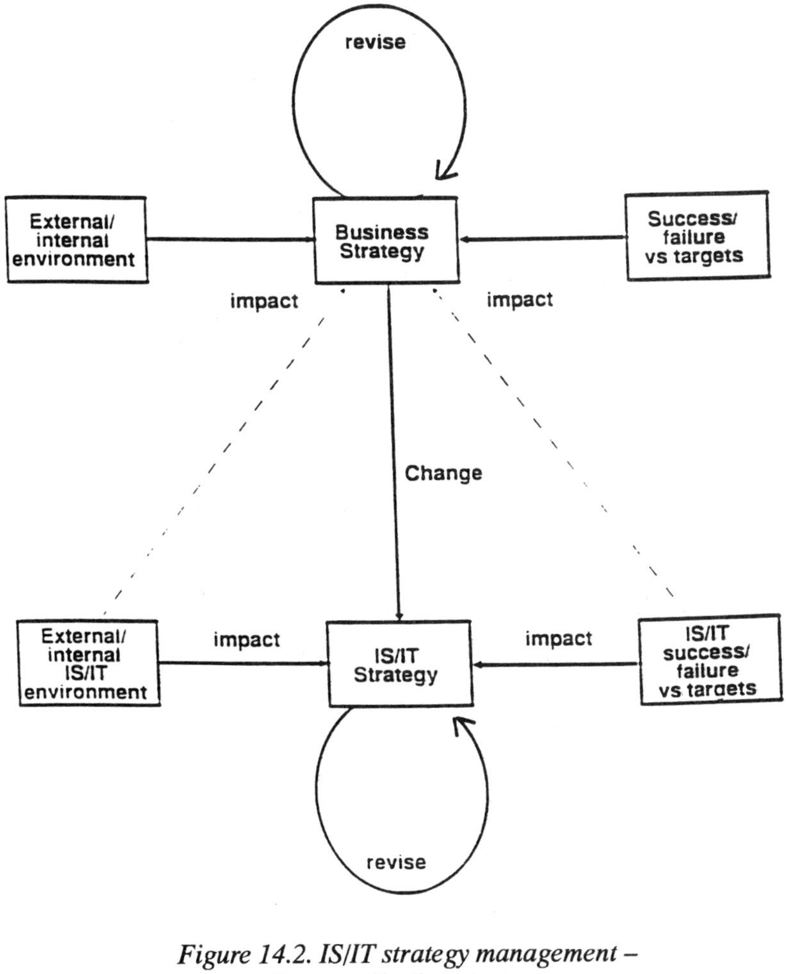

Figure 14.2. IS/IT strategy management – factors affecting strategy

14.4 IT SUPPLY MANAGEMENT – MANAGING THE APPLICATIONS PORTFOLIO

Having arrived at the IS/IT demand, expressed in the form of an application portfolio based on business strategy, then the IT supply requirements can be considered.

This usually involves the creation of a conceptual information architecture for the business, followed by proposals on applications, processing, networking and database architectures, together with policies, plans and organizational recommendations.

The remainder of this paper focuses on managing the applications portfolio itself, as so much of the IT supply side derives from this.

The systems comprising the existing and planned portfolios do not form a homogeneous set. An effective approach to managing the ever-changing portfolio requires some form of classification, where the members of the groups can be treated more or less similarly from a variety of perspectives. This approach is described briefly here, but is covered in much more detail in 'Strategic Planning for Information Systems' (Ward, Griffiths and Whitmore, 1990).

One of the most useful classification methods stems from work originally undertaken by McFarlan (1984) in which he categorized the whole portfolio of a business into one of four types. John Ward of Cranfield School of Management has also done a considerable amount of work on matrix-based approaches to IS/IT issues (Ward, 1988). In this instance he suggests that applications can be individually classified into the categories first advanced by McFarlan.

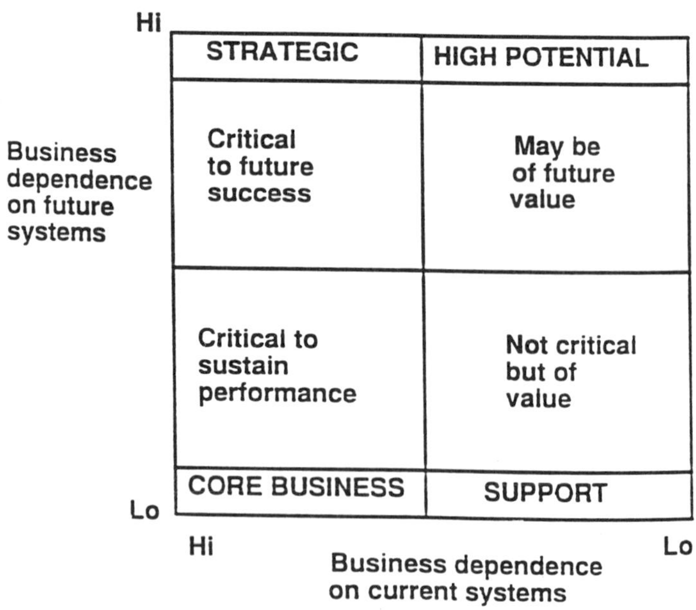

Figure *14.3. Classifying the applications portfolio*

Figure 14.3 illustrates the portfolio classified this way. The two axes relate to the contribution made by the application to current business success, and to the expected contribution from systems to the future business success. The four resultant boxes are labelled as :

- *Support* where business dependence on current and future systems is low. These systems are said to be of value to the business but not critical. They are usually the legally necessary systems, and basic financial systems. They can be seen to be correctly categorized by confirming that the business would not be seriously and immediately disadvantaged if they were not available. Their selection is dependent on cost effectiveness of IS/IT investment.

- *Core business (or factory)* systems are those which are critical to sustain current business performance, and indeed where the business would be severely disadvantaged if they were not available for even a short while.

- *Strategic* systems are those which are agreed to be critical to the future success of the business, either because they are directly delivering new strategic products or services for the business (as in many financial or data services), or because they are essential supporting components for delivering critical products or services (as in systems that link businesses together and in the process increase the collective value delivered).

- *High potential* systems are those where there may be substantial value to be derived from them, but they are as yet unproven. They may be exploring a new business idea and seeing how IS/IT can enhance it, or may be attempting to find the right way to exploit a piece of new technology.

A very simple expression of the underlying objective of each type can be overlaid onto this basic classification:

- *Doing the same – cheaper.* This means improving productivity. Here applications in the support box are only worth developing if they achieve the same aim for a significantly lower cost. Here for example would be the case where a payroll system costs a great deal in terms of operational and resource costs to keep it running and up-to-date with essential changes. A much cheaper alternative could be to switch to a standard package or to contract the operation of the payroll to a third party.

- *Doing the same – better.* Whilst there is often an element of improved efficiency of an individual process, the primary drive in the core systems box is to improve effectiveness in undertaking a task or set of tasks. This may be through increasing the value through improved linkages, reduced duplication or faster delivery of benefits, or providing better information as a by-product.

- *Doing something new and adding value.* This represents developing new applications to address new requirements that clearly add value to the business by meeting objectives, providing and sustaining competitive advantage, avoiding a competitive disadvantage, helping to manage or monitor strategy.

- *Doing something new to test its potential.* This is trying out new ideas as described above.

As mentioned earlier, the current portfolio is the starting-point for the evolution of the portfolio to its target point. So it is essential to evaluate the current systems and those under development to ensure that they are providing benefit to the business, and to assess whether their contribution could be increased, or indeed is at risk because of any current weakness or problem.

14.5 APPLICATIONS PORTFOLIO POLICIES AND TASKS

As stated earlier, the applications portfolio of an organization is very unlikely to comprise a homogeneous collection of systems serving the same set of business objectives, needing the same type of management or development approach, or justified in the same way. It is therefore practical to consider sub-classifications of the portfolio in determining appropriate application management approaches.

It is convenient to use the portfolio classification described earlier, and several aspects are addressed using this approach:

- Generic IS/IT management styles.

- Personal management styles.

- Economics and risk.

- Determining priorities.

- Development approaches.

14.5.1 Generic IS/IT Management Styles

In considering appropriate management strategies for the portfolio, it will be apparent that the approach suitable for strategic systems will be very different from that best suited for support systems. Parsons (1983) observed that there are six principal generic strategies for managing IS/IT. He called them linking strategies, referring to how businesses link the management of IS/IT with the corporate and business management processes. Each provides a different approach to setting IT objectives and policies, to the resourcing of the IS/IT function, to how projects are conceived and justified, and so on. He claimed that applying the appropriate strategy or set of strategies can help to ensure that the targets of the business are not impeded by incorrectly applied IT effort.

The six strategies described by Parsons are:

- Centrally planned.
- Leading edge.
- Free market
- Monopoly.
- Scarce resource.
- Necessary evil.

They are an evocative clutch of terms, which can readily be mapped onto the four quadrants of the portfolio (strategic, high potential, core business, support). A brief summary of the main characteristics of each strategy follows, together with the portfolio category they best support.

Centrally Planned

Responsibility for IS/IT strategy and its alignment to business strategy is centrally located at a senior level, perhaps the top management steering group. This group needs to be knowledgeable, having an understanding of competitive business opportunities and needs, and of the potential of IT to modify business strategy. Its remit is to identify and exploit creative IS/IT opportunities, and then to commit the resources of the business to achieving the potential.

This generic strategy is most suitable for managing strategic quadrant applications. Its main advantage is rapid and effective response to strategic IT opportunities. Its main disadvantage is that it requires a significant amount of senior management time, effort and commitment, which may not be acceptable to some organizations.

Leading Edge

Companies who adopt a leading-edge strategy are committed to use of state-of-the-art technology to create business opportunities. They are prepared to invest significant sums in R&D to explore technical potential, whilst expecting much of this investment to be unprofitable. Senior management commitment is necessary, but not their close involvement in the projects. A high degree of technical skill is needed in this environment, and also very effective working relationships between IT and business management to ensure that opportunities are directed towards business goals.

This strategy is most appropriate for high potential systems, but in some organizations where IT is generally acknowledged to be a competitive weapon, then the strategy can be adopted for strategic systems. The best solution may be to hand over high potential applications to centrally planned management once the project has been proven to have major strategic benefit to the firm. Its main advantage lies in its ability to translate technical potential into significant business advantage, but this is achieved at high cost, and must be carefully watched to ensure that it does not deviate from the paramount business interests.

Free Market

This strategy implies that users manage their own IS strategies, and make their own decisions about how to meet IT needs, either using in-house resources or going to external IT suppliers. Central management does not become involved, either in user issues or in internal IS/IT services. Alignment of IT with business strategy can only happen at the user level.

This strategy can be effective in either the high potential or support quadrants. In the former, users are sophisticated in their ability to identify IT needs and opportunities that could bring good value to their business area. In the latter, user investment will be governed by financial imperatives, associated with low-risk projects. Its main advantages lie in the possible alignment of IT alongside front-line business activities, and the improvement in internal services, prompted by the necessity to be competitive. Its primary disadvantages may lie in the danger of duplication of IS/IT effort in the business, and loss of potential synergy. Also there is a danger that inexperienced users may adopt the support-type portfolio rather than one which seeks to impact the business. It may also be very difficult to move on from a free market strategy once the users have established control over their own IT.

Monopoly

The internal IS/IT group are sole suppliers of IT services to the organization. Users are required to use the utility, and IS/IT are required to meet demand in the most cost-effective way, either through their own resources or by contracting services for the user.

It is an appropriate strategy for core business systems, and can be a suitable, if expensive way of meeting support systems. Effectiveness is measured by user satisfaction, and by meeting demands with a high-quality, cost-effective service. Duplication of effort is unlikely, but so is business innovation, since users perceive IT to be the responsibility of the monopoly. Providing user satisfaction implies a need for excess capacity in operational and skilled resource terms. It may be difficult to interest top management in playing a central role in aligning IS/IT and business if a monopoly has previously served the business effectively.

Scarce Resource

The organization's use of IS/IT is constrained by limiting the overall IT budget. Legally necessary systems are developed, but otherwise only low-risk, high-payback systems can be justified and are easily prioritized in order of best NPV.

This strategy is suitable for support systems. IS/IT is managed as a cost centre, and its greatest disadvantage is that it is very difficult to justify any systems without a sound ROI argument, which militates against strategic or high potential projects. It is also unlikely that users are satisfied, since the budget is always restricted. There may therefore be a tendency for free market strategies to spring up – perhaps for the wrong reasons.

Necessary Evil

This strategy is not really appropriate to consider in an environment where effectiveness and positive contribution from IS/IT is required. IS/IT expenditure is only considered when legally necessary to provide a very high ROI in terms of cost avoidance or displacement.

It is therefore a strategy only viable when considering support type applications. It can be a highly dangerous strategy to adopt or to fall into by accident, since staff turnover can rise dramatically due to low morale; skills fall sharply; and IS/IT management become over cautious and unable to return to a more balanced attitude to the role of IS in the business.

Historically, companies have tended to apply a single generic IS/IT strategy across their business. For example, most major corporations set up large-scale monopolies to provide IS/IT services to their companies. Some of these remain largely intact, although in many cases free market elements have been set up in the more IT-literate user areas, where they no longer considered that they had to use the sole in-house source. Also many private and public sector organizations began to offer their IS/IT services to external buyers as well as in-house. West Wiltshire District Council were one of the first local authorities to start up in this way. Others such as ISTEL became essentially a separate organization soon after they began to offer their services to external companies.

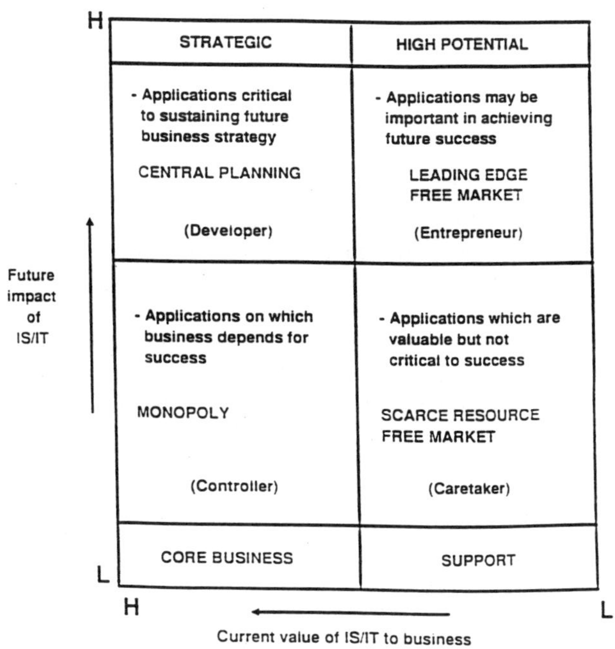

Figure 14.4. Application portfolio management tasks – generic IS strategies and management styles

In his paper, Parsons suggested the best fit for generic strategies on the basis that firms predominantly had applications portfolios that focused on one or another category, (strategic, high potential etc.). However, looking at organizations who are likely to have a portfolio with applications balanced more widely across the four categories, it is more useful to consider generic strategies from the point of view of applying appropriate generic styles to the different categories. See Figure 14.4.

They are useful in two ways:

- to describe concisely the way in which IS/IT is being managed at the time the current mechanisms are evaluated.
- to define application management supply strategies for the future.

An organization is likely to need to adopt a range of strategies to cover an extensive and balanced portfolio.

14.5.2 Personal Management Styles

As well as responding better to different generic IS/IT management styles, different styles of personal management are also required to successfully develop the various types of applications. As each application progresses around its life-cycle, then different management styles (and probably different management) will be needed. Ward (1988) suggests a set of personal management styles for each of the quadrants in the portfolio.

High potential applications demand an **entrepreneurial** style to champion the application, either to success, when they are taken up as a strategic initiative, or to abandon the attempt without the stigma of failure – in which case they are efficiently disposed of and useful lessons noted. This management style does not accept conventions and status quo, but seeks change and innovation. New challenges keep the entrepreneur happy, by nature a free marketer.

Strategic applications need a **developer**, who will ensure that the project gets the resources and commitment it needs. He thrives on achievement, which in this case means meeting organizational objectives. His style cannot be rigid, as he has to adapt to developing business needs, whilst keeping his eye on the goal. It is in his hands to ensure the reality of 'alignment' of business and IS/IT initiatives. He is not restless for new challenges like the entrepreneur, but sees his impact on the organization in a longer-term framework, fulfilling part of the central planning role.

Core business systems need a **controller**. He is there to ensure that risk is kept to a minimum through strict adherence to quality management, application of well-defined standards, and that the job is done right first time. Change control will be imposed and change discouraged. The controller will be the champion of effective software engineering principles applied throughout a rich system's development life-cycle methodology. He would be happiest in a strictly controlled monopoly.

Support applications need a **caretaker**. His satisfaction comes from keeping support applications going with a minimum of resources and no disruption to the business. He is entirely reactive, and proud of his flexibility, and ability to keep the 'show on the road', a natural scarce resourcer.

The roles are not readily interchangeable, but clearly all are important in the mixed portfolio.

14.5.3 Economics and Risk

Whilst it is difficult enough to quantify system costs, it becomes even more difficult when quantifying benefit. Parker and Benson (1988) offer several helpful suggestions. They describe five techniques for evaluating benefits:

- Traditional cost/benefit analysis, which addresses cost avoidance and cost displacement factors.
- 'Value linking' which quantifies improvement in performance resulting from improving one function and causing a 'ripple effect' improvement elsewhere, e.g. better information could reduce travel, telephone calls, fewer queries and complaints.
- 'Value acceleration', which considers value and cost effects of introducing a system which speeds up the delivery of benefits elsewhere, e.g. preparing invoices one day earlier.
- 'Value restructuring', which assesses the values associated with reorganizing a job or function.
- 'Innovation valuation', which puts a value on the introduction of new products, services or practices enabled by IS/IT.

A combination of these can then be applied in attempting to grapple with the economics of investments. They cannot offer the complete solution, since it is clearly impossible to put an accurate value on most intangible benefits.

Parker and Benson also propose several classes of value which can be assigned to different types of applications, namely:

- **Return on investment**, which is the most commonly utilized class, deriving from total cost of implementing applications, and tangible benefit analysis, together with assessments of intangible benefits. The techniques for evaluating benefits introduced above can be brought into use here.

- **Strategic match**, which refers to the value obtained by the business from supporting its primary objectives and critical success factors.

- **Competitive advantage**, which refers to the value obtained from introducing new products or services, or from changing the way business is conducted, and from which a competitive lead is established.

- **Management information**, which is the value derived by the business from providing information which is pertinent to the management process of the business area (i.e. improving management effectiveness).

- **Competitive response**, which is the value associated with avoiding a competitive disadvantage, by catching up with the leaders in the field.

- **Strategic IS architecture**, which is linked to the value of an investment in IS/IT which will benefit the business over a long period.

The role of the portfolio approach in assessing investments is to offer guidance to those putting the investment cases together, and to those evaluating them. This is especially so where purely financial cases have been the norm in the past. The classes of value introduced above are useful in ascribing value to a candidate system. Indeed they can be a useful check that a system has been correctly classified in the portfolio. For example, a support system that has elements of value relating to strategic match has probably been incorrectly classified.

Support Applications
The aim of these systems being primarily efficiency, the economic argument is most likely to revolve around justifying a sound return on the investment. This may be in competition for tightly controlled resources from a central fund, under scarce resourcing management, or in the hands of the local management to justify the expenditure within their own area when a free market policy predominates. Risk should be very low, and primarily financial.

Core Business Applications
Systems in this area can have a mixture of aims:

- The effectiveness of the operation and its management processes, where the classes of value addressed are both strategic match and provision of management information.

- Opportunities to extend integration across the business, addressing the strategic architecture class.

- avoidance of a competitive disadvantage of the system.

With such a mixture of aims there is likely to be an array of possible solutions, which need to be examined carefully before deciding which one to adopt. At that stage the economics of the alternatives and the risks, both financial and business can be considered by the business management. (See Figure 14.5.)

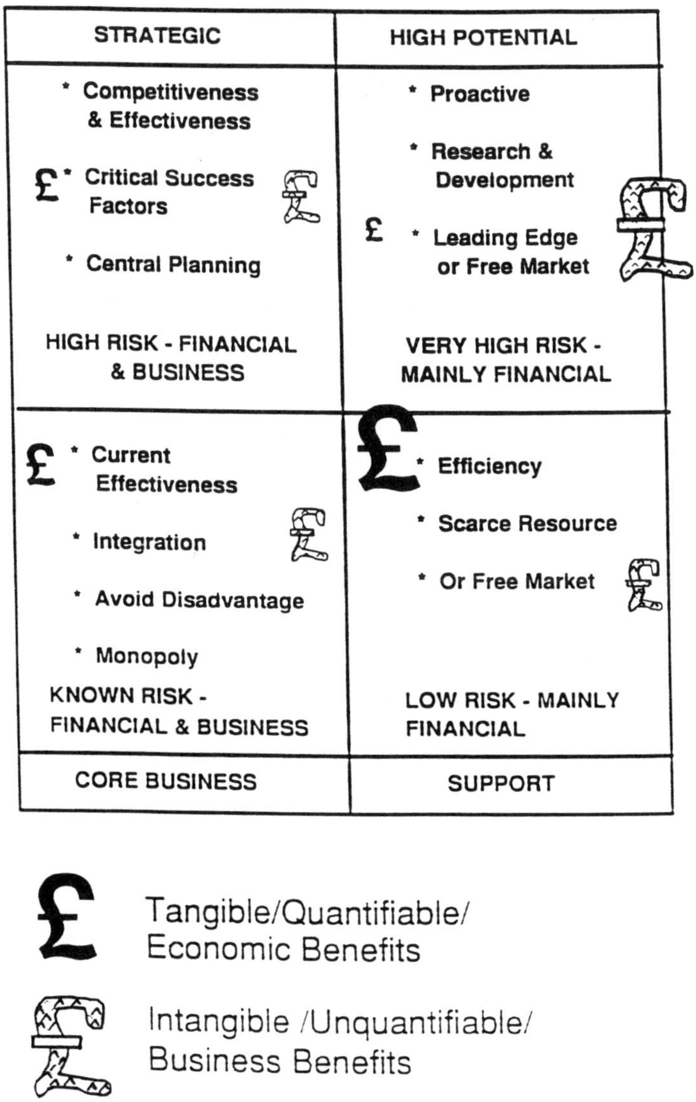

Figure 14.5. Economics and risk

Strategic Applications

Aims for these systems are closely tied to achievement of objectives and CSF's, strategic match, competitive advantage and also perhaps MIS. There is little opportunity to find tangible benefits and it is often difficult to quantify the intangible benefits, such as those associated with expanding a market, or delivering better quality and thus customer satisfaction. Given the intangible nature of the benefit, and the magnitude of the risks, both business and financial associated with the development, it is clearly important that a central planning strategy is in operation for these systems.

High Potential

The aim in this case is to find out if there are any benefits to be derived from the idea, which may be for any of the classes of value. Investment must be found either from a central R&D fund or from the user area championing the project. Risk is very high, in the sense that the project may have to be abandoned, with the commensurate waste of the investment.

14.5.4 Determining Priorities

Support Systems

Within the category, benefit is likely to be all tangible, and cost straightforward to quantify (doing the same cheaper). Similarly the risk of obtaining or developing the system should be very small and easily quantifiable. There can be little if any argument for experimenting with new technology, or with innovative business ideas here, so the risk is almost entirely based on financial considerations. Priorities can be assessed on a ranking of the net benefit to the business of introducing the system. The only case for deviating from this order would be where risk does have a bearing, such as when the existing system is in serious danger of failing.

Core Business

This is probably the most difficult area in which to assess priorities. Of the classes of value, named by Parker, there is probably an element of ROI, and strategic IS architecture (doing the same better). There may also be benefit derived from avoiding a competitive disadvantage, and these systems can be in support of objectives and their associated critical success factors, and thus providing the management information which measures progress towards the success factors. The only way to deal with this complexity, and get a rational measure of priorities, is to build up a table of 'scores' for each factor, weighing each according to subjective judgement. The weights can relate to ROI, contribution to the strategic architecture, avoidance of risk, and support for objectives and CSF's. Overall priorities should then be calculated by dividing the resultant score by the cost of providing the system.

Strategic

These systems can be scored relatively easily according to their contribution to 'strategic match', and assessed through association with one or more objectives and critical success factors, and then related to the resource consumption incurred. The scoring mechanism can become more precise by differentiating between levels of contribution. For example, a system may be assessed as contributing extensively to one objective, moderately to another, and marginally to a third. In addition, one objective may be deemed to be very important, whereas others are denoted as moderately important, etc. It can be seen that applying consistent weighting and scoring, a quantified, if approximate, view of the relative importance of a system can be achieved.

14.5.5 Development Approaches

A portfolio that contains an assortment of planned systems is likely to need a toolbox of development and project management approaches to suit the various requirements. Broadly-applied selection criteria would indicate that the best solutions for the four portfolio categories are:

Strategic systems. These are vital to the future success of the business, and are part of its business strategy. They are frequently linked to specific initiatives, often to attain a competitive lead. Traditional non-automated development methods are not appropriate here, since speed and flexibility are essential, and effectiveness rather than efficiency is important. Close working relationships are needed, between senior users who know the business need intimately, and very experienced IS/IT business analysts who can translate the business requirements into technical responses as they are evolving. Typically the system is not automating an existing business process, but breaking new ground. The system may have an external interface, and its objectives include delivering benefits to both internal and external agents. There is often a need to develop further increments along with extensions to business initiatives, and it must be easy and fast to revisit the analysis steps.

The information content of the business product is often crucial in strategic systems, whether it is part of the core product or is provided in order to boost delivered value or customer satisfaction. For example, when contact is made between a company and one of its customers, that customer should be treated as a known individual. He may need information about a range of services, and so all pertinent information relating to his customer history, the company's services, and any other information needed to make the contact as valuable as possible, needs to be available at the point of contact. To achieve this the level of internal information integration must be high.

The best design for the majority of strategic systems is probably a well-researched, analysed and structured core, encapsulating the essential business processes, surrounded by flexible user-driven modules. Fourth-generation tools or increasingly CASE tools are appropriate development vehicles here. Prototyping can also be effective in clarifying user needs. Relational databases containing the principal elements of a corporate database are frequently used in strategic systems, since they offer flexibility in viewing, manipulating and accessing business-wide information. Interconnectability rather than integration may be a temporary goal here, in order to assess the long-term value of the strategic systems, whilst protecting the installed base of core business and support systems.

High potential systems. The need here is for independent, rapid, low-cost development, which can be abandoned without wasting massive resources, since risk is high, success far from certain and cost control essential. Prototyping software is appropriate to use for these systems, although if they are testing out new technology, they may well employ knowledge-based software or other technologies. Integration and data management are rarely considered in the first place, although they may become important in any emerging strategic or core business systems that develop after the prototype has proved of value. There is a danger that users may become attached to an unsuitable prototype, which then gets adopted along with all of its defects. The other danger to be avoided is of the R&D developer getting carried away on a technical joyride. The right style of personal management can avoid that problem.

Systems in this quadrant may be developed by a user on his own or with an IS/IT professional. Such systems may start life as single-user PC developments, which are later redeveloped with a broader production environment in mind.

Core business systems. These are critical to sustaining business performance. They need to be well designed, efficient, robust and with a long cost-effective life. There is often a need for integration with other primary systems and so they benefit from adhering to global data management standards, and from complying with any emerging systems and information architecture. They can sometimes be satisfied by well-built packages, or bought-in core software, but this often precludes them from effective integration, resource sharing and data management, and so this approach is only worth considering when development resources are not available or time is pressing. They are usually developed using traditional project management and systems development life-cycle methodologies, increasingly automated with CASE tools. Old systems showing the debilitating effects of age and excessive maintenance could well be candidates for reverse engineering.

Support systems. If support systems need replacing or acquiring, the most appropriate solution could be to purchase a sound standard package, provided it meets the business need as closely as possible and requires little maintenance or 'interference', especially if there are few if any requirements for integrating the system with others in the portfolio. In comparison with the development demands of other candidate systems, it is unlikely that an organization can justify the resources to develop a system of this type. However, the amount of resources to implement a package should not be underestimated, and a viable alternative may be to consider contracting the operation outside the organization.

14.6 KEEPING THE PORTFOLIO ALIGNED TO BUSINESS NEEDS

Some of the management factors that need to be considered in setting out or confirming application management policies were put forward in the early paragraphs of this paper. For the portfolio to then be maintained in close alignment to business requirements, a number of other conditions need to be met.

Good communication and feedback mechanisms are needed. These include the obvious, but not always competent, methods of communicating business objectives and strategies through the organization. Then each function needs to broadcast its own objectives, initiatives, tactics and detailed plans. Equally important are the feedback routes where plans at each level are fed back up the business, and ultimately measures of effectiveness are also conveyed. Other external and internal information is also needed, which should include monitoring external impacts and any observed trends, threats or opportunities. In addition, each function in the business will need to monitor its own special areas of interest. Thus, the external IS/IT perspective is a key consideration of IS/IT focus, and user needs, views and satisfaction are the principal internal factors. Further communication lines may be important, for example cross-functional links (e.g. marketing to IS/IT, or inter-company links with trading partners) and marketing the role and potential of IS/IT broadly to the business.

However, strategy management and maintenance must be more tangible than that. Responsibility needs to be vested in several bodies in the business, and procedures set up to ensure that the strategy retains its value to the business. The business strategy needs to be monitored to measure achievement, for any changes made to business objectives and for variations in the business's strengths and weaknesses, any of which may cause the change to the business strategy, although it may be more difficult than that to identify.

That change to business strategy should prompt a review of the IS/IT strategy to assess the impact of the change, and if necessary cause a revision to the IS/IT strategy and thus portfolio and action plans. Other factors can cause change to the IS/IT strategy. One of these derives from monitoring achievement of targets associated with IS/IT initiatives. Over- or under-achievement here may cause a rethink of the IS/IT strategy and plans. Similarly, changes in the external technical environment, or in the internal capacity or capability may impact the strategy. Finally, changes in achievement, IT opportunity or ability to meet the business IS need should be reflected back to the business strategy in case it causes a reaction there.

This continuous monitoring and feedback represents one of the responsibilities of the steering groups set up to implement and manage strategies, set policies, initiate planning, and continuously ensure that IS/IT contributes appropriately to the business. The shape, constitution, location and responsibilities of the various groups will vary from organization to organization. Ward, Griffiths and Whitmore (1990) propose a set of steering groups.

The top-level group are responsible for ensuring that the IS demand and IT supply strategies are correctly interpreting business needs and risk factors. They are also responsible for setting IS/IT policies, and for resolving any conflicts and setting priorities where subjective management decisions are needed. Their commitment to IS/IT being a key business resource, and to considering innovative ideas for exploitation of IS/IT, is essential.

The business IS planning groups will represent strategic business units in the business, or other self-contained business areas. They are responsible for producing and maintaining the IS demand strategies. They must therefore continuously monitor business needs, priorities, justification and achievements. They take full responsibility for the systems 'owned' by their part of the business, and liaise with other business areas when applications have interfaces. They also assume responsibility for their business information, and where information is corporately owned, share that responsibility across business areas. Where organizational change results from implementation of applications, they are also responsible for the effective management of those changes. Where there are certain critical applications being developed on behalf of one or more business areas, they may introduce temporary application management groups.

The application management steering groups mentioned above are user-led groups responsible for all aspects of the planning justification, development and implementation of applications including any management of change in the user area, or user training. Such groups can report to a number of business area groups, and as such must be wary of unresolved conflicts, which may need top management arbitration.

The IS/IT planning and strategy maintenance group have to ensure they can respond to what may be several IS/demand strategies, without compromising business needs and priorities, and IT supply capabilities. They defend the IT supply strategies and policies. They are also the group responsible for keeping abreast of technical trends and external IT usage, and for assessing and managing technical risk.

Technical management groups are responsible for the hard technical aspects of the supply side – the hardware, systems software, database management, telecommunications. Their role being to respond to defined needs, manage change and monitor achievement and technical capabilities.

Service management groups are responsible for the other aspects of the supply side, the provision of services to the business, through development, operations, network services, end-user computing services and data administration functions.

All these groups, as well as implementing the policies and requirements defined by the higher level groups and maintaining effective peer-to-peer relationships across the business, should also feed back information on effectiveness, and unexploited potential, as well as any innovative ideas for improving the service delivered by IS/IT to the business.

14.7 SUMMARY

One of the main deliverables from strategic IS/IT planning is the portfolio of applications, comprising the existing portfolio and the required portfolio.

The existing portfolio has been classified, assessed and its contribution evaluated, and any necessary changes noted. The required portfolio has also been classified and prioritized, and incorporated in the IT supply strategy.

It is essential that the portfolio is well managed, if an effective IS/IT service is to be provided, and it may be worthwhile thinking of the portfolio as the hub of the IS/IT wheel. (See Figure 14.6.)

Its spokes link the business, the IT supply, and the information and systems architecture. Business demands and opportunities, expressed in terms of information, systems and sometimes technical aspects are fed into the hub, and the applications and information are passed back to the business.

Components of the existing and required portfolio of systems are the building blocks of the information and systems architecture, from which the migration plans for developing applications and databases are derived.

All IT supply needs are resolved into the IT services and infrastructure. The wheel is not static, and all its components need to be kept in balance with one another, meeting business requirements and taking advantage of business and technical opportunities when applicable and justifiable.

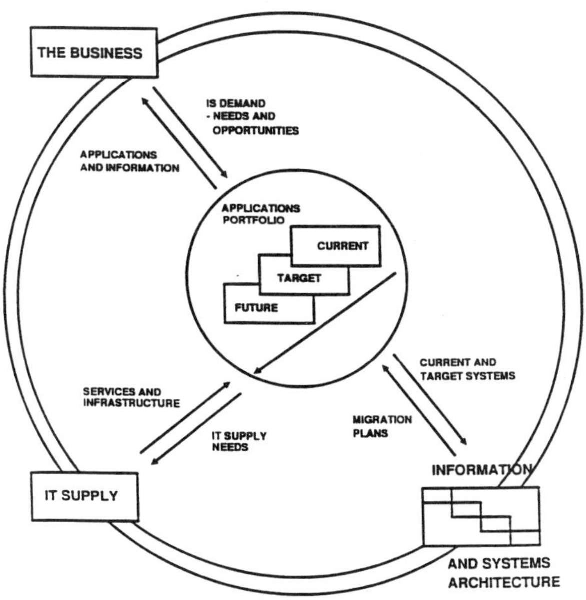

Figure 14.6. The applications protfolio – at the hub of the wheel

REFERENCES

McFarlan F W (1984) Information Technology IT Changes the Way you Compete, *Harvard Business Review*, May/June issue.

Parker M M, Benson R J, and Trainor H E (1986) *Information Economics*, Prentice-Hall International Editions, 1988.

Parsons G L (1983) Fitting Information Systems Technology to the Corporate Needs: The Linking Strategy. *Harvard Business School*, Teaching notes 9-183-176.

Ward J M (1988) Information Systems and Technology: Application Portfolio Management – An Assessment of Matrix-based Analysis. *Journal of Information Technology*, Vol. 3, No. 3, December issue.

Ward J M, Griffiths P M, and Whitmore P (1990) *Strategic Planning for Information Systems*, John Wiley.

15 Creating and developing a practical IT strategy

C. Holtham
City University Business School

15.1 INTRODUCTION

Many of the key decisions on how to use Information Technology in organizations are strategic decisions. Often strategic decisions are either not taken or are not taken within an appropriate framework (Aeh, 1990). One of the key responsibilities of directors and senior managers is to create that framework. There are four key components to the framework:

- Vision
- Systems
- Information Technology
- People

all of which must be considered (see Figure 15.1). In particular the interaction between all four needs to be carefully reviewed. In many organizations one or more of these components are not in fact given full consideration. For example, many organizations have a strategy which focuses heavily on the Information Technology or the applications components, but which has no link at all with the business decisions, or which do not adequately take into account the impact of Information Technology on people (Dockery, 1990).

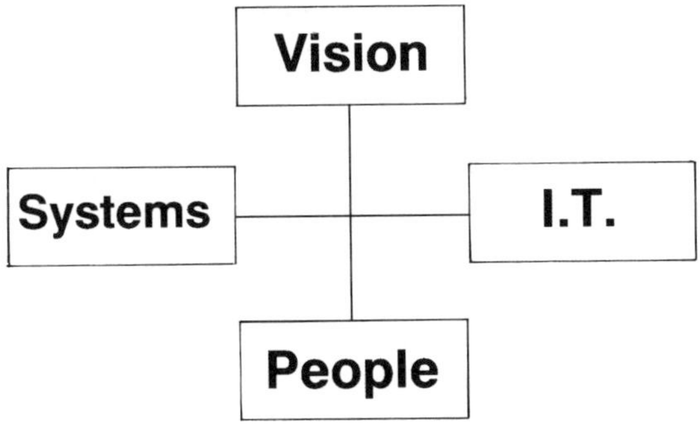

Figure 15.1. The four elements of strategy

In Figure 15.2 the four components of the diamond are defined in slightly more detail. It is no accident that the question of vision in achieving business success is shown as the top component. This is the link between a business's overall strategy and how it needs to deploy Information Technology to achieve that strategy. The word 'vision' is used not to suggest some long-term or fanciful approach but rather the need to emphasize a very small number of key beliefs or objectives which are set by the directors and top managers of organizations and contain what they believe to be the key to driving the organization forward. Visions can almost always be encapsulated in a few sentences, rather than in a 100-page corporate plan.

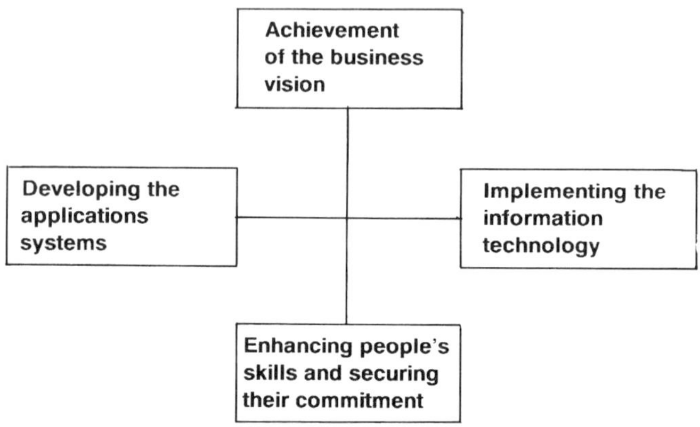

Figure 15.2. The four elements

Many people would correlate an Information Technology strategy with the second component in Figure 15.2 which is the physical implementation of Information Technology. Information Technology is what you can actually see – the hardware and communications systems that physically make up computing systems. In fact, in most circumstances the actual Information Technology is a secondary factor to business vision and normally should be the secondary factor to the third component in Figure 15.2, which is the applications software which needs to be developed or introduced – that is the underlying reason for acquiring the hardware.

The fourth component of people is a critical one. The people side of Information Technology systems is often only taken into account as an afterthought. There is often insufficient investment in the people side of Information Technology and there is often insufficient attention given as to how to gain people's commitment when a particular Information Technology strategy is under development. Each of these components will now be considered in more detail.

But before doing so it is necessary to identify the need for caution; not all the claims made about IT strategy after the event are always what they seem. A considerable amount of literature has grown up around strategic information systems, but not all systems that have actually been strategically successful were necessarily designed as such. For example, the McKesson company's systems have been well documented (e.g. Wiseman, 1988). However, in what amounts to a deconstruction of such classic cases, Clemons (1991) points out that the McKesson Economost system was originally implemented to save costs:

> it is interesting that a system that we now believe was a strategic necessity – instrumental in saving the drug wholesale business from pressures created by chain stores – was justified on such prosaic grounds. Impact on the industry was never considered. Competitor response also was not considered.

Indeed several authors argue that it is increasingly difficult to use information technology for what Latham (1990) graphically describes as 'strategic strikes'.

15.2 WHAT VISION?

Putting these reservations to one side for the present, it is first useful to review the vision component, about which there are a number of basic questions that need to be asked. How do we go about actually generating a business vision? Much will, of course, depend on the type of business. It is a very different matter defining and shaping a business vision for a small company with a handful of employees than for a giant multinational. Also the market or sector of the economy or type of product of the organization critically affects the time-scale for achieving the vision. In some organizations even one year may be a long time. In others, particularly where large capital intensive investments are involved, then a planning time-scale of as much as ten years may be quite common. Often a time-scale of between two and five years would be quite typical as the period within which the business vision can be achieved.

One of the things that should be asked during the 'what' exercise is how changes in technology can themselves affect the business vision, or the ability to achieve it.

One of the techniques which many directors find extremely useful for coming to conclusions about their business vision is to use scenarios – to paint alternative pictures of the future and then to work through the implications of achieving some or all of those alternatives. Through this technique the theoretical desirability of certain alternatives can be tempered by more practical considerations on their achievement, or on deciding what needs to be done differently in order to be able to achieve them.

15.3 WHO?

It is not always obvious exactly who should be involved in driving forward the business vision. The conventional viewpoint is that this should always be done by the board and be a top-down exercise. However, certainly in larger organizations, senior executives may well take a central role in at least drafting the vision, although one would always expect it to have the endorsement and positive approval of the board.

Use will often be made of small groups to generate ideas on business vision, and great importance needs to be placed on the environment for discussing and taking decisions on visions. Looking at the fundamental purposes of an organization and where it wants to be in two to five years' time are not really suitable items for the average board meeting. The physical environment of the long central table is simply not conducive to thinking through alternatives. Many organizations now recognize this and will set up the physical environment for discussion of strategy at a hotel or a conference centre where the room layout and style of meeting is SEEN TO BE very different from the conventional board meeting.

Contributions from even quite junior managers and staff to the business vision exercise should not be ignored; indeed wherever possible a contribution of some nature from at least a small number of middle and even junior managers should be sought – as their perspective of the organization and where they think it should be going is often a valuable one even where it may be limited by their own relatively narrow perspective.

15.4 HOW?

Elaborate processes for generating a business vision are worthless unless certain core questions can be asked and answered:

- Where are we now?
- Where can't we go?
- Where do we want to be?

There are really no magic techniques for answering these questions. The answers to these questions depend on the business intuition of the executives or directors who are involved in examining the vision in detail. At the heart of the process is actually deciding what are the key areas of choice faced by the company. There is no textbook that can guide the director on this area, and the key areas of choice may well be very different even for two apparently similar organizations.

Part of the conventional wisdom of drawing up a strategy for the use of Information Technology is that the company should first of all go through its business strategy in detail and draw out the issues which impact directly or indirectly on Information Technology strategy. The problem with this approach is that many organizations simply do not have business strategies in any explicit form that could be reviewed for this purpose. Only a minority of companies and other organizations have explicit strategies and probably only a minority of those are in a form that could be used to generate a list of strategic Information Technology issues.

15.5 BALANCE

The four components are important in themselves, but it is also essential to consider the interaction between them. We summarize the variety of interaction between them as 'balance'. Achieving balance between the four components is an absolutely critical role for top management and board of directors of any organization. It is also commonly believed to be a somewhat neglected area. Too often, Information Technology strategy and plans to develop new systems are generated without full or adequate consideration of, in particular, the business vision and people aspects.

The ideal way of achieving a balance between the four components is in fact to work strategic Information Technology thinking into all the existing management and high-level decision-making processes of the organization. It is a preferable solution to setting up some separate process. For example, Information Technology systems should be woven into the basic strategic planning processes of the organization. But even today this happens insufficiently often.

The human resource department should explicitly take into account the demands and issues arising from the use of Information Technology, particularly on the skills side. It is perhaps surprising that even the operational planning of Information Technology itself often fails to take into account strategic Information Technology thinking. Those responsible for managing Information Technology on a day to day basis are sometimes not best placed to inject a strategic dimension into Information Technology operations.

A key area is how Information Technology projects are evaluated. Ideally they should be evaluated on the same basis as all other significant investments of time or effort. In particular there should be no creation of special rules for Information Technology, or the suspension of normal business judgements and disciplines simply because the expenditure is of perhaps a different type to other capital investments. Equally, account does have to be taken of some of the special features of Information Technology; in certain sectors this relates to the speed of obsolescence of systems technology in particular. Finally, the budget-making process should always take into account Information Technology plans and strategies.

The ideal theory therefore is to work Information Technology strategy into existing processes. This may be in many practical circumstances just a theoretical ideal. It requires having many different people in the organization changing the way they do their jobs if it is to be achieved. Obviously this can be done with clear central leadership and direction. One of the widely quoted examples (Hildebrand, 1990) is Lithonia Lighting which has developed Lightlink, a group of integrated network systems tying together different elements of Lithonia's business. Here the vice-president for information systems has had very close links with the development of company direction.

But in many organizations there may be a variety of obstacles in the way of doing this and therefore it may be more convenient or appropriate to set up a special additional process for reviewing Information Technology strategy for achieving a balance between the four key components.

An important question is 'who should be involved in this process for creating an

Information Technology strategy?' Historically, developing a strategy has often been left to those who have been directly or professionally involved in the use of Information Technology. This is often a source of problems. It is essential to broaden the involvement to those who are responsible for planning and operating the main lines of business of an organization. So there should be a wide involvement to generate a balance between vision and strategy. There should in principle at least be a commitment to fairly extensive consultations on the proposed strategy.

Some managers and directors believe that there is an incompatibility between decisive management and consultation. However, in the area of Information Technology strategy many of the mistakes of the past have arisen through driving ahead thinking about technology – often in a quite decisive way – without taking the time to make the linkages to the business itself. Kraut, Dumais and Koch (1989) correctly stress that:

> technological change extends beyond hardware and software, and includes the wider, intrinsic changes in organizational design and work procedures that are embedded in the context of work technology, of which the computer technology is only one part.

Certainly in larger organizations an important element in canvassing views is to create some sort of consultation document on the strategy. This document may be used as the basis for consultations and an approach that many organizations take is to set up some form of 'road show' where those responsible for initiating the alternative scenarios for the strategy can actually go out and talk directly to the 'customers' of the strategy about the scenarios and listen carefully to the ideas and views on various opportunities.

15.6 THE ROLE OF INFORMATION IN MANAGEMENT

Inappropriate Information Technology strategies concentrate almost completely on technology. A relevant strategy must take into account a wider range of considerations. These considerations will vary from organization to organization but can be at least discussed under the broad heading of the 'role of information in management.' Why, after all, is information important to an organization? Too often this question is not stated or avoided and the absence of thought about it can lead to some very inappropriate directions and decisions.

Paul Strassmann (1990) validly argues:

> My way to understand ... is to attribute business performance not to computers but to management value-added. Since the management of information is inseparable from management's general roles I view the processing of information by electronic circuitry as an extension of traditional management roles by other means. (p. xvii)

Although it is not possible to generalize about the areas of relevance, it is possible to give examples or illustrations of some of the questions that could be asked. For example, how far does the organization want to promote a centralized or decentralized approach to management, or indeed some combination of the two? Modern Information Technology can support a whole variety of styles of management. Those designing systems and prioritizing them need a clearer model of the preferred decision-making style of the organization than is actually available to them.

How far does the organization want to promote at least amongst its managers and executives, an open or closed style of management? In some organizations, pride is taken on the sharing of information and management reports amongst a quite broad group of managers. In other organizations a narrow perspective is taken. Neither is intrinsically right nor wrong, the real question is deciding what is appropriate to the particular organization and then actually developing systems and procedures that efficiently deliver what is required.

Too few Information Technology strategies at the moment make an adequate link between technology and business objectives. For example, in an increasing number of companies great emphasis is being placed on quality of service. In theory Information Technology could play a very important role in improving and achieving quality, but all too often those producing Information Technology strategies are either not sufficiently aware of core business objectives, or lack the business perspective needed to work through how these objectives can be achieved through the use of technology.

One area that is likely to be of growing concern is how technology can actually be applied to improving customer service. The vast majority of systems aiming at improving customer service are actually based on an inward-looking view of what the customer's needs are. There is very little experience of, for example, involving the customer directly in the design and evaluation of a system and thus of systems being developed from a 'customer perspective'.

In the next decade we might expect much more to see what might be described as 'customer-led information systems' or less emphasis on introverted solutions and much more on a realistic understanding of customer expectations, needs and opinions.

One of the areas in which appropriate Information Technology is currently making a major contribution is to take account of the uncertainties of the future. Unfortunately, all too often Information Technology systems seem to have a rigidity which actually makes flexible responses to this issue very difficult (see Puttre, 1990). As the environment for many companies and organizations becomes increasingly fast moving and increasingly uncertain it is essential that the design of computer systems takes on board much more sophistication through being flexible and responsive.

Finally, in looking at the role of information in management, account needs to be taken of the particular organization's attitude to risk. Information Technology is itself extremely expensive. How far are the risks of these kinds of investments evaluated? And how far can Information Technology itself contribute to minimizing or at least reducing some of the risks which are intrinsic in normal business operations?

It is very noticeable that in the financial services sector, for example, a lot of effort is now going into designing computer systems that can at least assess and quantify the amount of risk and exposure that the financial services company is open to at any particular time.

15.7 DEVELOP GENERAL INFORMATION TECHNOLOGY STRATEGY ... NOT A PROCUREMENT PROGRAMME

Many organizations have documents called 'Information Technology Strategies'. Simply giving a document this name does not in any way guarantee that it meets the definition of a strategy set out and summarized in Figure 15.1, for example. In reality the great bulk of so-called Information Technology strategies are simply procurement programmes. They set out to quantify and justify the need for Information Technology and are often drawn up to lead into an organization's budgeting or capital investment plan process. Such documents should never of course be decried *per se*. The objection to these documents is that they claim to encompass strategic thinking within the organization when, in fact, they are looking only at the operational plans for the procurement of hardware and sometimes software.

A genuine Information Technology strategy has to be completely rooted in the underlying business strategy. Whether that exists formally or not it has to take account of the role of information management in the organization. It should set out clearly the priorities for the development of systems and software as these are what are actually used. In addition to setting out the technological requirements in a general sense. It is increasingly important in smaller and certainly the larger organizations that explicit policies on networking and communications. In the next few years networking and communications in many organizations may become dominant in defining the scope and alternative ways of implementing Information Technology (Keen, 1986). Finally, proper consideration needs to be given to the human resources aspect of developing systems.

15.8 STEPS FOR DEVELOPING AN IT STRATEGY

Figure 15.3 sets out six steps which need to be gone through in order to develop an Information Technology strategy. Firstly, a business vision needs to be generated. Secondly, there needs to be the type of balancing exercise referred to earlier. Thirdly, the physical resources of the organization, whether financial, people or technological, need to be organized so that the strategy can be delivered. An important element in this is securing commitment at a variety of key points throughout the organization. Having organized the resources it is then necessary to actually implement the strategy which can of course have the longest time-scale of any of these steps. Finally, after the strategy has been implemented, there should be a formal procedure of reviewing what was actually done compared to the original intentions. Unfortunately this type of review is rarely or sufficiently carried out.

Steps

- **Generate**
- **Balance**
- **Organise**
- **Secure Commitment**
- **Implementation**
- **Review**

Figure 15.3. Six steps in strategy development

15.9 STEPS AND STAGES

There is often a great confusion between the steps needed to develop an Information Technology strategy and the physical documents which have to be produced to that end. In Figure 15.4 it is argued that there are potentially three distinct types of document for the planning process which need to be gone through for generating an Information Management strategy. In practice these three documents or processes may be combined. This does not matter as long as it is recognized that there are two distinct processes which need to be gone through.

The first type of process is the exercise involving vision, the linkage of business and Information Technology strategy, the generation of order of priorities and the achievement of balance. In Figure 15.4 this could be represented by an Information Technology strategy plan. Though this might be a physical document, particularly in a small or medium-sized organization, this could simply reflect the outcome of various brainstorming meetings, and never actually be set down in a written form at all.

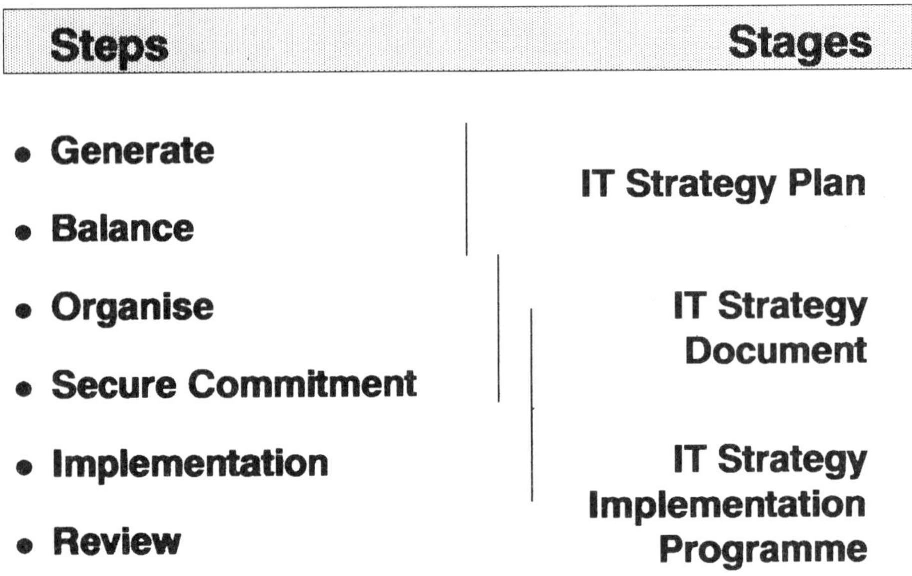

Figure 15.4. Steps and stages

The second stage of the process is concerned with taking the strategic thinking and then organizing resources to implement that throughout the organization. This is the stage that was discussed earlier with particular reference to going out and seeking opinions, consultations and perhaps in some organizations a 'road show'. This stage would much more appropriately be implemented through the use of an Information Technology strategy document. It needs to be emphasized that this would be a draft document rather than a finished version which line managers were simply being told about.

The third stage partly overlaps the second in that it is still concerned with securing a commitment but now it has also got a heavy focus on the physical implementation of the strategy change after consultation on the strategic document. A phrase that might be coined to describe this phase might be an Information Technology implementation programme. This would be very action-orientated in contrast to a strategic document, yet even in its emphasis on action it should still take into account the strategic plans and issues which were earlier identified. Fusfield (1989) identifies several of the elements which need to be present in such a programme.

15.10 SPENDING LESS MONEY ON SOME IT ...

IT is important to many top managers. It is clear that there is some concern and probably an increasing amount of concern by top managers at the levels of spending on Information Technology in their organization. In fact, there may be a variety of methods through which, by the implementation of strategic thinking through Information Technology planning, it is perfectly possible to spend less money on certain aspects of Information Technology.

Firstly, by actually insisting on a clear link between Information Technology strategy and business strategy, it may well be possible to focus Information Technology spending on those areas where there is the biggest pay off. Secondly, there needs to be very clear accountability for Information Technology projects. They are often complex, involving a variety of functions or departments and certainly involve at least one line department and the Information Technology function itself. Many projects fail to achieve their stated objectives through a lack of clarity and accountability and insufficient or inappropriate project leadership. Special efforts need to be made in the case of Information Technology projects to ensure that there is good project management and clear accountability for achieving results.

Many Information Technology systems are over-elaborate. They try to encompass all the current and even past information requirements of middle managers. These could be called '100%' solutions. In very few other areas of business operations would theoretically ideal solutions be so vigorously pursued. In areas of business such as buildings, transport and procurement there is a lot of experience in understanding the trade-off between ideal solutions and high cost. In these more traditional areas there is generally good understanding of what is essential and the areas of less essential spend. Unfortunately these similar disciplines do not always apply to Information Technology areas and this can be particularly difficult as the less essential areas may actually consume a disproportionate amount of the costs of Information Technology.

One of the roles of directors and top managers of an organization is to keep a very close eye on whether Information Technology is being applied to essential or less essential areas. Some organizations in recent years have actually set out to ban '100%' solutions – in other words the emphasis is on only meeting the essential business requirements through Information Technology.

One of the more promising areas for being able to effect a reduction in spending in Information Technology without sacrificing quality is through the use of international information technology standards. The idea behind standards which are laid down by independent organizations is that they force the suppliers of computer hardware and software to compete with each other not in relation to differences in their products but by actually ensuring that there is commonality and compatibility between their products, particularly encouraging price competition.

Particularly in large organizations there are often very long times taken in developing systems and one technique that is being increasingly looked at is to shorten development times, perhaps dramatically from a three-year average to less than a 12-month average and this is closely linked with the banning of the '100%' solution.

Finally, the need for a strategic review of Information Technology strategy after it has been implemented has already been touched upon; it is also important that individual projects or schemes developed are themselves subject to individual review after implementation. Future development of Information Technology should be based on an understanding of the reality of Information Technology systems today in a particular organization. In many organizations the reality which would be revealed by post-implementation reviews is very different from the theory that was embodied when the ideas of a particular system were first conceived.

15.11 ... AND SPENDING MORE ON OTHER AREAS

Even if it is possible to reduce the overall costs of Information Technology through some of the techniques just described, there are a number of areas where there will almost certainly have to be an increase in spending.

First of all much more management time and effort, and where necessary cash expenditure needs to be devoted to approving 'adequate' solutions. Those who cut out frills and concentrate on basics will be rewarded whilst those who seek over-elaborate and over-complex solutions will not.

In almost any study carried out into the failure of Information Technology systems, it is very common to find that those involved highlight a major reason as being a lack of awareness of Information Technology (e.g. Northcott, Christie and Walling, 1990; McClatchy, 1990). This can apply at all levels within the organization from the strategic right down to the implementation phases and also a lack of training of those who have to use the systems. In many cases there seems to have been no investment at all in the area of training and so it is hardly surprising that systems and many of their features are never implemented properly due to lack of staff awareness and understanding.

Another area of traditional under-investment is project management. Major projects demand good project management and it is unrealistic to make already busy managers find a few minutes every day or week to be part-time project managers.

In the short history of developing Information Technology systems those who are best at developing such systems place much emphasis on listening to the customer whether he is an external or more typically an internal customer.

Unfortunately good practice is not introduced in all organizations and a considerably greater emphasis needs to be placed on many of those professionals involved in Information Technology in developing skills necessary to become a better listener.

A very important question is the organizations attitude to technological innovation and technological risk-taking. Very few organizations could or should see themselves as innovating across a broad range of information technologies. But if they did not have some innovation going on they are firstly unable to learn about the issues involved in innovative Information Technology, and secondly competitors do not necessarily stand still: they can increase their own capabilities to develop new and innovative systems and can gain some competitive advantage through this. An appropriate stand for many organizations would be 'focused innovation'. In other words, a conscious decision is made to innovate in a particular area and carefully analyse the results of that essentially research and development type exercise but without necessarily taking a major risk across the board (Holtham, 1989).

15.12 COMPETITIVE INFORMATION SYSTEMS – SOME CONCLUSIONS

Sager (1991) reached a number of conclusions on competitive information systems derived from work carried out in Australia. This work does not accept much of the 'conventional wisdom' on competitive information systems, much of this conventional wisdom having been developed in a North American environment. He concluded that competitive information systems are independent of technology, and are better at defending positions than attacking them. It is important to stress that competitive information systems are in fact largely independent of information technology. Their really distinctive feature is the way they are routed in business strategy and in the developing of technology to meet that business strategy rather than technology lead themselves.

It certainly has to be recognized that competitive information systems are a complex phenomena: this is precisely the point made in the diamond in Figure 15.1 when considering the balance between the four components.

It is becoming increasingly clear that as many organizations within a particular market sector increase their spending on Information Technology, and their ability to develop Information Technology, it is becoming harder and harder for any one organization in that market sector to gain sustainable competitive advantage through the use of Information Technology. The other players in the market are sufficiently aware of the capabilities of technology that they can quickly develop computing products. More and more it would appear that companies are spending significant amounts of money on competitive information systems rather less from an attacking viewpoint and rather more from a defensive viewpoint. What they fear is that if they fail to spend money on technology they will be put at a competitive disadvantage, rather than believing that they will gain a relative advantage over their competitors.

15.13 WAYS AHEAD

Moving now to the conclusion, it is first of all essential that there is some type of formal information system or information management planning. This does not need to involve vast quantities of paper and bureaucracy but it should have at least the following elements:

- There should be adequate involvement particularly of those who are responsible for the business vision.

- There must be a comprehensive commitment to developing an awareness and understanding objective.

- There must be a broad scan of the business and technological opportunities available, and the building of at least a limited number of scenarios. In the light of that...

- An Information Technology strategy is as much about creating a shared purpose within an organization as it is about buying hardware and software.

- It is possible to over-emphasis the importance of a strategic plan as a document; what is really needed is a strategic planning process that filters throughout the organization.

Secondly, a major area of concern is in ensuring that Information Technology contributes to a more flexible and responsive organization, rather than consolidating or reinforcing the status quo.

Given that many organizations do not in fact have explicit business plans and strategies, one of the questions which often arises is 'can information systems planning lead business planning?' There is, of course, no right answer to this question: before the Information Technology business evolved, there could be little doubt that in any organization it would be better to use Information Technology strategy as a reason or even an excuse for breaking into business planning rather than to delay the production of an Information Technology strategy by waiting for a possibly hypothetical business strategy exercise.

There have been a variety of organizations of different sizes that have actually broken into business strategies through developing an Information Technology strategy. There are often great complexities in the appraisal and review of Information Technology projects and proposals, particularly those at a strategic level within the organization, where there is often an absence of explicit financial measures. This topic is a difficult one – often inadequate attention being given to the way these types of schemes are appraised. It is suggested here that the very difficulty of the exercise should focus the intensity of effort to try to come to some form of resolution of the problem rather than to avoid the problem altogether.

Developing Information Technology strategies and indeed developing Information Technology systems is essentially a human process rather than a technological one. In this process the relationship between Information Technology professionals and line managers is absolutely critical. It is fair to say that in the past there have been problems on both sides, line managers are often reluctant to commit on paper business vision and business understanding to the Information Technology professional, and the Information Technology professionals are often seen as being more concerned about the technology than achieving the business objectives. What is needed in the future is to find line managers who have a much better understanding of the reality of Information Technology and its management, and similarly Information Technology professionals themselves who have an understanding of business issues.

Top managers, including company directors, are often far too little involved in key decisions on Information Technology strategy and management. Top managers and directors are critical of the integration of Information Technology with the broader business objectives. There is just as much a need for top managers and directors to increase their understanding and awareness of Information Technology as there is for middle managers to be more personally involved in individual systems.

One of the endearing features of the Information Technology industry, which is still a very young industry, is that it has developed what can only be described as a certain element of fun. It has more in common in its product launches with the most glamorous parts of the car industry or of the music business than most other capital-intensive industries. It is not uncommon to see products launched with celebrities, dry ice and fanfares of music. This climate of excitement and hype is harmless enough; the problem arises when it leads to a suspension of normal business disciplines and judgement. One question that needs to be asked is who are actually the theorists in relation to Information Technology?

Very little of the theory of Information Technology actually derives from the academic world. Most of the theory of Information Technology derives from hardware and software suppliers and many of the consultants. Academics spend most of their time researching the reality of Information Technology which, as indicated earlier, may well be at odds with both the hype and the theory as espoused by those who have significant vested interests in the area. We need to actually understand reality better and promote greater amounts of both internal and external research. We need to develop techniques of Information Technology management that are more geared to piloting projects, prototyping projects and to understanding the risks involved in various Information Technology approaches and strategies.

In conclusion, the successful management of Information Technology depends heavily on the overall knowledge and capabilities of an organization. Implementing Information Technology strategies and plans is not just a question of technological understanding, it is a broad-based managerial challenge and it in fact represents a challenge to the organization as a whole going from top to bottom and across all the various functions within the organization.

BIBLIOGRAPHY AND REFERENCES

Aeh, Richard K. (1990) 'Does IS have technophobia?' *Journal of Systems Management*, October, v41 n10 p23

Clemons, Eric K. (1991) 'Evaluation of strategic investments in information technology', *Communications of the ACM*, January, v34 n1, pp22-36

Dockery, E. (1990) 'The development of information technology strategies in banking firms and building society organizations', City University Business School Working Paper

Earl, Michael (1989) *Management Strategies for Information Technology*, Prentice-Hall, Hemel Hempstead.

Fusfield, Alan R. (1989) 'Formulating technology strategies to meet the global challenges of the 1990s', *International Journal of Technology Management* v4, n6 pp601-612

Hildebrand, Carol (1990) 'Lighting up IS in business', *Computerworld* 9 April, v24 n15 pp55-56

Holtham, Clive (1989) 'The challenge of information technology and its management', *Journal of Information Technology*, December

Keen, P.W.G. (1986) *Competing in Time: Using Telecommunications for Competitive Advantage,* Ballinger

Kraut, Robert, Dumais, Susan, and Koch, Susan (1989) 'Computerization, productivity, and quality of worklife' *Communications of the ACM* , February v32 n2 pp220-238

Latham, Randall W. (1990) 'Systems architecture: identifying strategic strikes', *Journal of Systems Management*, October v41 n10 p28(3).

McClatchy, Will (1990) 'Reengineering the CEO; companies are sending their execs to computer-literacy school', *Information Week* , November, n294 p34(2).

Northcott, Jim, Christie, Ian and Walling, Annette (1990) *Information Technology and Management Awareness: Advanced Information Technologies*, HMSO, London

Puttre, Michael (1990) 'Centers of competence can keep MIS informed; MIS must keep up with industry issues as well as technology', *MIS Week*, March, v11 n13 pp29-30

Sager, Michael T. (1991) *Managing Advanced Information Systems*, Prentice-Hall International

Scott Morton, M. (1991) *The Corporation of the 1990s*, Oxford University Press, Oxford

Strassmann, Paul A. (1990) *The Business Value of Computers*, The Information Economics Press, New Canaan, Connecticut

Targowski, Andrew (1990) *The Architecture and Planning of Enterprise-wide Information Systems*, Idea Group Publishing, Harrisburg PA

Tomlin, Roger (1989) Clues to Success: *Information Technology Strategies for Tomorrow*, Supplementary report; revised European edition. Amdahl Executive Institute, Hartley Wintney

Walton, Richard E. (1989) *Up and Running: Integrating IT and the Organization* Harvard Business School Press, Boston

Ward, John, Griffiths, Pat and Whitmore, Paul (1990) *Strategic Planning for Information Systems*, John Wiley & Sons, Chichester

Wiseman, C. (1988) *Strategic Information Systems*, Irwin, Homewood, Illinois

Zuboff, Shoshana (1988) *In the Age of the Smart Machine – The Future of Work and Power*, Heinemann, Oxford

16 Information Systems you can rely on

M. Kapp
Kapp and Partners

By the year 2000, there will be twice as much IT around as there is today.[1] Much of this vast inventory will be interconnected in one form or another. When a customer places an order for goods or services, a stream of information will begin to flow – nearly all of it in electronic form: from customer to supplier; internally within the supplier; from the supplier to secondary providers of goods and services; and, to complete the cycle, between the banks of the various parties involved as payment is made for the items involved.

This scenario is not based on supposition: advanced users of IT are using IT in this way today, driven by the need to stay in touch with Japanese levels of performance – Japan already being a more intensive user of IT than its western counterparts (Figure 16.1).

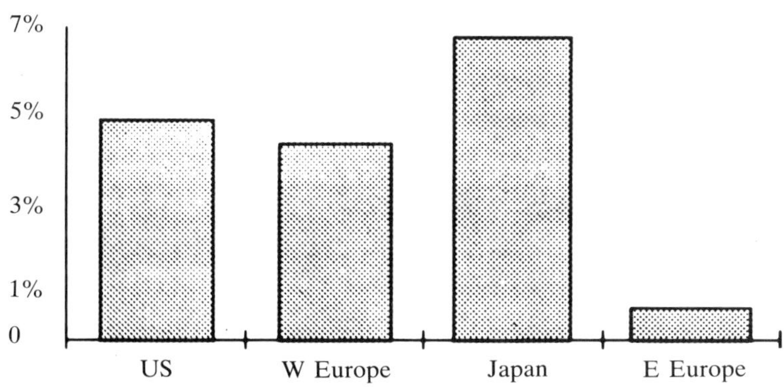

Figure 16.1. Penetration of IT (IT spend as % of GDP)

And where leaders go, others follow – partly due to fashion, partly because leaders will make electronic links with their suppliers a condition of trade.

The key force for change, however, is that all the parties involved stand to gain from using IT in this way. Individual consumers get the products and services they want, more quickly and cheaper; companies enjoy a range of benefits including:

1 Author's estimate based on combined growth rates for worldwide computer shipments (source MACE, 1989) and published forecasts of the Japanese Electronics Industry Development Association (source JEIDA, 1989)

- faster response to customer demands
- elimination of manual errors
- lower administrative costs
- reduced stock and work-in-progress
- improved cash flow
- improved profitability.

Indeed, given the nature and scale of benefits, it is difficult to see how any company can hope to prosper in the decade ahead unless it actively participates in the sort of 'electronic trading community' outlined above, except in very special circumstances. One company, for example, already operating in this way reports a 96% reduction in administrative costs per transaction; an insurer reports that it can turn round a proposal in minutes or hours rather than in days.[2]

There is, as ever, a catch. Put simply, it's this: if economic activity is going to be mediated by IT-based information systems, such systems will have to be much more robust than the ones we have today.

16.1 THE PROBLEM

At first glance, there is no reason to doubt the dependability of IT: in day-to-day use microelectronics routinely achieve remarkably high levels of reliability in terms of mean time between failure.

But IT systems are more than just collections of chips. They contain software – notoriously prone to behave in unexpected ways at the slightest provocation; they are made up of sub-systems, commonly from multiple suppliers – which often do not work perfectly together; people are involved in their development, operation and use and people tend to get things wrong, often by accident, sometimes by design; systems are physically extended and – through their extensive use of telecommunications links – accessible from a distance. These factors together make them susceptible to a wide range of disruptive events.

The result is that, at present, as systems get larger and more complex, their dependability goes down. Moreover, it's not just that the *chances* increase of things going wrong; as the use of IT intensifies, the *consequences* become more serious.

In the main, the source of the problem is not technical, although technological developments are needed. Rather, it is that the rapid rate of exploitation of IT has exposed users to new dangers which are not well understood, for example:

- When traditional forms of communication are superseded by streams of binary digits:
  - familiar cues which people rely on such as tone of voice, headed notepaper and human signatures are no longer available; human judgement and intuition can no longer be applied to all transactions;

2 Case studies conducted by the European Security Forum, 1990.

  - well-established legal frameworks may no longer apply to the new 'electronic' processes of trade;
  - control may be vested in a smaller number of key individuals than with traditional arrangements.

- Familiar sources of error are being replaced by new opportunities for getting things wrong, e.g.:
  - sending transactions twice in error;
  - corruption or delay of transactions in transit;
  - inadvertent mis-routing of messages in transit.

- New opportunities for fouling things up are being inadvertently created, and exploited by a growing fraternity of individuals with the desire and know-how to harm IT users:
  - 'viruses';
  - 'hackers';
  - deliberate jamming of data lines.

- Spiralling complexity and interconnection is increasing the likelihood of:
  - changes to one part of a system having unforeseen knock-on effects elsewhere;
  - weaknesses in one company's systems having a knock-on effect on others;
  - responsibilities being difficult to assign when things go wrong.

Although, in principle, all of these aspects can be dealt with, the fact is that, today, developments in the use of IT have outstripped the development of the practices, techniques, technology and regulations needed to keep risks within acceptable limits.

16.2 FIXING THE PROBLEM

Alarmed by the growing incidence of unwanted events, a flurry of activity has been recently initiated by governments and the IT industry with the intention of accelerating the development of more trustworthy systems.

A notable example is ITSEC.[3] This covers the development of a standardized set of criteria for evaluating the security of IT products and systems. In principle, the ITSEC criteria provide a yardstick for assessing the level of trust that can be properly given to existing systems or products; they also give a lead to designers of new systems and products. Although originated by a four-nation group of governments (UK, France, Germany and the Netherlands), ITSEC is set to be endorsed by the European Community as a whole and the intention is for it to be harmonized with equivalent initiatives in the US and Japan.

3 Information Technology Securiuty Evaluation Criteria (ITSEC), 1991; Commission of the European Communities.

Much work at the technical level (well over 80 projects[4]) is also going on under the auspices of the International Standards Organization.

At the international policy level, attention is being given to the development of a new framework for policy-makers covering the rights and obligations of governments, companies and individuals in the 'IT age'.

These developments are important and, in time, will make it easier to build and operate systems that can be relied upon. But the time-scales are long – it takes years to develop new technical or regulatory standards and years more for these to be generally adopted. In the meantime, companies planning to intensify their use of IT need to take matters into their own hands to keep risks under control.

16.3 ACTION BY INDIVIDUAL COMPANIES TODAY

So what should an individual company do to ensure that it can rely on its critical information systems, in the context of developing a new strategy for information systems? The following four-step approach is commended:

Step 1: Preparation
Recognize the risks of systems misbehaving are real and understand the key principles and concepts involved in dealing with them.

Step 2: Fact gathering
Establish (a) what risks the organization is currently facing and how the strategy under development will change them; and (b) what arrangements are in place to control IT risks and what additional controls are needed to counter the increased level of risk.

Step 3: Policy formulation
Make key policy decisions which will apply during the period of the strategy under development.

Step 4: Planning
Ensure that the strategic plan takes account of the activities required to make the company's systems as dependable as needed.

Each of these steps is discussed below. The weight of discussion is on the first of the four steps because there is overwhelming evidence of confusion at the conceptual level. The rest of the discussion assumes that a company has an existing portfolio of systems up and running and has managed to identify what systems it needs in the period covered by its new strategy for information systems. The intention is not to provide detailed advice but to outline an agenda covering what needs to be done

---

4 European Security Forum; 1990 report on security in Open Systems Interconnection (restricted circulation).

by those engaged in putting together a new information systems strategy and wishing to improve the dependability of new and existing systems.

16.3.1 Step 1: Preparation

> *Recognize the risks are real and understand the key principles and concepts involved in dealing with them.*

It's surprisingly difficult to get solid statistics on how much lack of system dependability is costing companies. The reason is not so much that organizations are unwilling to talk about incidents they have experienced as the fact that few, if any, keep comprehensive records of them or find it easy to evaluate the full impact they have on their business.

A study published in 1988 (Kapp, Stanley et al.[5]) indicates that annual losses by UK business in 1991 are likely to be of the order of £1.5 billion. A more recent study[6] looked at a sample of 172 incidents experienced over the course of a year by a group of 44 leading users of IT in Europe. Analysis indicates that technological breakdown (software and hardware malfunction, loss of telecommunications, unsuccessful changes to systems, and system overload) and invalid data input are regarded as commonplace – a feature of processing in many installations. Most incidents had a modest financial effect. However, some (20%) incidents had a major impact (i.e. leading to losses of more than £100,000). These included cases of fire, flood, natural disaster, vandalism, sabotage, theft and strikes by key personnel (e.g. computer operators). Thefts of equipment (typically PCs) were not as costly as incidents where systems had been misused in order to steal valuables controlled by the systems (e.g. cash).

The pattern of incidents confirms that even in the best run organisation lack of dependability is dissipating the potential benefits of IT. Although most incidents are minor the cumulative effect of a collection of minor events may be substantial. The chances of a major loss being suffered are significant. In both cases, profitability is eroded and, at worst, the continued existence of an enterprise may be called into question.

While the risks are real, in practice few business managers (or IT professionals) fully appreciate what is at stake or how to control the problem. This is largely because *information* is an asset like no other. Of itself, it is pervasive yet intangible; it flows around organizations and outside them; people share it; one piece of information can be assembled with another into a new piece of information; ownership is often unclear; the creator of information may be unaware of the uses to which it is put. Moreover, when in electronic form, information may be highly concentrated; it can be accessed from anywhere in the world without regard to jurisdictional boundaries; it can be stolen without depriving its owner of possession and improperly altered without obvious trace.

5 Kapp, Stanley et al., The Security of Network Systems, 1988, Coopers and Lybrand, London

6 European Security Forem; 1990 survey of members; restricted publication.

Because information is becoming such a frontline resource it's important that both business managers and IT professionals understand the key concepts and principles involved in practising safe computing in the 'IT age'.

Key Concept 1: Types of loss
An information system can harm an organization in two ways:

- *consequential* loss can, and normally will, arise when the system fails to perform as intended;
- *direct loss* arises when the system itself suffers loss or damage.

The indications are that, on average, consequential losses are much larger than direct losses. Accordingly, it is on consequential losses that attention should be focused by business managers.

Key Concept 2: How consequential losses arise
Although systems vary enormously, it turns out that – irrespective of the type or scale of the information system involved – consequential losses always arise when one or more of three key properties of information are compromised:

- availability, i.e. response time and up-time;
- integrity, i.e. accuracy, completeness and validity (validity meaning that the information results from an authorized business process);
- confidentiality, i.e. access to the information is restricted to authorized individuals or processes.

It follows that attention should be concentrated on preserving the availability, integrity and confidentiality of the *information processed by a system* rather than on simply protecting the *information system itself.* (As it happens, if everything necessary is done to protect against consequential loss, protection against direct loss is conferred as a by-product. The converse, however, does not hold true.)

Key Concept 3: How to evaluate consequential losses
To put a figure on actual or potential consequential losses to a business, all types of possible losses need to be considered. Analysis of incidents provides the following checklist of possibilities:

- *loss of goods, funds or other tangible assets;*
- *loss of valuable information;*
- *loss of competitive advantage;*
- *reduction in cash flow;*
- *loss of orders;*
- *loss of production efficacy, effectiveness or safety;*
- *loss of customer or supplier goodwill;*
- *public embarrassment and/or loss of business credibility;*
- *penalties suffered as a result of breaching some statutory obligation(s).*

Key Concept 4: How direct losses arise

Direct losses arise when one or more components of an information system are destroyed, damaged or stolen, i.e.:

- *hardware*, i.e. processors, workstations, printers, disks, tapes and telecommunications equipment;
- *software*, i.e. systems software and applications software for all hardware components;
- *system information*, i.e. specifications, drawings, user manuals, operating procedures, computer programmes, parameter files;
- *physical environment*, i.e. equipment rooms, air-conditioning and power supplies and similar items;
- *people* , i.e. operators, managerial, technical and support staff, and users.

User's data is not listed here as a component of an information system but is often considered as part of the system in practice.

Key Concept 5: Disruptive events

There is no limit to the variety of things that can happen to make information systems go wrong. But experience shows that the following are common sources of disruption:

- *fire, flood and other natural disasters;*
- *vandalism and sabotage by staff or outsiders;*
- *breakdown or malfunction of software, hardware or physical environment;*
- *invalid or incorrect changes to existing systems;*
- *loss of telecommunications services;*
- *overload;*
- *invalid data input;*
- *loss of key personnel;*
- *strikes by key personnel;*
- *unauthorized access (including 'hacking');*
- *deliberate or inadvertent introduction of 'viruses';*
- *theft of software (unauthorized copying);*
- *theft of hardware.*

Key Concept 6: Multiple perspectives

In discussing what goes wrong with information systems people tend to mix up quite different things in the same breath. This often obscures the real issues and leads to confusion. It's easy for this to happen because when people talk about things going wrong with an organization's systems the chain of events they are trying to describe can be quite complex (Figure 16.2).

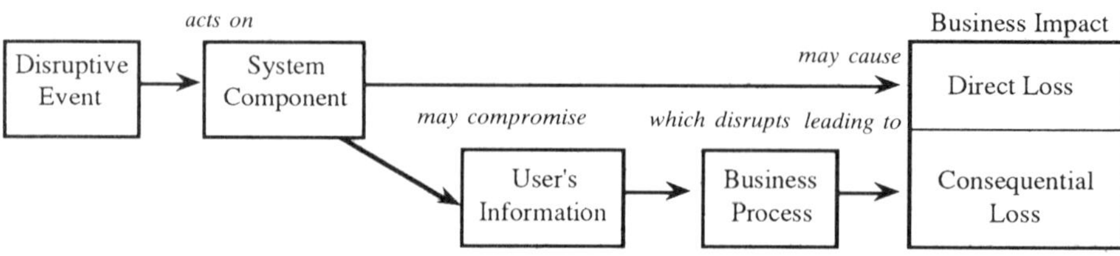

Figure 16.2. How information sytems fail in operation

The events also look different from different points of view: to an IT professional what matters is the impact a disruptive event has on the system for which he or she is responsible. To a line manager, what matters is what the event may do to the business process he or she is responsible for. To top management, what matters is the overall impact on the business. Forming the overall picture is thus essential, at least to top management, but impracticable unless the different parties involved share common terminology and concepts.

Key Concept 7: Countermeasures

It's not possible to make a system 100% robust, and even if it was it would rarely repay the effort. But it is possible to build a set of countermeasures that control the risks involved and keep them within acceptable levels. Countermeasures (also referred to as controls) are devices, procedures, policies, methods or programmed mechanisms used to:

- *prevent* disruptive events materializing as far as possible;
- *detect* such events as do nevertheless occur;
- allow an organization to *recover* from disruptive events which have occurred, within acceptable time and cost.

Examples of countermeasures are 'no smoking in computer rooms', fire detectors, halon gas fire suppression systems, contracted backup sites, and insurance.

Diagrammatically, the different types of countermeasures come into (and control) the chain of events as shown in Figure 16.3.

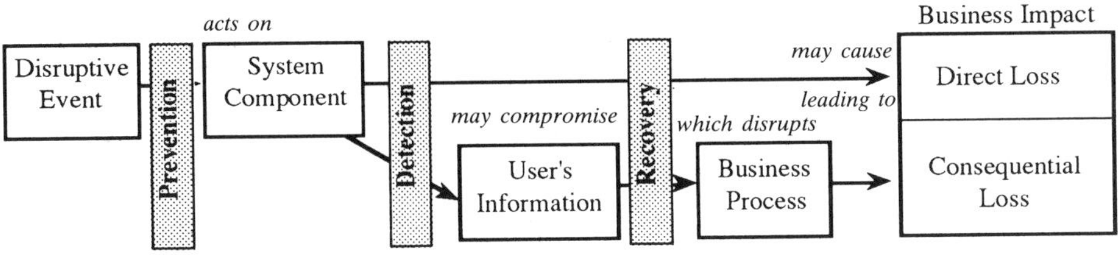

Figure 16.3. Where countermeasures fit in

Key Principles

To put the seven key concepts outlined above into effect, experience shows that certain key principles should always be observed:

- *assurance*: means should exist to provide business management and other interested parties with a well-informed view of the level of dependability that they can realistically expect from their information systems and the adequacy of arrangement for achieving this target.
- *proportionality*: the strength of countermeasures deployed should be proportionate to the risk involved.
- *responsibilities*: responsibilities for achieving a target level of dependability should be clearly assigned and all parties concerned should be aware of who is responsible for what;
- *coherence*: the different elements of an organization's countermeasures should work well together with no gaps in important areas;
- *ethics*: individuals should be aware of their rights and obligations as regards the organization's information systems and of such sanctions as may apply to improper use.

16.3.2 Step 2: Fact gathering

Establish (a) what risks the organization is currently facing and how the strategy under development will change them; and (b) what arrangements are in place to control IT risks and what additional controls are needed to counter the increased level of risk.

Experienced users of IT almost always act as though they know what risks they are facing and have a reasonable degree of confidence that risks are matched by a sound set of controls. Such confidence is hardly ever justified. Consider: for the most part companies build up their portfolio of systems over time with no one person monitoring the overall picture in any detail; the amount of information flowing through systems changes over time as do the underlying technologies in use, the technological opportunities for disruption, responsibilities for system development and operation and the links between one system and another. Many companies do not have a schedule listing all systems that are in current use. In some companies, extremely important systems are running on single PCs.

Given this background, a periodic re-assessment of risks and controls can be expected to throw up surprises.

To carry out such an assessment is not difficult if it's tackled in the right way. But you need a sound approach and good fact-gathering instruments (ie proforma checklists and questionnaires). In the context of an information systems strategy, here's what needs to be done:

- *Charter*: you are going to have to collect information from the IT function and from user departments, so you need to get a charter to act and to persuade others to cOoperate. The higher you go to get it, the better.
- *Scope*: you need to be very precise about what you are going to cover in your review and what you are going to leave out. This is particularly important if you are aiming to provide management with an overall assessment and recommendations which they will be encouraged to act upon. You need to ensure that they are aware of what you have looked at and what you have not.
- *Risk assessment*: in principle, every system will have its own unique set of risks and these should be assessed on a case-by-case basis. In practice, this is rarely feasible or necessary. What you need to establish is whether a given system should be treated as 'normal' or 'high' risk in the context of your own organiZation (some companies are more risk-averse than others). The easiest way to establish the relative risk of different systems is ask the people responsible for the systems in question to indicate: (a) which types of consequential loss would be suffered if the availability, integrity or confidentiality of their information was compromised; and (b), against each possible type of loss, to rate the maximum possible impact on the business on a three- or five-point scale (e.g. 0 = no impact; 5 = the business would not survive). This should be done using a pre-prepared proforma for a cross-section of existing systems and for all new systems being considered for inclusion in the information systems strategy. This process will allow two end-products to be produced:
  - a schedule of systems classified by risk;
  - a commentary on the overall level of risk facing the organization highlighting, for example, whether any systems are sufficiently important to threaten the existence of the organization should they go wrong.
- *Controls assessment*: proforma can also be used to establish what controls are in place, any weak points in the organization's control arrangements and any

areas that need to be strengthened in the light of the new systems covered by the information systems strategy. To be useful, the proforma needs to divide the field of IT into control areas and break each area down into the next one or two level(s) of detail. There is no single right way to identify control areas but, as a guide, the proforma needs to get down to around 100 individual points of assessment to be both comprehensive and useful. For each point, the minimum objective is to establish the existence of control measures. It is obviously even better if you can also establish the strength of such controls as do exist. Thus a three– or five-point scale may be usefully incorporated (with the extremes signifying 0 = *no control* and 5 = *very strong* control respectively). The proforma should be filled in by the people responsible for each control area. Possible control areas could be, for example:

– systems development;
– computer and network operation;
– user procedures;
– change management;
– system administration;
– access control.

The assessment should cover the main datacentre(s) and important subsidiary sites when information systems are developed and/or operated. A sample of PC/office systems should also be assessed.

The pattern that is likely to emerge is that the organization has a very variable pattern of control: strong in a few areas, very weak in a few areas and medium in all others. This pattern is likely to have emerged by default rather than design and is unlikely to make good business sense.

16.3.3 Step 3: Policy formulation

Make key policy decisions which will apply during the period of the strategy under development.

By pulling the results of the risk assessment together with the controls assessment, you should be able to establish an overall picture of what needs to be done to make the organization's systems more dependable.

Some aspects will undoubtedly warrant treatment as policy issues. These include matters concerned with:

- top management's attitude to risk;
- arrangements for reviewing high-risk systems;
- responsibilities for information 'ownership';
- responsibilities of system users, developers and operators;
- ethical standards for all employees.

If the organization already has policy statements in these areas they should be reviewed to ensure they remain current; alternatively, clear statements of corporate policy should be developed for endorsement by top management. Any organizational changes needed for the future should also be considered at this time.

16.3.4 Step 4: Planning

> *Ensure that the strategic plan takes account of the activities required to make the company's systems as dependable as needed.*

Where control weaknesses have been identified, these should be scheduled for rectification, in the same way as any other project. Individual items can be usefully separated into two classes:

- *Baseline controls*: i.e. those controls which apply to 'normal'-risk systems and which will be implemented in the general IT environment, e.g. main datacentre(s) or network(s). The costs of these may be impossible to assign to any one user and they should therefore be considered as individual 'overhead' items. They will need to be costed, prioritized, justified and scheduled for implementation in the same way as other 'overhead' items.
- *System-specific controls*: these are additional controls required by particular systems to counter risks which are specific to that system. These should be costed, developed and implemented as part of the overall plan for the system(s) concerned.

16.4 CONCLUDING REMARKS

The discussion above distils experience gained from looking at the dependability of information systems in a wide range of environments, and detailed studies of the problems that exist and the best way of overcoming them. While many of the things that need to be done to make systems dependable are relatively inexpensive, others will require substantial outlay and all of them demand continuing management attention.

In companies where time and resources are in short supply, these realities may amount to a justification for inaction.

But systems will not 'come right' by themselves. As the head of IS strategy in one of Europe's largest users of IT puts it:

> *'We've failed to meet our operational targets 18 times in the last three months. Our systems are too complex to understand and operate.'*

Overall, discrimination, thoroughness and the determined avoidance of unnecessary complexity are the keys to success. In the 'IT age', if you want systems that will keep your business up and running, you have to put in the effort up front to make sure they won't let you down when you most need them.

17 IT strategy at Nationwide Anglia

B. Davis
Nationwide Anglia Building Society

17.1 INTRODUCTION

This section deals with some of the practical issues which arise when trying to coordinate IT and business strategies. It is based on the real activities and experiences of the country's second largest building society. There is no suggestion, however, that this provides the definitive methodology and rather it describes an approach which is still subject to change – reflecting, of course, the changing business issues for the society in a very competitive environment. Although essentially the views of a practitioner, the case study approach serves to illustrate key underlying principles and it is these, at the end of the day, which must be applied to a particular organization's own circumstances.

The primary need is, not surprisingly, for cooperation between the IT and direct business providers. This has to stem from an understanding of each other's concerns and the clearest possible definition of responsibilities, but without compartmentalizing people. How you organize to maximize the cooperative input of your people will depend on each business's own particular culture.

17.2 WHAT IS THE BUSINESS?

Whilst not wishing to bore the reader with a lengthy definition of the business of a building society it is important to understand this before it is possible to show how the business and IT strategies can be coordinated. Although a building society is used as an example this serves to illustrate two key, general, points:

- We need to know the business strategy first (although this may be modified in the light of IT capability).
- The business is not always as straightforward as outward appearances might suggest.

Building societies used to be simply providers of mortgages and a safe haven for personal savings. They were part of a pricing cartel and competition was limited. Strategies were focused on a simple service concept but one in which the customer was still the poor relation. But building societies can now offer a wider range of services, from personal banking through unsecured loans and on to estate agency. The cartel no longer exists and competition is fierce – the customer is now king.

But this still does not describe what is happening. The increased sophistication of customers and the introduction of additional financial services legislation means that individual transactions are more complex. The multiplicity of payment mechanisms and the wide availability of different types of savings and current accounts have increased the sheer volume of transactions at a remarkable pace. And now there is Europe on the horizon and the possibility of even greater competition, and, perhaps, the need for multi-currency operations.

Furthermore, there were over two thousand bulding societies at the start of this century; now there are fewer than 100. This ongoing merger activity adds a further dimension which needs to be considered in any strategic planning.

In summary, a bulding society today is a highly complex, fast-changing operation which is the backcloth against which the business and IT strategies have to exist. So, although the business strategy can be condensed into 'the provision of excellent personal financial services', the practical ramifications are certainly more complex.

17.3 BUSINESS AND IT OBJECTIVES

True business objectives relate to the provision of new services, standards of operation, and the desire to deliver a long-range vision. These will vary by business type and philosophy but frequently there are some common second-order issues which, again, need to form part of the backcloth for ongoing strategies. This illustrates another key point:

- There are always practical constraints which must be borne in mind when formulating strategy.

In another context this is a bit like saying that it is pointless setting a goal to put a man on the moon if you haven't yet invented the rocket – unless you take an exceptionally long-term view. And even 10 years was tight for a nation that already had.

For most financial institutions some of these constraints will be the need to ;

... continue to add/change functionality of existing activities
... handle an ever-increasing workload
and ... keep going while making the changes!

It is in the context of this last point in particular that we can examine a practical example of a business objective, born out of a particular business strategy, and the way the IT strategy needed to be pursued.

17.4 MERGING NATIONWIDE AND ANGLIA BUILDING SOCIETIES

The business strategy for the two precursors indicated a need to increase the size of the business in order to be able to influence the market and to compete more effectively using economies of scale. The objective then became to merge the two societies. At this point the constraints started to become important, particularly for the IT people whose starting position was about as far from ideal as might be imagined.

Pre-merger Technology

	Nationwide	*Anglia*
Mainframes	Sperry	ICL
Card processors	Tandem	IBM
Branch	Burroughs	Nixdorf
ATMs	NCR	Nixdorf
Workstations	PCs	OPDs

In trying to find a way forward it was imperative that any solution allowed the business not only to continue, but to start to provide a demonstrably better service from day one of the merger.

The first step was to question the business users. They very easily determined that the ideal solution was a combination of the best parts from each of the existing systems, by which was meant part of Sperry and ICL together rather than choosing one from each technology category. At this stage the users were not aware of the obvious systems constraints but rather saw it as shuffling two packs of cards together – it's a little tricky, but you soon stop dropping things.

The technologists were naturally able to take a more practical view but, here again, an unexpected constraint arose. Prior to the merger, each group of technical staff had always been keen to point out the shortcomings of their particular suppliers – possibly as a way of deflecting a disgruntled user towards a common enemy. However, as soon as they realized that their 'beloved' machine might be a casualty of the merger, it suddenly acquired virtues that even the manufacturers didn't know it possessed.

Strategically, another key issue in the coordination of business and IT strategies was being realized:

- Realism and a belief in the greater good of the final strategy are more important than strongly held personal desires.

This objectivity was achieved and represented the clear ongoing theme of bringing all parties together to share the strategy and devise the practical implementation plans. Multi-discipline project teams met in convivial surroundings and quickly recognized the strengths and weaknesses of each other's arguments. Most interestingly, the solution needs to be described by adding a further, business, dimension to the table:

Post-merger Technology

	Nationwide Anglia	*Business Process*
Mainframes	Sperry	Banking and Savings
	ICL	Mortgages and Insurance
Card processors	Tandem	
Branch	Nixdorf	
ATMs	NCR	
Workstations	PCs	

The resulting multi-vendor strategy has significant advantages in that it provides the optimal machine for the job, together with resilience (since not all services are located on a single machine), and vendor competitiveness for adding new applications.

To some extent this describes a planning process that was brought about by necessity. The alignment of the business and IT strategies can normally be determined following a more well-thought-out, but nevertheless equally practical approach.

17.5 ALIGNING THE BUSINESS AND IT STRATEGIC PLANNING PROCESSES

It is important to have a basic framework which, in theory at least, will provide the marrying of the business and IT strategies. As stated previously, the business directions need to be delineated first and many organizations will be familiar with a 3-5-year corporate planning process.

The broad corporate view is then refined into more detailed business plans for the various functions that make up the organization. At this point, or even before, the particular development needs – both IT and for other areas – start to become more focused. It is here that the joint ownership, user plus IT, is crucial. It is all too easy for one party or the other to have thought there was a mutual understanding until the project delivery date and specific functionality is debated, by which time it can be too late.

Before illustrating this with some examples there is one further aspect of the planning process that should be mentioned. That is the need to prioritize projects on the basis of some form of logical reasoning. Even in the most efficient and large IT functions it is common nowadays for the business to think of many more ways that IT can be used than it is practically possible to deliver. Typically, the IT director ends up having to play god and has the unenviable task of informing some users of what they cannot have – no wonder they are sometimes seen as unhelpful.

Interestingly, most people seem to agree that some form of ranking based on cost/benefit analysis provides the best method, until you examine how this works in practice. It certainly used to be the case that the IT function was poor at estimating the cost and time-scale involved in delivering a project. However, these failings have now been largely overcome and it is the issue of project benefits which is often most difficult to assess accurately. Some broad categories can be helpful:

Assessing Project Benefits

Category	*Benefit*
Essential/legal	Avoid jail
Efficiency	Cost control
Strategic	Survival
Nice to have	Happiness
Research	Unknown

c.f. McFarlan

Clearly this not sufficient detail to draw up a definitive project order of merit but it is not intended to delve further into this here. Suffice to say that there is considerable scope for an improved methodology which will work as well in practice as it does in theory.

The all-time classic example of how one group, in this case the IT people, essentially misled their users, is office automation. Most projects will have a complex benefits picture with at least some items appearing under most of the above headings. For office automation the following diagram illustrates what it was expected to deliver.

Office Automation	*Projected Benefits*
Efficiency	Save paper and postage. Better access. Fewer typists.
Strategic	Faster. EDI. Improved quality.
Nice to have	Diary.
Research	Electronic storage. Composite documents.

In reality, it achieved few of its expected aims and has probably done more for printer technology than anything else. Certainly, it hasn't eliminated paper and there aren't fewer typists. Electronic diaries are in limited use and the research for storage and composite documents is still in its early stages. Quality is about the only thing that has been improved (before OA an average of two drafts of a document were produced – the average now is more than 5).

To set the record straight let's look at another example, directly relevant to the financial services industry, which did come through the planning process and which did deliver: the introduction of ATMs.

ATMs	*Projected Benefits*
Efficiency	Save counter staff.
Strategic	Better service. Defensive.
Nice to have	Fast cash.
Research	Passbooks. Smart cards.

The research has yet to deliver fully but has been demonstrated in principle – but that's the one category that can be a little late! In all other aspects, the planning and delivery have been superbly executed and ably demonstrate what can be achieved when cooperation is at its best.

17.6 FLEXIBILITY

The theme of business and IT partners working together does not mean that every single aspect of coordinating the strategies has to be physically tackled together. As the strategy for the business is clarified, with due regard for IT and other constraints, certain aspects can now be handled in some degree of isolation.

The setting-up of an IT infrastructure is one such aspect.

It is becoming increasingly popular for the user community to take an active interest in computer applications, even building them themselves (particularly in the PC arena), but it is equally acceptable that users should not need to know the details of how the basic operating or network control systems operate. This is analogous to telephone users not needing to know how their call is routed and connected, although they could easily invent a new telephone-based service organization. Similarly, a car driver does not need to understand anti-lock braking to be able to use it effectively when needed.

Unfortunately there is, perhaps inevitably, a Catch-22 situation inherent in enabling one group to go off and set up their part in isolation. That is the issue of flexibility.

No business strategy is perfect and new opportunities are bound to arise which were not predicted in the plan. The job of an infrastructure is to provide a means, not only of enabling current and foreseen activities to be carried out, but to provide enough scope to cater for the unknown. This is, not surprisingly, an impossible task.

The more flexibility is required, the greater the cost and the greater the time to implement. The analogy here is of road planners who know that a two-by-six-lane motorway would probably meet most needs for some time to come, but are told it would cost too much and take too long to build. They build it smaller and are congratulated for solving the immediate problem and coming in under budget. As traffic grows the road clogs and the 'hindsighters' expostulate about the poor planning and so forth. The M25 springs to mind ...

For financial service industries which rely on computer systems so heavily, a flexible infrastructure is essential. Flexibility to connect different users to different computers; flexibility to add new functionality to a 'finished' system; flexibility to provide new information systems that were definitely not needed; flexibility to cope with the latest advances in technology; flexibility – well, just flexibility.

It is ironic that the one thing which aids the ability to provide this flexibility is the provision of standards. If all computers adhered to standard protocols for communicating with display terminals, it would be a relatively simple process to provide different computer systems on different computers displayed at a user's terminal. This is why some organizations find the single vendor-approach attractive since at least that vendor's equipment should be compatible with itself – but even this is far from perfect as technological advances cannot be anticipated, and sooner or later a solus supplier will need to introduce new standards.

Nevertheless, there are some opportunities and, for example, Nationwide has introduced an X.25 standard network to interlink all the different computers. This clearly supports the business strategy of wishing to be able to use the best machines available, since practically all manufacturers can be connected over such a network. Similarly, many organizations now use 'standard personal computers' with selected software packages throughout their organizations which enable new applications or data files to be transported easily from one user to another.

In terms of key issues, flexibility must be on the planning agenda.

- Flexibility is a desirable goal but cannot be perfectly planned for and needs to be understood in the context of the business and IT plans.

17.7 MORE PRAGMATISM

17.7.1 Cost Management

All planning involves the optimization of costs and benefits. Usually, however, it is necessary to provide an initial estimate of the likely costs without a full appreciation of the expected business outcome. This is part of the iterative process in building up a plan.

It is important, therefore, to understand that large parts of IT costs are essentially fixed – something most business planners would ideally wish to avoid. It is relatively easy to understand how the costs of a building are mainly fixed and that unless the whole building can be emptied it is difficult to reduce the running costs. This is also the situation for most mainframe users in that a partly used computer will still cost almost as much to run as a full one.

Similarly, there is an 80/20 rule which needs to be considered when attempting to outline new applications. The business direction requires a new application but it often happens that 80% of the benefits are achievable from the first 20% of the functionality specified for the application. For example, a word processor that enables only part of a page to be viewed on screen in a basic font will be a vast improvement over a typewriter, but could be 'written' as a computer application very much quicker than the sort of fully-fledged word processors with multi-page display, multiple fonts, line justification, mail merging, etc.

- Care needs to be taken not to overspecify an application as costs will soon start to outweigh benefits.

Cost management also needs to be applied to another crucial planning activity, that of projected business volumes. Again, particularly for mainframe users, costs will increase in quite large, discrete steps as a new piece of equipment is added.

This means that capacity utilization will be at a low point immediately after a purchase and it is important to recognize that small-volume increases can sometimes push the organization into the next purchase step, even though it will be a considerable time before the full capacity is utilized. This can be expressed as another key point:

- Capacity management needs to be an integral part of strategic planning to avoid carrying unnecessary, under-utilized equipment.

Other cost management issues tend to be focused on the day-to-day practicalities of running the business and, as such, can usually be delegated to the management of the IT function. Strategic planning hardly needs to concern itself with the decision to use BT or Mercury for example, although this may well be important in the detailed cost planning for the IT function itself.

17.7.2 Contingency

Strategic planning for the business may easily overlook the importance that the business places on its IT systems; seeing them simply as a means to an end. But many businesses conducted on a large scale, and financial services are a perfect example, are wholly dependent on their computer technology. If the systems are not available for even a short length of time the business will be in jeopardy and will probably fail.

Duplication of crucial elements, or the availability of alternative facilities, are essential but can easily be overlooked at the planning stage – particularly when this may push the costs to a level which actually militates against carrying out the activity.

Contingency arrangements also need to be applied to the business processes since, in a worst-case scenario, if the computers survive but the people don't you still will not be any better off. This is one that the business and IT managers really can tackle with a common interest.

- Contingency planning needs to be an integral part of business planning.

It is also prudent, referring back to an earlier point, to provide some funds to cater for the unforeseen – this may be used for R&D, but if a sudden problem arises, the careful planner will have made at least some provisions on which to call.

17.7.3 Maintenance

In a nutshell, all systems, just like buildings or motor cars, need maintenance. But similarly, there can come a point where the maintenance costs outweigh the costs of starting afresh.

Maintenance is a large 'fixed cost' element which is generally not well understood. It is very difficult to pin down since many small system additions can often be described as either maintenance or enhancements. This is an area which most organizations could profitably attempt to cover in more depth in the planning process, but it will not be easy.

- Maintenance activity needs to be assessed vis-à-vis the alternatives of rebuilding.

17.7.4 Development Backlog

Earlier in the text reference was made to prioritizing projects using a simple set of initial categories. In practice, many more applications will be suggested than can possibly be handled. Even more of a problem is the fact that all of these will have good justifications in terms of return on investment, payback period, etc.

The business planner may then be lured into recommending that IT resources are increased so that all the projects can be carried out – since this appears to make good business sense. The IT function may be tempted to agree with this approach, since they will have more funds; will not have to keep saying no to people; and will increase their power base in the organization.

This is, of course, a trap for the unwary.

It isn't simply a case of increasing resources. First of all, it is likely there will be financial reasons why this is not tenable, e.g. cash flow (not all projects have an instant return, and too many investments with insufficient deliverables will require a very strong source of funds as backing). But there are also considerations of a more fundamental, practical nature.

Increasing staff to carry out more projects requires a recruitment drive; this takes time and costs money; it may lead to an overall increase in salaries as the need arises to pay new recruits above the basic rate to attract them from competitors; it needs more management; more space is needed; and so forth.

Also, the old adage of too many cooks spoiling the broth may come into play. Few systems are isolated from one another, and the complex interactions can be magnified if too many different projects are all trying to interface with each other at the same time. Complexity in these situations seems to follow a 'square rule' and can quickly become unmanageable. In the planning process it is important to recognize the practical management constraints which may mean turning away good projects, but may also save the business from collapsing under the weight of its own enthusiasm.

- Over-expansion can be equally important in regard to IT projects as it can for the business as a whole.

17.8 PEOPLE

It is stating the obvious to say that people are the most important element when organizing to bring IT strategy in line with the business strategy. Nevertheless, it does need saying along with a few more specific statements of what this means.

Firstly, there are important characteristics of technical experts, as indeed of most experts, that should be borne in mind. Someone who is good at building a computer system is not necessarily a good manager or a good communicator. Business users are, almost by definition, better on the whole at making their case for a particular action. This can lead to tension and, more importantly, to poor decisions being forced through. It is essential to recognize this tendency when putting a plan together and to accommodate for the relative strengths and weaknesses in the constituent members of the planning teams.

Also, technical personnel are typically seen as the 'backroom boys' or the 'boffins' and seldom receive credit from the public when things go well. It is all too easy to turn on these people when something goes wrong rather than looking a little deeper into the underlying reasons.

Secondly, many computer departments contain a particular group of managers who are well trained, both in the theory and through practical experience of project management. Few other functions possess such in-depth knowledge. Typically, however, new application projects are recommended to be managed by the user – thus ensuring ownership of the final product. While this is essentially correct, it can be a worthwhile practice to ensure that the technical project manager is kept close to the action as he or she will certainly be able to assist in the process.

Thirdly, round-table discussions between users and IT staff do not often happen by themselves. Some form of structured meeting arrangements are necessary. And it is a particularly good practice to have an ongoing review process and not concentrate such discussions in a last-minute, once-a-year, planning meeting.

People work well in teams when they understand each other's abilities – but team-building across organizational boundaries needs to be worked at. It is not a natural phenomenon.

- Understanding people's skills is important and obtaining the best from people needs a sympathetic and continuous management process.

17.9 SUMMARY

Throughout this section various practical issues have been highlighted and the following list is a summary of the key points:

- We need to know the business strategy first (although this may be modified in the light of IT capability).
- The business is not always as straightforward as outward appearances might suggest.
- There are always practical constraints which must be borne in mind when formulating strategy.
- Realism and a belief in the greater good of the final strategy are more important than strongly-held personal desires.

- Flexibility is a desirable goal but cannot be perfectly planned for and needs to be understood in the context of the business and IT plans.
- Care needs to be taken not to overspecify an application as costs will soon start to outweigh benefits.
- Capacity management needs to be an integral part of strategic planning to avoid carrying unnecessary, under-utilized equipment.
- Contingency planning needs to be an integral part of business planning. Maintenance activity needs to be assessed vis-à-vis the alternatives of rebuilding.
- Over-expansion can be equally important in regard to IT projects as it can for the business as a whole.
- Understanding people's skills is important and obtaining the best from people needs a sympathetic and continuous management process.

Strategic planning is not a perfect process but is a prerequisite for an ongoing business. Some of the practicalities that need to be considered when coordinating the business and IT strategies have been exposed and it is recommended that these are taken into account as part of any planning process.

Part Five

Future Realities

18 IT strategies: issues and prescriptions

K. H. Macdonald and C. Yapp
ICL (UK) Ltd

18.1 INTRODUCTION

While many organizations are starting down the road to develop IT strategies, there are some organizations who have many years' experience with IT. In this paper, we will explore the lessons that can be learned from the successes and failures of others.

Hugh Macdonald was the ICL sponsor representative for five years in the 'Management in the 1990s' research programme at Sloan School of Management at MIT. This five-year, $6 million collaborative effort between MIT and twelve US and UK sponsoring organizations developed a number of models and concepts to assist in the understanding and planning of IT in organizations from the perspective of management and not the technical specialist.

The purpose of our paper is to discuss the issues that affect the benefits derived from IT investment and to identify the key business management issues that must be addressed if an IT strategy is to be taken from 'paper' to implementation.

It is now over ten years since the first examples of strategic use of IT arose. Why after ten years have we not all learned the lessons? Indeed, why do there still seem to be so few really good examples around? These two questions need to answered if we are to convince organizations that IT has a significant role to play in the 1990s.

18.2 THE MANAGEMENT CONTEXT OF IT

Over the past few years there has been an increasing dialogue in the IT industry on achieving the benefits that IT has promised, but often failed to deliver.

Many directors will point to the large and growing expenditure on IT within their organizations but find it hard to demonstrate an impact on 'the bottom line'.

To address this issue, there have been frequent calls for the appointment of IT directors, the creation of 'hybrid' managers and calls to address the 'technophobia' that affects senior management in many companies.

What has received less attention in this debate is the question of what is 'owned' rather than who should 'own' IT.

Consider, for the moment, the following proposition. If the board of a large organization were all PC literate, would they be able to run their business better because of this knowledge? Our answer would be a definite maybe. The argument for the proposition is essentially that lack of confidence in the capabilities of IT could best be addressed by personal experience.

Against the proposition are some powerful arguments. First, the rapid change in the economics and capabilities available in the IT market place would make redundant any such knowledge very quickly. Second, a little learning could be dangerous. Seduced by the technology it could be easy to lose sight of the business.

What needs to be owned by senior management is the implications of IT not the IT itself. To understand these implications we need to understand what the management task is and how IT affects management work. In the next section we will explore the management in the 1990s model of the management task, the MIT90s paradigm.

18.3 THE MIT90s PARADIGM

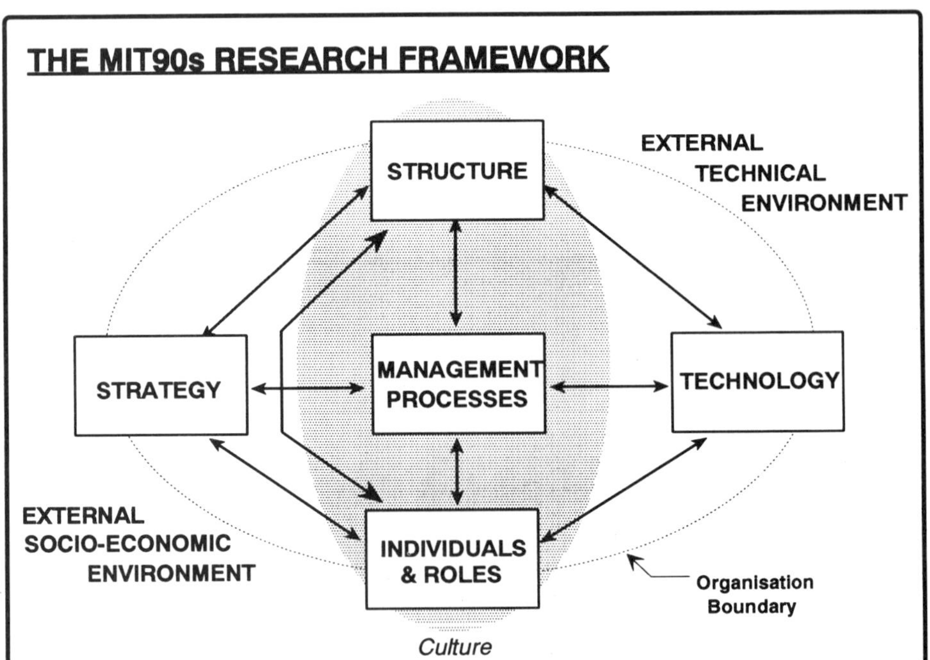

Figure 18.1. The MIT90s paradigm

Rockart and Scott Morton (1991) created a research framework for the MIT90s programme, which over the period of the research has proven to be very robust in understanding IT and its implications.

The aim of the MIT90s study was to develop an understanding of the management issues of the 1990s and propose tools, techniques and models to aid in the diagnosis and prescription of these issues. The research, conducted at Sloan School of Management was concerned with IT, but from a business perspective, not a technology perspective.

The first point to note is that the paradigm consists of five interdependent components, bound together in the external environment.

It is one of the truisms of business today that the only constant is change, but even that is changing. The pace of change is accelerating. Turbulence, in social, political, economic and technological arenas is a fact of life. However, many organizations still behave as if the external turbulence can be ignored. It is rare to find an organization that not only recognizes the turbulence but proactively seeks out change, seeing the opportunities as well as the threats.

It is our contention that organizations will need to be more 'extrovert' than has been past practice. Those that prosper in turbulent times will seek, not react, to change. In this we are supporting the messages of Tom Peters (1987).

However, it is important to understand that IT has an intimate link with this turbulence. IT is both a cause of turbulence and a potential ally in 'thriving on chaos'.

The ability to transfer capital electronically in seconds over a global network-from Tokyo to London and to New York makes possible instantaneous overreaction to news events, with potentially destabilizing economic effects.

Equally important, instantaneous news coverage of important events, the use of electronic mail within companies shrinks the world to Macluhan's 'Global village'. Old views of hierarchical control and dissemination of information are inadequate to prevent 'us' making up our minds about an event before 'they' tell us the official position.

Given that we live in an increasingly turbulent world, what should and can we do about it? The answer that we are proposing is not comforting to managers. *We must rethink the nature of management work.*

In the paradigm, the five components identify the changes that we are proposing. Let us consider each in turn.

• *Strategy* has been accepted as a traditional part of the management task. However, to the traditional role we can now see examples of organizations implementing strategies that would be impossible without IT. Examples include point of sale in retail, automatic tellers in banking and the airline reservation systems.

• *Structure* is again an accepted part of management work. The choice of organizational design is key to success. Should we organize on product lines/market lines or customer lines? Should we organize geographically? How much responsibility do we devolve? Are profit centres or cost centres the right approach? All these are traditional and still important questions. We must now add some more for the 1990s.

Traditional spans of control in organizations are recommended in the range of six to ten. However, there are now examples of organizations running with 60 to 100. What spans of control should we be seeking and how do we make them work?

The use of electronic networks makes it possible for 'teams' to work together where in the past geographical separation would have been a barrier to productivity and coordination. This creates a potential for 'ad-hocracy' as a response to turbulence. However, as has been seen by the slow growth in 'telecommuting', managing these arrangements is not easy. Can we make 'electronic teamwork' a reality?

In the nineteenth century, the emergence of railroads and the telegraph transformed the structure of enterprises. The vertically integrated businesses we know today are the product of these innovations. One impact of IT is that it is becoming possible for production and coordination to be managed across organizational boundaries through the use of IT, starting with electronic trading but extending to electronic integration of businesses. There are a few examples of this type of integration, but we expect this to become increasingly attractive during the 1990s. We call this style of business 'the virtual corporation'.

• *People and roles* again are recognized management responsibilities. Managers traditionally have hired and fired, trained and been responsible for people.

There has been much talk about 'people are our no. 1 asset' in many organizations. There is a recognized need to move from a 'personnel' culture to a 'human resource' culture.

It is here that IT has some of its most significant effects. Past technologies have generally been used to 'deskill' work, to improve work through automation. The general focus has been on the removal of the human impact through labour substitution by technology. Even where technology has been implemented to enrich work there has been a tendency to narrowing work scope.

Also, past technologies have either had their impact on 'production' as with machine tools, or with 'coordination' as with the typewriter.

IT can be used both to impact production and coordination. Here, the creation of information as a by-product of production is biting into traditional supervisory work, where supervisors acted as 'data integrators' for management. The newer technologies such as expert systems may well encroach further into management work during the 1990s than has been our experience in the past.

By far the most important change is on work design. IT can be used to deskill or enrich work. The decision lies in the hands of management. Sadly, the decision is often taken to automate by default.

Many of the IT 'disaster' stories can be traced to a failure to manage the people aspects of the business. Our organizations of the future may well run with fewer people and more machines, but success will accrue to those who get the human factors right.

• *Information Technology* is recognized by some organizations, but by no means all as a key component of the management task. Where it is recognized, it may be because of the growing costs of the IT rather than because of some strategic factor.

In the next section, we shall review some of the arguments for elevating information and Information Technology to be a corporate resource.

• *Management processes* are a growing focus of management work. In manufacturing, through the growth of 'just in time' techniques, the importance of rethinking processes has become a management issue. There has been a growing interest or concern in the West with 'total quality management'. Faced with global competition, notably from Japan and the Pacific Rim, the West is learning to compete on quality and price, rather than the traditional belief in quality or price. It is notable in the development of Edward Deming's work on quality that the traditional view of process and statistical process control has moved from the manufacturing processes to all aspects of business. Neave (1990) provides a readable and thorough review of the Deming philosophy.

In summary, the corporation of the 1990s needs to be more externally focused than ever before to cope with the accelerating pace of change. In doing so, the whole is more important than the five components.

It is our belief that those organizations which have a conscious competence in the management of their processes are those best able to survive and thrive in changing times. The role of managers must change from owning the 'structure' to managing continuous process improvement.

An important lesson to learn is that the business value of IT can only be satisfactorily measured in a management context. Management expectations of IT tend to shape the outcome. In particular, those organizations that recognize and tackle the people issues tend to reap higher rewards from IT than those who do not.

Let us move now to the question of the strategic role of IT.

18.4 A STRATEGIC ROLE FOR IT

During the 1980s, there arose the concept of 'IT for competitive advantage'. In this section, we wish to explore this concept and get a handle on what it means. From this, we would like to explore the issues that organizations need to address to achieve business benefit from investment in IT.

Early work on IT and competitive advantage identified a number of organizations whose use of IT had achieved significant boosts to their competitiveness. The case studies are well known: American Airlines SABRE, Thomson TOPS, McKesson, Baxter Healthcare.

Over the years since these first appeared, many of the case studies being ten or more years old, why have more not appeared? Some would argue that these are special cases and not applicable to their own organizations. Others would argue that the IT part in these stories has been overdone or misrepresented.

While it is true that a system like SABRE is 'IT enabled', the fundamental truth is that it is what you do with the IT and not the IT itself that provides competitive advantage.

Some organizations have attempted to copy the successes of IT, and floundered. The natural tendency has been to lay the blame firmly at the door of IT.

We would argue that both the successes and failures have been misunderstood and frequently misrepresented. Success or failure are contingent. There are a number of factors which are important to get to grips with, if the real lessons are to be learned. These factors can broadly be summarized as follows:

- *Economics.* The rapid change in IT costs is not well understood.
- *Processes.* IT is a tool for automating procedures. However, the relationship between IT and organizational processes is rarely explicit in organizations.
- *IT and competition.* The increasing pervasiveness of IT is having an impact on market and organizational structure. With this there is a need for organisations to review their competitive potential with awareness of IT.
- *Alignment.* Business success tends to arise from organizations managing a requisite balance between internal and external factors. Internally, the balance between strategy, structure, reward systems, people systems and processes can be critical. Failure in any one can damage excellence in the others. IT compounds the problem if misunderstood.
- *Organizational culture.* As organizations move from 'structural' to 'process' thinking there can be considerable cultural resistance. While culture became a 1980s buzzword, many organizations may recognize its importance, but fewer are confident in managing the implications of a culture.

Putting these together, IT as a factor tends to increase interdependence within the different aspects of a business. To solve IT problems requires systemic or holistic skills rather than functional or reductionist attitudes.

This is perhaps too abstract an argument. The old phrase that 'the whole is greater than the sum of the parts' reflects the paradigm's implications well. To illustrate this, consider the following parody illustrating the competitive potential of IT.

Two organizations, ABC and XYZ share a market between them. If both ABC and XYZ buy the same hardware, software, consultancy and services from ICL can one achieve competitive advantage from its use of IT. There are two classical factors which can be significant. First, the 'first-mover advantage' and, second, a scale factor. Because of the rapid change in IT costs, a second mover may be able to copy the first implementation at lower cost. This factor may give some benefit but we see little evidence that it is sustainable. A scaling factor would occur if ABC's market share were the larger initially and identical investments gave greater benefit, for instance, on an 'order-for-order' basis. Again, we see little evidence that IT *per se* causes the change.

Much more significant is the following. Consider the case of a sales-order processing system. On a good SOP system, there will be useful information about average size of an order, frequency of purchase, associated purchases etc. This information is highly valuable to the marketing function. Consider the dialogues between the sales directors (SD) and the marketing directors (MD) in both ABC and XYZ.

- ABC

  MD: 'We need to improve our marketing planning. The information on your system is exactly what we need. How do I get at it?'

  SD: 'See my technical chappie. Have another sherry old boy. Jolly good idea!'

- XYZ
  MD: as above.
  SD: 'Leave the customer to us. Get your own system! We do the selling, you do the marketing.'

In the case of XYZ, marketing either operates from little information, which is not unheard of, or builds its own system. Meanwhile ABC has a sales and marketing operation operating from common data.

It is not difficult to envisage a situation where XYZ is spending more money on IT and has fragmented inconsistent data which may itself exacerbate the tension illustrated in the two-line dialogue above.

What we hope this illustrates is that the benefit achieved by ABC over XYZ is contextual. It is a moot point as to whether this is a case of 'IT for competitive advantage' or 'culture for competitive advantage'.

Let us analyse this situation in a little more depth. In both ABC and XYZ, the IT is used to *automate* the sales-order process. Zuboff (1988) has coined the term *informate* to illustrate the impact of IT. Information is created as a by-product of the automation of sales. In ABC, this is used to enhance the capability of the organization, where this is ignored by XYZ.

This problem has long been recognized in the capital appropriation request procedures or their equivalents in many organizations. When assessing the cost benefits of a particular investment, what benefits are to be included? When those benefits lie outside the department or division requesting the investment how do you ensure the realization of those benefits? A good encapsulation of this issue is to be found in Hayes, Wheelwright and Clark (1988).

IT has some unique properties that tend to enlarge the scope of the problem. There is a strong tendency for the costs and benefits of IT to fall in different parts of an organization. The benefits of automation tend to be easily copied by competitors so any early adoption of a technology provides short-term differential advantage. On the other hand, the benefits of informating tend to be hard to copy because they are dependent on the organizational culture.

The significant moves made in many organizations to devolve power within their organizations, such as the creation of internal profit centres and managers being told 'to treat it as your own business', seems to be in contradiction to achieving the above benefits.

It is not that we are arguing for centralization. Far from it! There is no longer a centralization/decentralization debate that makes sense. There is no centralized model that is stable. It is much more useful to consider a feudal versus federal axis for the new order. There are many models of federalism which make for a rich variety of implementation. In devolving decision-making in organizations we would suggest that we have tended to concentrate on devolving structures, i.e. hierarchy, and created feudal organizations. Although difficult, we believe that IT benefits are best reaped by a federal organization. The key lesson is that organizational integration is a precursor to IT integration. To use IT as a substitute for appropriate organizational integration may well be a high-risk/low-reward strategy.

The challenge for organizations in moving from a feudal to a federal model is to move from seeing the organization as a structure, the management tree, to identifying the core processes of the organization that contribute to its health and wealth.

In moving to a process culture among management we are calling for a move from the 'independent' to the 'interdependent' style of manager, from lone star to team player.

This will not be easy, but to meet the quality needs of the 1990s it will be necessary. IT will not be a substitute for management teamwork. 'Teamwork' is in danger of getting a bad name through overuse and under-explanation. The parody that we used earlier in this section illustrates how the MIT90s' paradigm provides a measure of the state of organizational integration within ABC and XYZ. How does your organization fare?

So far, we have barely touched on the role of information itself as a corporate resource. One of the key impacts on the IT-user community is that information and IT is increasingly becoming part of the products. Otis Elevator have used microprocessors to create smart lifts. Panasonic are creating vacuum cleaners using fuzzy logic, Minolta are doing the same with cameras. In many areas, the ability of IT to manage scale and complexity is allowing for new opportunities for those with the vision to take them. As market segments seem to be shorter and smaller than ever before, the opportunities for using IT to manage 'mass customisation' or to manage 'segments of one' grow.

So, ultimately why should IT be managed as a strategic resource? It is both a cause of change and a means of effecting change. Without strategic ownership of IT and increased management teamwork the risk is for IT to become the problem rather than a solution to the problem.

In the remainder of this paper, we shall consider the individual aspects of the 'ownership' question, looking first at the economics of IT.

18.4.1 The Economics of IT

Let us pose the question: 'If silicon is free, why is computing getting so expensive?'

We can illustrate this by looking at an example of the change in price-performance of IT over time. Consider the case of a 4.5 MIPS mainframe. Rather than look at cost, consider the cost relative to the cost of labour, the economists' term being the capital equivalency ratio.

4.5 MIPS mainframe

1970	2000 salaries
1980	210
1990	2
2000	0.125 (expected out-turn)

The detailed figures may be different, but a general principle can be illustrated here. In the 1970s, the focus was on the capital cost of computing. IT tended to belong to the finance director for two reasons. First, finance was an early automator of its procedures. Second, the capital cost of computing was very significant.

Why has this erosion in the cost of computing not been matched by a decline in DP/MIS expenditure. There are a number of reasons:

- A massive explosion in the number of computers within organizations, particularly during the 1980s with the arrival of the PC.
- New applications including systems software has become increasingly complex requiring more power, storage and communication capability.
- While the capital cost of computing has been eroding, the operating cost has been rising. The early targets for computerization were justified on labour substitution and could provide high payback. While labour substitution looks increasingly attractive from a capital viewpoint, the new areas for investment may have lower payback and a relatively higher operating cost.

Market research on the external spend of IT users has shown a steady decline in the percentage of IT spend on hardware moving towards software and services. This shift is also fuelling the move to facilities management or 'outsourcing'.

As the capital cost of computing has fallen in relative terms, the cost of ownership of IT in many organizations has risen. Many organizations have not adjusted to these changes or feel powerless to act, calling into question the whole value of their IT spend.

A few years ago, there were calls for organizations to spend 'x%' of sales on IT or equivalent measures. Unfortunately, these types of measures for determining the 'correct' level of IT spend area are likely to cause undesirable effects as they are to add value to the business.

The important question we must ask to determine the correct level of investment in IT is: 'What are we trying to do with the business and what role should IT play?'

To answer this, we must return to the topic of process and discuss a model for relating the business to the use of IT from a process perspective.

18.4.2 Management Processes: The Key to Value

Traditional views of organization about structure may reveal a lot about status within an organization, but relatively little about activity. In a stable world this is of little consequence as each department or division of an organization learns its part and knows where it gets work from (inputs) and who receives the work it produces (output).

It may even have a clear idea of the skills it has and the source of value-added that it provides to the business. In a changing world this view ceases to be adequate.

For instance, department A sees its role as making goods that are easily maintained by department B's engineers. Now a new competitor arrives whose vision is to produce goods that don't break down. A classic example of this is in the development of the colour television market. If A and B seek to maximize their contribution individually in response to the competitive threat both will ultimately fail.

Unfortunately, the literature is full of such behaviour. One approach organizations take to address this competitive situation is to automate to reduce headcount.

If there is slackness in the system there may well be temporary respite in this course of action, but computerization in itself is not the long-term answer.

The key issue to be addressed is whether the value-added within the business can be re-created or shifted by redesigning the business. This is what we mean by redefining the core of the business. Adding to the traditional question of 'what business are we in?' we are proposing 'how are we in the business?'

It is important here to draw a distinction between process and procedure. Where there is work to be done, a task to be accomplished, there is a process. Procedures are required where there is a need for consistency in the output. Examples include design for safety, component manufacturing, orders and invoices, and audited accounts.

There are other tasks where a higher degree of human input is required or where greater discretion on the part of an individual is needed. Very crudely, PROCESS = PROCEDURE + PEOPLE.

In many organizations this distinction is not clear. Work may be designed to allow no human discretion. It is frequently observed that people spend their time trying to get round the system rather than make it work or improve it. We will return to the people issues later, but meanwhile consider the process issue.

Venkatraman (Scott Morton, 1991) has developed a model which opens up the relationship of IT to business. The model he has created opens up five levels of IT-induced business transformation.

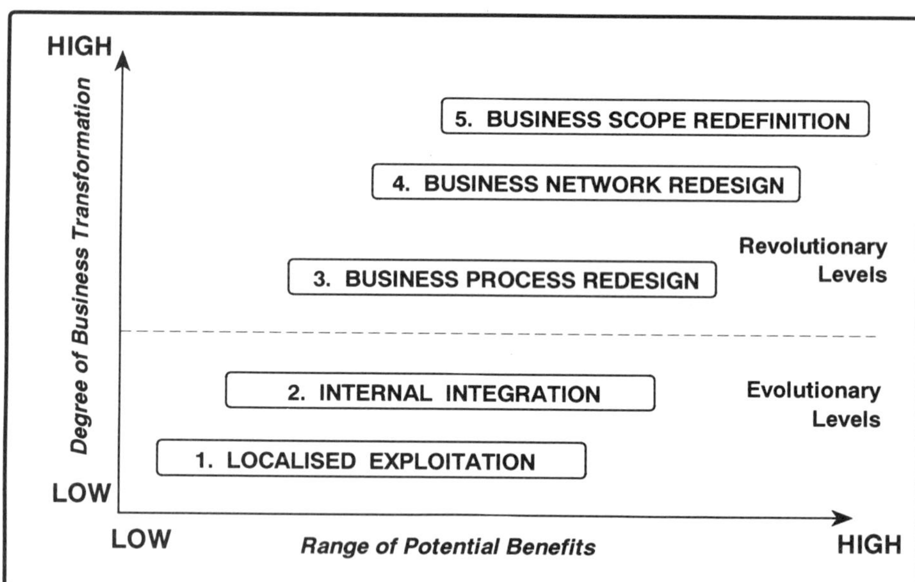

Figure 18.2. Five levels of IT-induced business transformation

These levels explore the degree of business transformation (vertical axis) with the range of benefits available (horizontal axis).

As we move from level 1 to level 5 along the horizontal axis, the range of benefits increases though there is considerable overlap at all levels.

As we move up the vertical axis, the role of IT within the organization changes. At level 1 we are describing automation as the dominant role. As we move through levels 2, 3 and 4 we are changing the balance from automation to informating. Level 5 adds a new concept, that of the transformation of the organization. By this we mean that an organization at level 5 is at such a state of development, that its IT is so central to its success, that the strategy of the business and the IT strategy have become interdependent. We shall return to this later.

Let us consider each of these levels briefly before looking at the management issues associated with changing the view of the role of IT from automating through informating through transformation.

> *Level 1.* The first level, called *localized exploitation*, is one most organizations should feel comfortable with. It is here that much of IT implemented in organizations resides. When personnel implements a payroll system, or finance a ledger system these are generally 'localized' systems supporting a particular function. The main justification is cost-benefit. The costs and benefits are generally only those concerned with the function being automated. However, some organizations may take into account other metrics, notably quality and service.

> *Level 2.* This level, *internal integration*, sees some important changes. A devolved organization may discover that it has a number of networks supporting parts of the business frequently serving many of the same locations. Cost savings may be available through rationalization and creation of a corporate network. Also, the introduction of electronic mail to enhance communications and improve organizational responsiveness is an example of the activity of level 2. As an organization seeks to establish this type of capability, the importance of technology standards grows. These standards may cover the physical network, computer-operating systems, databases, programming languages, methodologies and the Human-Computer Interface, HCI.

The central technology role is the creation of an IT platform, with standards providing an overall architecture for the implementation of IT. This is an important area and still presents some difficult choices for the IT professionals. However, it is frequently heard among the managers involved in creation of an IT platform, 'Why should I pay when he benefits?' This reflects the issue we raised earlier, that the costs and benefits of IT may fall in different places within an organization.

There are two essential challenges to management in creating a level-2 platform:

- The articulation of the logic for organizational integration.
- Making the organizational processes explicit.

The two levels discussed so far make up what Venkatraman calls the evolutionary levels. They are evolutionary because they essentially automate the existing practices of the organization. There are opportunities to extend the business by creating an IT platform at level 2. A case in point is the US Internal Revenue Service and the tax preparation business described in Scott Morton (1991).

The top three levels are the 'revolutionary' levels. Here the focus shifts from improving the efficiency of the business to addressing the effectiveness of the business through the redesign of the core processes. This is increasingly widely becoming known as re-engineering the business.

- *Level 3. Business process redesign* is essentially internally focused. We do not aim to change the source of value-added within the business. Instead, we buy the same inputs and make the same outputs but we redesign the processes by which we convert inputs to outputs. We may achieve added flexibility by simplification of processes which enables us to manage a greater range of outputs in an economic manner. JIT is a good example of level-3 implementation.

It is with changes of this scale that we are asking the management and workforce to accept changes to existing practices and even power relationships. The challenge for management is to consider the shifts in the skills required in the new organizational design and to address the people issues early in the implementation rather than wait in the hope that problems will not arise.

- *Level 4. Business network redesign* is in many ways the most significant shift in thinking. Here we begin to redesign the processes of the organization but step beyond our traditional organizational boundaries. This embraces the area of electronic trading but extends this into electronic collaborations.

With electronic trading two organizations may exchange orders, invoices and payments electronically. We can extend this further. Consider for instance placing a Computer-Aided Design, CAD, workstation into a client organization allowing the client to design or customize a product before transmitting the design into the manufacturing plant of the supplier. Here we are beginning to achieve process linkage across organizational boundaries. It is with this step that we see the capability for discrete organizations to behave in a united manner in the market place, the 'virtual corporation'.

The potential arises for what we have termed 'process invasion' through the increased permeability of organizational boundaries. This can have a significant impact on the competitive capability of an organization which we shall address in the next section.

- *Level 5. Business scope redefinition* arises once the network is in place. The scale of investment in IT and the availability of an electronic 'channel' into suppliers and client companies provides a means to utilize the network to offer a broader array of products and services. In this way the centre of gravity of the business may be shifted through the constructive use of IT. The SABRE reservation system is such an example. What was once a system to help shift seats on aeroplanes has mushroomed into a general reservation system including hotels, hire cars and sports events.

The aim of any model should always be to assist in understanding, so it is worth clarifying a few points at this juncture.

Many organizations may recognize parts of their organization to be at different levels. We are not advocating that there are level-1 or level-2 organizations for instance. The important issue is to understand where the organization is and why.

The critical issue for many organizations at level 1 is the question 'Can I go straight to level 4?' The evidence of the research is that level 2 is of vital importance. The creation of the IT platform, articulating the logic for integration and making the organization's processes explicit is a necessary step.

Without this step, the risks associated with the scale of the changes being wrought in the organization may be too great for comfort. Once the IT platform has been created at level 2, the decision to move to levels 3, 4 or 5 can be made in the context of the business and competitive pressures or opportunities.

We have illustrated the changing role of the technology in the different layers of the model along with some of the management issues. It is worth extending these changes to look at the relationship between strategy and IT and the IT investment case.

At the bottom layers of the model we have the following characteristics:

- The IT vision is process automation.
- The management requirement is efficiency.
- The investment is mainly justified on cost-benefit.
- The IT investment is as an 'administrative expense'.
- IT is essentially independent of strategy.

As we move up through the middle layers, the following emerge:

- The IT vision is organizational integration and informating.
- The management requirement is effectiveness and efficiency.
- The investment case needs to include business metrics not solely cost-benefit.
- The IT investment is as a 'business expense'.
- IT is reactive to or dependent on strategy.

As we reach the top layers, we find:

- The IT vision is extending the business, i.e. transformation.
- The management requirement is 'new businesses'.
- The investment case is determined by revenue not solely on the cost of the IT component.
- The IT investment is as a 'business investment'.
- IT and business strategies become interdependent.

One reason that organizations who have set out to emulate the famous 'IT for competitive advantage' cases find them so hard to emulate is that they focus on the IT too hard and too soon. It is not untypical to see an organization wishing to create a level-4 impact, but with a management style and metrics more appropriate to level 1.

18.4.3 Competition and IT

We have mentioned earlier that the costs and the benefits of IT have a strong tendency to appear in different places. Our example of the sales-order processing system in companies ABC and XYZ illustrated the point.

IT does have some unique features which need to be understood in a competitive context. IT has the capacity to eliminate the economic consequences of distance and time. As an example, a marketing department in New York could co-ordinate with a factory in Hong Kong over a computer network in real-time using the geographic separation and the time difference to advantage where, prior to the availability of networked computing, these two barriers would have been significant.

Once we cross organizational boundaries as in level 4, we need to understand how this may change the market place in which our organization competes.

An interesting effect is seen as JIT and EDI spreads within a manufacturing community. As we place orders electronically on our suppliers, and managers increasingly focus on timeliness, there is a tendency for the benefits to drift downstream, i.e. to the customers and the costs notably inventory drift upstream, i.e. to the suppliers.

If our organization exists in a market place with powerful buyers, it is not uncommon to find that the successful organizations get more business, but by manipulation of stock-holding levels a powerful customer may become more powerful. Traditional adversarial relationships between suppliers and buyers may become exaggerated by an electronic market place.

To redress the balance there is a need for suppliers and buyers to move from traditional (win/lose) confrontation toward more cooperative (win/win) relationships. Again, we are treading on ground where Deming has gone before us. Carlisle and Parker (1989) and Neave (1990) provide powerful arguments for this important change in Western business practice.

There are further significant implications of IT in relation to competition to which the reader is referred to Saloner and Rotemberg in Scott Morton (1991).

18.4.4 Strategic Alignment. Making it Happen

The 'jewel in the crown' from the MIT90s program is undoubtedly the Strategic Alignment Model (SAM) of Henderson and Venkatraman.

Having established the need for a new model or paradigm for the management task in the light of IT potential, the 5-level model provides a framework within which to consider the role of IT in relation to business strategy, but this begs the question, 'How do we make it happen?'

Let us consider first the approach that has been advocated by the various methodologies available to aid in the alignment of business and IT strategies.

The essential core of most methodologies is that the IT strategy should be derived from the business strategy. This is done usually by decomposing the business strategy into objectives, critical success factors and similar measures. IT projects are then related to these objectives etc. Increasingly, some form of IT architecture and statements of standards for operating systems, databases and communications will be incorporated within the IT strategy to maximize future flexibility for interconnection and interoperability of systems.

There are a number of issues that arise in the majority of these approaches which we believe to be inappropriate for the business climate of the 1990s.

The first of the deficiencies is that most of the approaches are linear one-shot approaches. By this we mean that there is little feedback from the IT strategy to the business strategy. This is particularly important for organizations moving up the 5-levels model, especially above the evolutionary/revolutionary boundary.

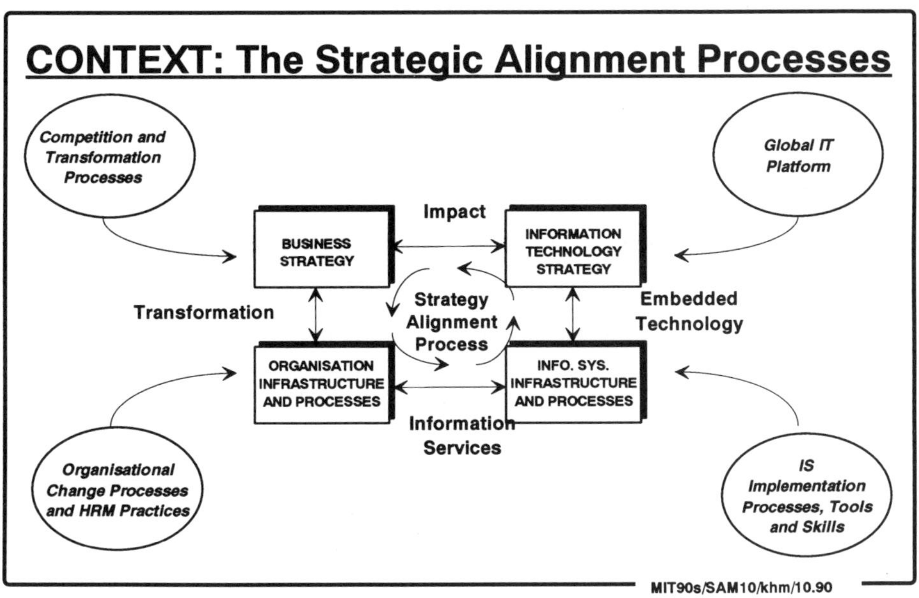

Figure 18.3.The Strategic Alignment Model

This linearity is also indicative of an assumption that the external environment is stable. It is our fundamental belief that iteration is an essential part of any process model that is to assist organizations in the management of issues in turbulent times.

When managers are asked about their information requirements, these requirements tend to be either difficult to extract or produce data that might conceivably be needed. In the latter case it is frequent to end up with DP/MIS and the business coming to unhappy compromises.

Line managers then complain that IT is trying to determine the business, rather than the other way round and MIS bemoans the ignorance of the line managers.

With few exceptions most approaches we are aware of only look at processes in too narrow a context and too late.

The too-narrow context is essentially the procedure rather than process issue raised earlier.

In this paper, we cannot explore fully the ramifications of strategic alignment for which the reader is referred to Scott Morton (1991). We would, however, like to draw out the essential issues of where do we start and what are the steps in alignment?

As with most methodologies, starting with the business strategy is the recommended approach. This can, however, be overridden in certain circumstances should this be necessary. The circular nature of the process has an advantage in this respect.

The critical component of SAM needs a little explanation here. First, it is not adequate to align IT and business. The interactions between the components of the paradigm need to be considered if alignment is to occur.

From the business strategy the direction around the Strategic Alignment Model that we advocate is anti-clockwise.

Given the business strategy, the following questions are an essential precursor to an IT strategy:

- How shall we organise to deliver the strategy? By product or market, geographically or customer?
- What are the key processes of the organization, i.e. those needed to ensure delivery of the strategic goals?
- What skills do we need to support the strategy?
- What training and reward systems do we need in place to deliver the strategy?

This list is not exhaustive, but is essential. It is at this stage that there is need for agreement between the line and DP/MIS over processes.

The core processes, once agreed, provide clear guidance as to the information needs of management. Explicitly, the key information for management is that which gives measures on the performance of core value-added processes.

Once the processes have been agreed we need to consider the existing IS infrastructure and test for the level of support that this provides to the business strategy and the organizational arrangement developed to deliver the strategy.

It is from this that we develop the IT strategy which takes us up the right-hand side of SAM.

Finally, with the IT strategy in place we complete the loop. Now that we have an IT strategy and systems in place, how can we use this to develop the business?

An organization at level 2, on the 5-level model, i.e. internal integration, might wish to move to redesign its business (level 3) or redesign its role in its supply chain (level 4). It is the link from IT strategy to business strategy that provides IT input to the developing strategy. Note that we are not advocating IT leading the business but in providing input.

The critical step in the whole process is the translation of the strategy into organization. Crudely, ORGANIZATION = STRUCTURE + PROCESSES + PEOPLE.

In automating or informating, it is the interaction with the structure and the people that is too often ignored by IT strategists. The benefit of SAM is that it makes these links explicit. Also, the focus on business processes provides a route for even technophobic line managers to get involved in IT.

By our definition, senior management 'ownership' of IT means the recognition and explicit management of the organization's processes. The MIS role is as 'process consultant' to the business in the strategic role and as automator/informator in the implementation phase.

15.5 FINAL THOUGHTS

Some readers having got this far will undoubtedly feel let down that we have not produced some metrics for IT benefits.

There still appears to be a desire to find the IT equivalent of NPV or ROI. The 'giant managerial pill', some formula for calculating the correct IT spend or for measuring IT benefits, seems to be desired by many organizations. Life would indeed be simpler if it existed, but it doesn't.

The costs and benefits can only be derived from the strategic context. The 5-level model provides a good starting-place to look at the role IT is playing within an organization. From this model an individual organization should attempt to determine the 'value' of IT in the transformation of the business. General guidelines can sensibly be derived, but industry-wide measures seem some way from being available.

The issue of translating IT costs and benefits into accounting data is a thorny one. The move from 'structural' to 'process' operations within organizations creates challenges to current management accounting practise. Johnson and Kaplan (1987) have observed the weaknesses of much management accounting practise in relation to process control. Their ideas need to be taken on board if we are to obtain relevant and usable information on the cost-benefits of IT investments.

It is worth commenting here on 'best practice' benchmarking in relationship to IT spend. If an organization is spending 3% of sales revenue on IT and its main competitor 5% what can we learn? Again, from the ratios very little. However, using the ratios along with an understanding of how the spend is being apportioned can be very revealing. For instance if the competitor has an IT platform and is investing in redesigning its processes while our organization is content to stay with localized exploitation then the spend figure may well be very significant!

Finally, we must return to the topic of process. The attitude change that we believe is required for organizations to maximize the benefits of IT is significant, but the rewards are more than commensurate. In the turbulence of the 1990s, we must learn to organize to deliver process, rather than have procedures to support organization.

In the introduction, we posed two questions. To these questions we would answer that IT can be a powerful tool in transforming an organization. However, IT for 'competitive advantage' is misleading. Competitive advantage comes from the business, not from IT. It is engineering the business in the light of IT potential that is the trick the innovators learned. Others have found it hard to follow because they tend to see the IT implications and focus on these, rather than see IT from a business perspective.

In turbulent times, survival is not compulsory. Knowing what business you are in has never been more vital, but knowing how you are in the business is the secret of the winners.

REFERENCES

Carlisle, J A and Parker R C, (1989) *Beyond Negotiation*, John Wiley & Sons, London.

Hayes, R H, Wheelwright, S C and Clark, K B, (1988) *Dynamic Manufacturing*, The Free Press, New York.

Johnson, H T and Kaplan, R S, (1987) *Relevance Lost*, Harvard Business School Press, Boston.

Neave, H R, (1990) *The Deming Dimension*, SPC Press Inc., Tennessee.

Peters, T, (1987) *Thriving on Chaos*, Macmillan, London.

Scott Morton, M S (Ed.), (1991) *The Corporation of the 1990s*, Oxford University Press, Oxford.

Zuboff, S, (1988) *In the Age of the Smart Machine*, Heinemann, Oxford.

19 Future alignment realities

K. Macdonald
IT Partners Ltd

19.1 INTRODUCTION

There is no lack of literature extolling the value of alignment of an organization's strategy with its use of Information Technology. There are numerous methods offered for achieving this desirable state. There are case studies that claim to demonstrate how a particular method is effective, although the examples are often trivial and a large dose of hope is implied. There is a growing body of case material that demonstrates how IT systems have failed to deliver their promised benefits, how failure to build alignment has led to failure to exploit IT effectively, and even how serious efforts to achieve alignment have failed. Whatever point is to be made, a document or case study is probably available to demonstrate its validity or invalidity! It is hardly surprising that management is confused and frustrated, although they probably have only themselves to blame for this condition.

Successful alignment is dependent upon an appropriate management vision, both of the organization's strategies and of the role that Information Technology plays in the execution of those strategies. Successful alignment is assisted by the use of an appropriate process, particularly one that reflects implementation realities. Both vision and process rely on shared understanding, which includes a common vocabulary. Unless all these elements are present, alignment is impossible to achieve.

At the same time, it is essential to recognize that achieving alignment within an organization is not a simple and quick task. It is difficult and can take a lot of time, both elapsed time and applied effort by many people. It is the responsibility of the organization's management to achieve alignment, and this applies across the organization and not just to the IT management. Many failures stem from the simple mismatch of expectations to realities and the erroneous perception of alignment as the responsibility of the IT organization. Processes, that should have worked, were expected to yield instant alignment, and, when this did not happen, the determination to persist in the face of organizational, technical and personality problems was lacking. General management often leaves the task of building alignment to the IT organization or to consultants, assuming that it is a technical issue rather than a business issue. If alignment were easy to achieve, then the subject would not attract so much attention and there would be much more of it evident!

19.2 MANAGEMENT VISION AND THE ROLE OF INFORMATION TECHNOLOGY

We know that, where the use of Information Technology (IT) relates to simple **local** improvements in efficiency (usually through the automation of a function and the reduction in the cost of the function through labour substitution), the problem of alignment is relatively trivial. This does **NOT** mean that alignment is unnecessary. If the local management, who are responsible for the function being automated, are not convinced of the value to be gained from the use of IT (and prepared to obtain the active support and participation of the operational personnel), then the application will not succeed. The problem becomes more serious as the IT application cuts deeper into the local processes and begins to affect the **quality** of the functional output, in terms of accuracy of satisfaction of demand or the timeliness of delivery.

As the scope of IT applications increases, and there is an impact on the performance or operation of the organization as a whole, similar issues arise. Unless senior management supports this wider role for IT in an effective way, it will not be successful and there will be widespread disappointment as conflicting personal and organizational agendas cannot be satisfied. Whereas it was relatively simple to resolve the causes of problems with a limited local application (and to apportion blame for failure), this becomes much more difficult, or even impossible, as the broader scope leads to a diffuse situation. It is then often convenient to blame the IT organization because it is not perceived as an **essential** contributor to the health and wealth of the organization as a whole.

It is argued elsewhere (Venkatraman, 1991) that the rapid technological developments and growing capabilities of IT, together with the increasing importance of information in the management of organizations and as a component of products, are combining to elevate IT to the role of a strategic resource. It is clear that real acceptance of this concept is an essential prerequisite of effective use of IT as a contributor to the achievement and preservation of competitive advantage. 'Acceptance' means much more than simply agreeing with the proposition, but must imply action as well. The belief needs to be visceral, and associated both with a sound appreciation of the capabilities and implications of IT and with a commitment to involvement and success. Management needs to view IT as an issue that is far too important to be left to the IT professionals. The IT professionals need to recognize that this interest is for their own good, and they must help management achieve the understanding necessary for the relationship to be productive.

Management's 'vision' must also include the 'strategies' that the organization is pursuing. These strategies must be shared with the people, and must be both understandable and real. Keeping strategies confidential, lest they 'tell our competitors how we are thinking', means that the employees must follow blindly. Those who must provide support for the organization's execution of its strategies will need to fumble around to determine what they should provide. Strategies expressed in high-flown words or jargon impress only their authors. Strategies that are so detached from reality that they are no more than pious phrases fool only their authors. Without a clear vision of the way ahead, it is impossible to build an organizational capability, including IT capability, that will relate to the future opportunities and challenges that the organization must face.

It is sometimes claimed that turbulence in the business environment leads to so many uncertainties that strategies are unhelpful and only tactical responsiveness is relevant. This misses the essential point and presumes that 'strategies' are either medium- or long-term goals, or actions. Strategies should really describe the **positioning** that the organization wishes to achieve in its chosen markets or business environment (see Porter, 1980 and 1985). An organization's business strategies must cover:

- the scope of the business,
- the distinctive competencies on which the business is based, and
- the style of governance to be adopted.

To illustrate this, there is nothing wrong with a strategy expressed in very general terms as 'flexibility and rapid response' in a market that is volatile and unpredictable. The implications include some reasonable boundaries of business activity, building resources and an organization that can correctly interpret market situations and react rapidly to opportunities, and establishing a business style and relationships with other organizations (suppliers, channels, collaborators, etc.) that help to achieve this responsiveness.

19.3 WHAT IS STRATEGIC ALIGNMENT?

Like beauty, strategic alignment is hard to define but easy to recognize. It is a condition of harmonization of various essential elements of business operation. It implies that the organization is viewed as an integrated and inter-related system, in which changes in one part are understood to be the source of changes elsewhere in the system. This organizational tuning is not confined to establishing consistency between strategies as viewed from headquarters and strategies as implemented within operational units. This is indeed one dimension of alignment that may reflect the harmonization of choices relating to positioning in the organization's product/market arena with choices relating to strategic positioning in the IT market place. Alignment must also take account of strategic choices of organizational arrangements, including the need to design management processes, develop appropriate skilled resources, and a structure within which these processes and skills can be applied to the achievement of the strategies.

Figure 19.1 shows the two essential dimensions of alignment. Unfortunately, it is often the simple (horizontal) harmonization of business strategy and IT strategy that is pursued; this may be interesting but is seldom particularly useful. It fails because it presumes that IT strategy derives from business strategy, and does not reflect the possibility that IT strategy, and the capabilities that can be offered, can influence business strategy through the enhanced organizational capability that can be provided by IT. At the simplest level, the linkage must, at least, be bidirectional.

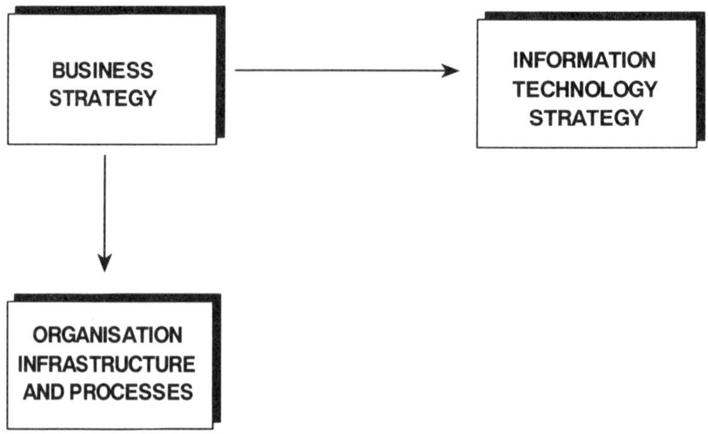

Figure 19.1. Basic alignment concepts

The (vertical) linkage reflects building an organization that can implement the business strategy. This is really the more important form of harmonization. However, the one-way linkage implies that the organization infrastructure and processes are unconstrained and derive from the business strategies. In practice, these depend on the availability of essential skills. If resources with these skills cannot be obtained, or afforded, or will take time to be obtained, and if the required organization infrastructure is not in place, then the strategies may be unrealistic and may need to be reconsidered. Fighting with ghost divisions may be a good game but it contributes nothing to the welfare of the organization.

The organization as a whole, with its top-level strategies, organization infrastructure and processes, can be regarded as the summation of the strategies, management infrastructure and processes of all the separate 'businesses' or 'divisions' that form the organization. This is shown in Figure 19.2. It can be helpful to regard the IT organization as a 'business within the business' or as a distinct 'division'. In this way it is clear that harmonization of the organization with its IT activity needs to include both the strategies of the organization and the strategies of the IT activity, together with both their respective organization infrastructures and processes. Alignment must cover both what is to be done (the strategies), and how it is to be done (the management infrastructure and processes). In the latter case, issues of resourcing, skills availability and affordability arise, both at an overall level and at a local level covering only the IT activity.

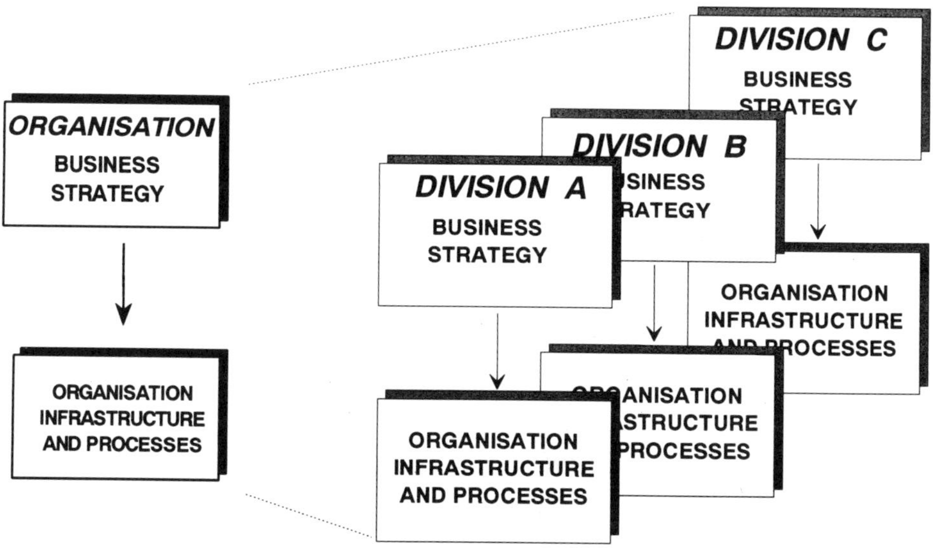

Figure 19.2. Hierarchical strategy relationships

If we concentrate on the issues of alignment as they relate to the business as a whole and the IT functions, the diagram can be simplified, as shown in Figure 19.3. This representation is the Strategic Alignment Model (see Henderson and Venkatraman, 1989 and Venkatraman, 1991). This model reflects several additional points that may assist understanding:

1. The two strategy elements at the top relate to **external** factors, the external positioning of the organization and of the organization's IT function. The two infrastructure and processes elements relate to **internal** issues, choices about internal organizational arrangements.
2. The two 'boxes' on the left relate to the organization's **business domain**, while the two 'boxes' on the right relate to the organization's **IT domain.**
3. The vertical relationships reflect **strategic integration**, whereas the horizontal relationships reflect **functional integration**.

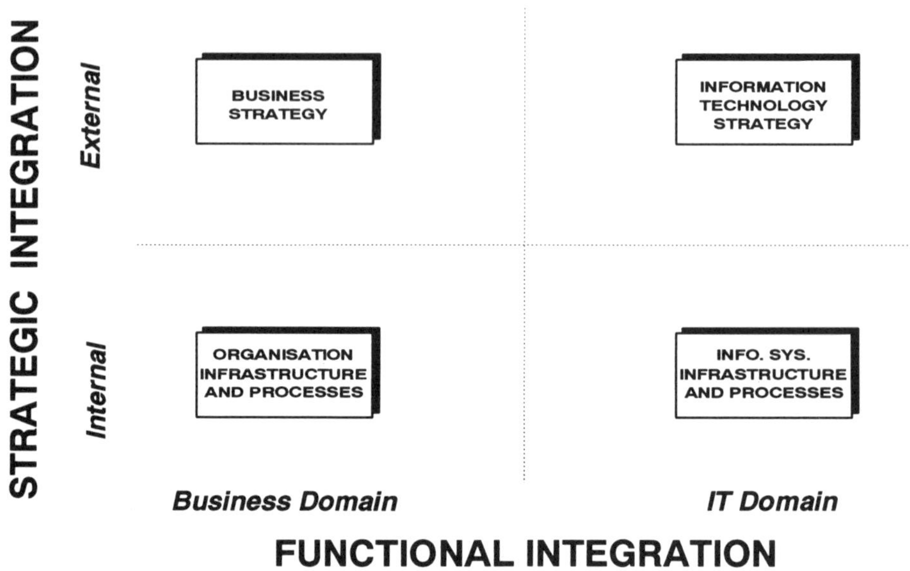

Figure 19.3. Alignment components

Building strategic alignment is essentially the process of harmonising the relationships between these various elements, eliminating any mismatches between them, and then maintaining this alignment as the various elements change in response to internal or external factors.

19.4 STRATEGIC ALIGNMENT RELATIONSHIPS

The relationships between each of the elements in the Strategic Alignment Model (SAM) reflects a down-to-earth view of business issues in the real world, as shown in Figure 19.4. These issues, which reflect information about (harmonized) relationships, are as follows:

Business products and services – this is the capability that the IT strategy contributes to the organization's business strategy;

Business transformation – this is what is achieved by the harmonization of business strategy and the organization infrastructure and processes;

I/S products and services - the enabling of the organization infrastructure and processes by the IS infrastructure and processes;

Technology transformation – this reflects the exploitation of Information Technology delivered by the IT strategy to achieve the required IS infrastructure and processes;

Automation – this is the contribution to businessefficiency and/or business effectiveness of the organization infrastructure and processes by the IT strategy; and

Linkage – the contribution of the IS infrastructure and processes to the achievement of the business strategy.

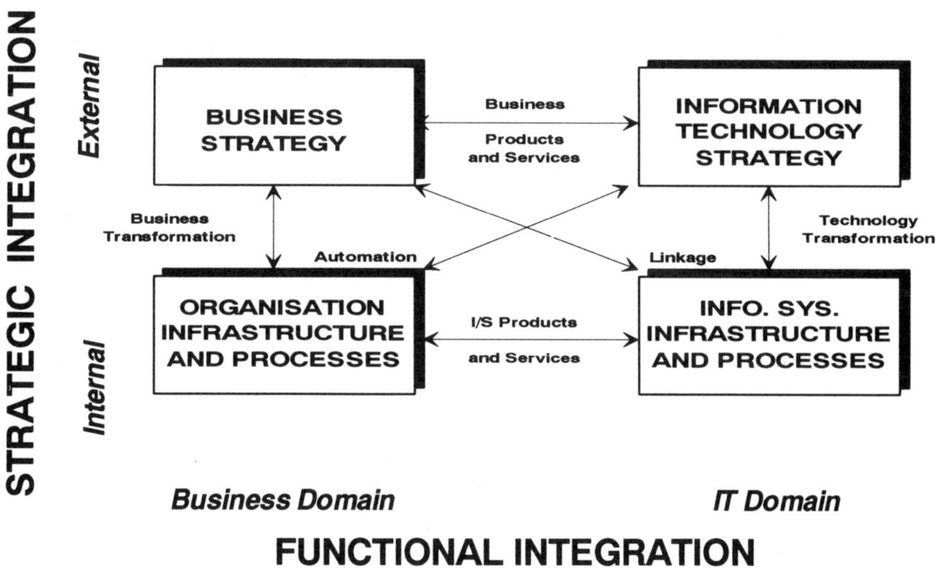

Figure 19.4. Alignment relationships – information

The descriptions (information) that an organization develops to express the relationships in the Strategic Alignment Model (SAM) are not easy to create in isolation. Unless the organization has in place the range of processes needed to construct the content of each 'box', the development of any alignment is of no value. Unless the 'boxes' reflect reality, and can be related to what is actually happening within the organization, mismatches cannot be identified for any useful purpose. For SAM to help in the building of alignment, there needs to be 'something' to align, and this implies that SAM must exist in the context of a number of operational processes. Each element of SAM must be supported by information and processes that can be used to create that element and to review the element in the event that organizational realities make complete alignment impossible. Figure 19.5, (Macdonald, 1991), illustrates this.

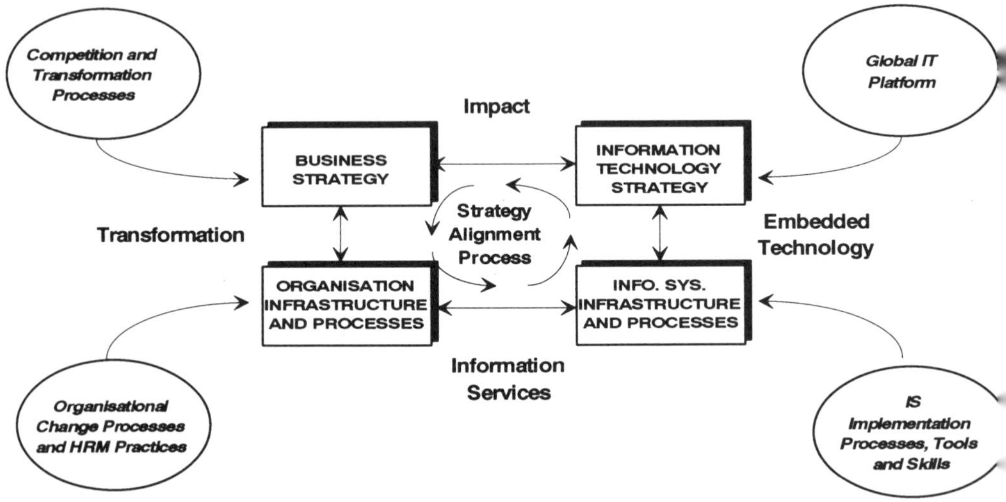

Figure 19.5. Alignment relationships – supporting processes

The sort of capabilities that are required are indicated below:

Business strategy must be supported by a set of planning processes that will create it, including market research, competitive analysis, assumption surfacing, strategic options generation, decision conferencing, etc.;

Organization infrastructure and processes requires that structure derives from some approach to organization design, that the organization's key business processes are known and documented, that human resource management processes exist to obtain or train the required skilled resources, that mechanisms for communication and motivation exist, and so on;

IS infrastructure and processes depend on tools, and resources and the necessary mechanisms to obtain these, and apply them in order to build IS applications to support the organization;

IT strategy implies that processes exist to ensure awareness of the global IT platform capability, the likely development of this platform, and the decision mechanisms whereby the organization can build its own IT platform, including make-or-buy decisions and the management of the necessary investments.

In each case, what is needed must include the facility to take the necessary decisions to achieve what is required for each element ('corner' or 'box') of SAM. In practice, most organizations have processes that are used for producing strategies, key business processes and critical success factors, structures, recruitment and training, investment decisions, etc., and for adjusting these in the light of experience and changing circumstances. Neither SAM nor SAP imply a great new edifice of planning processes. If the planning processes do not exist, then that is a significant issue, but this relates more to intrinsic survival of the organization than to the use of strategic alignment! SAM uses processes that are already available, or should be available if the organization is properly managed. However, SAM does provide a means of reviewing the range of existing processes, ensuring that they contribute value, and identifying requirements for changing the planning processes. SAM provides a means of identifying opportunities for improving an organization's effectiveness and then managing the implementation of the improvement and the continuation of improvement. SAM is **NOT** an elixir that will solve the problems of an organization in terminal decline – it may make it abundantly clear why the patient is dying, but it then depends on management action to apply essential organizational medicine.

19.5 BUILDING ALIGNMENT – THE BASICS

It will be observed that at the centre of Figure 19.5 are a number of arrows surrounding the words 'Strategic Alignment Process'. This, SAP, is the new kernel process that builds alignment, and it depends on the surrounding elements of the Strategic Alignment Model and the supporting processes that are used to create or change the elements. It cannot be emphasized too strongly that without this essential infrastructure, building alignment is just too difficult.

Since harmonization of the organization as a whole is what is being pursued, it is hardly surprising that this is not a trivial task. Because of the scope of the exercise, it cannot be delegated to junior management, technocrats or outsiders. Top management have to be involved, and this involvement is necessary over a long period. During this time it is very likely that the circumstances affecting the organization will change, and top management needs to be involved to ensure that these issues are addressed. Organizational problems and conflicts will be exposed and these too will need to be addressed. It may be tempting to obscure the difficulties because of a fear that their exposure will result in the issue of alignment being 'too hard' to get the attention of senior management for the long haul. Non-involvement of senior management is the most common cause of failure of alignment exercises. Just agreeing that the issue is important and then offering to 'bless' the results is not enough; it does not build commitment and this abdication means that the hard issues are 'fudged'.

To apply the Strategic Alignment Process (SAP) requires documentation describing the various elements of SAM as related to the organization. A number of proforma are required to record input information and conclusions, and these can usually be derived from existing planning processes; they will not be described here. Getting the information may prove a challenge because SAM exposes inconsistencies and the inadequacies of existing processes. Getting the right people involved is vital and is probably by far the most important issue.

Because the achievement of alignment is actually difficult because of the scale and scope of the issues, addressing the total problem is not productive. Instead, SAM must be 'decomposed' into a number of more manageable steps, which can then be undertaken in sequence. This is done by breaking SAM into a number of 'triangles', each comprising three elements, and then building alignment for each triangle. The four triangles, each based on a 'corner' of SAM, thus cover all the interrelationships between the elements. The basic idea is represented in Figure 19.6.

Each triangle relates to a 'problem domain' and the intention is to build alignment within this domain, while ignoring (or 'holding constant') the fourth element of SAM (see Venkatraman, 1991 and Macdonald, 1991). The element at the right-angled corner is called the **domain pivot**. The principle is that one adjacent corner, called the **domain anchor**, acts as an 'input', and its contribution to improving or stabilizing the domain pivot is considered. In doing this, possible changes in the domain pivot generate impacts on the other element of the triangle, the **impacted domain.**

Ignoring for the moment the questions of the starting-point for this process and the direction of progression (both of which will be addressed later), the process can be described as follows:

> *Taking into account the constraints and contributions of the domain anchor on the domain pivot, determine what changes can or must be made to the domain pivot, confirm the content of the domain pivot, and determine what impacts any changes may demand of the impacted domain.*

In practice, there can be 'feedback'. Constraints may be unacceptable or contributions unnecessary, so that there is feedback from the domain pivot to the domain anchor. Likewise, it may be evident that the demands for change on the impacted domain are just not acceptable and so the changes to the domain pivot may be impossible. This feedback must be considered, but the important point, which will be much clearer after the whole process has been considered, is that the strength of 'forward impulsion', based on reality, must be much stronger than the feedback. If this condition is not satisfied, then alignment is impossible. There is no point in pursuing an unrealizable situation, although a robust approach is needed to ensure that what is claimed to be impossible really cannot be achieved. Management involvement is needed to maintain this impulsion.

The lower half of Figure 19.6 shows an alternative representation of the triangular process, although in this case the triangle has been 'unfolded'. There is no difference in the process implied, although this representation may help to emphasize the forward impulsion that is needed.

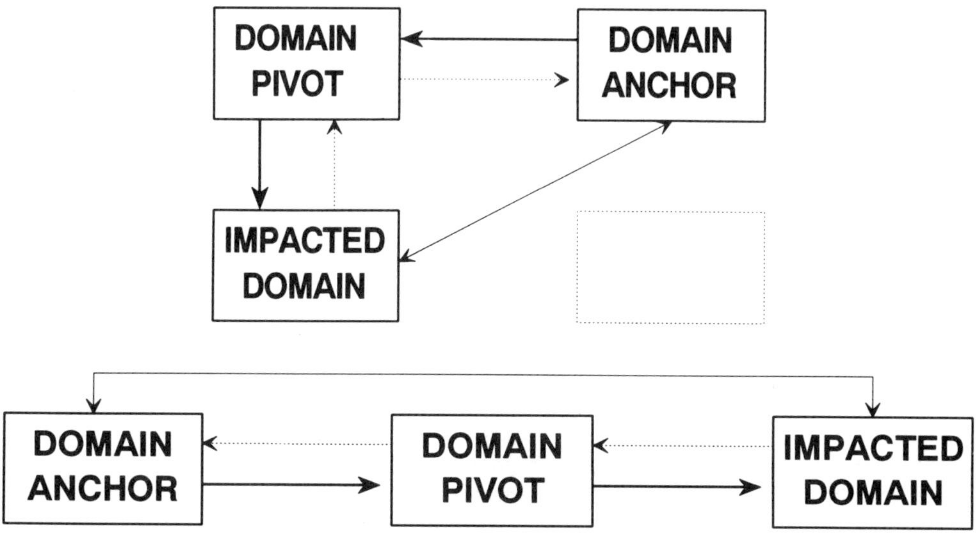

Figure 19.6 Alignment Process Triangle

The complete Strategic Alignment Process is made up of four triangular processes, and these are each applied in sequence, proceeding around the Strategic Alignment Model. After one triangular process has been completed, the domain pivot from that triangle becomes the domain anchor in the next triangular process stage. The impacted domain from the first stage becomes the domain pivot in the next stage, and so on. In this way, the SAP 'cycles' around SAM. The issues are: starting-point, direction and finishing point.

In theory it is possible to start with any triangle. In practice, having the **business strategy as the domain pivot** is the most useful place to start. There is merit in the principle that external business issues are the most important, and thus confirming the business strategy as a starting-point is logical. Since IT is normally an 'enabler', it is not appropriate to give IT strategy the influence that is acquired by being the starting-point. SAP will correct the impact, if IT strategy is the starting-point, but the 'convergence' may be slightly delayed by this choice.

As has been argued earlier, the prime alignment that must be achieved is in the business domain, relating business strategy to the organization infrastructure and processes, i.e. building the organization that can implement the positioning implied by the business strategy. Thus if the starting-point is confirmation of the business strategy as the first domain pivot, then the organization infrastructure and processes should be the impacted domain, and **a clockwise rotation is implied.**

SAP 'cycles' around SAM in a clockwise direction, and should continue until a practical level of alignment has been achieved, as represented by the removal of unsatisfied impacts from each domain pivot on each impacted domain. At the very minimum, all four triangular processes must be completed. Experience shows that the first cycle leaves many unresolved feedback issues – these are the reverse feedback items implied in Figure 19.6. These must be passed to the supporting processes to re-examine the SAM elements, explore the unresolved feedback, resolve the impacts, etc. Then a second cycle is needed to consider the changes that the first cycle generated, which have now been explored, and to confirm resolution of the impacts. When SAP is first undertaken, convergence is slow, and several cycles may be required, although senior management may need to engage in some constructive 'head banging' if a reasonable level of agreement has not been achieved after three cycles. Once the process has been established, and the participants have understood what is expected of them, two cycles are usually sufficient.

Figure 19.7 illustrates the first alignment triangle, in which business strategy is the domain pivot. What is being determined here is the **competitive potential** of the organization. In the second triangular process, the organization infrastructure and processes are the domain pivot, and the **business value** that the organization is trying to achieve is derived. When the IS infrastructure and processes is the domain pivot, the issue is the **service level** being provided by the IS function. When IT strategy is the domain pivot, the **technology potential** of IT for the organization is developed. The completion of the cycle introduces the potential of IT to influence the business strategy and thus achieve the progressive harmonization and interdependency that is required by the whole organization.

Does the Strategic Alignment Process ever finish? Not really, because SAP becomes a way of life! One of SAP's particular virtues is that the resolution after each cycle relates to a manageable step towards improved alignment. The organization can use SAP to iterate towards an ultimate but unachievable alignment. This is a practical situation that reflects the increasingly turbulent business environment. It contrasts with other alignment processes which imply unrealistic long-term stability of the original strategy, or imply a major exercise which, when finished, is likely to be as far removed from reality at that time as was the case when the exercise started!

Because SAP addresses complete organizational alignment, and not just alignment of business and IT strategies, it relates to operational business issues. Thus management must be involved, and the organization gains from this involvement. progressive functional integration of the business (organization infrastructure and processes), and IT (through the IT infrastructure and processes), develops in a manageable way. Business management and IT management become productively associated.

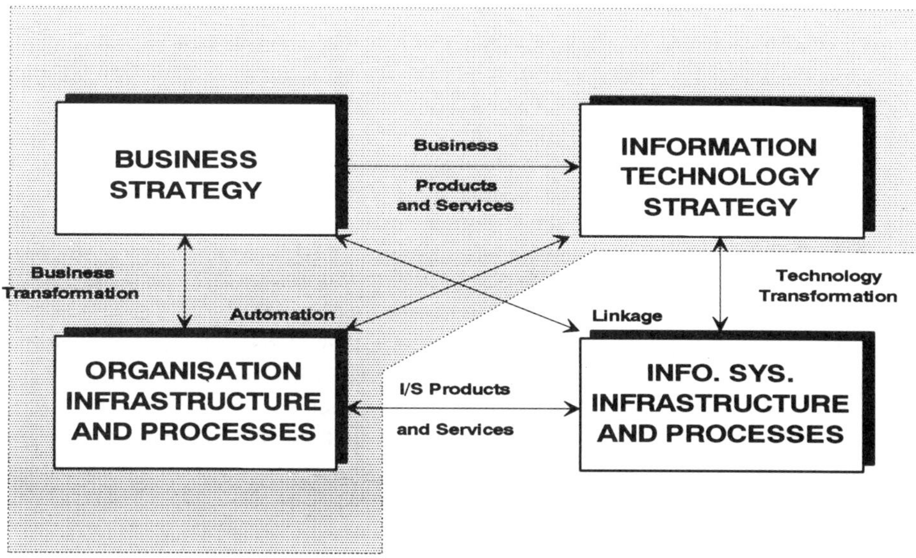

Figure 19.7. Process example – competitive potential

19.6 BUILDING ALIGNMENT – THE WIDER CONCEPTS

The process that has been explained in section 19.5 depends on considerable preparation, some of which is indicated by the surrounding supporting processes discussed in section 19.4. In practice it is not possible, or sensible, to start building organizational alignment without these supporting processes, without having 'something to align', and without a clear understanding of the nature and implications of the 'journey' upon which the organization and its management are about to embark. Education is obviously one essential preparatory step.

Management may conclude that the scale and scope of the exercise is such that the 'journey' is not worth starting. The initial learning phase is difficult, but once the concepts are understood, their application can proceed at a pace that suits the organization, subject only to the need to transform the organization to intercept or respond to turbulence in the external environment. That management must transform their organizations, including rethinking the core of the business, making effective use of IT as a strategic resource, and so on, should not be a matter for debate. If these issues are not accepted, then the only possible response is that nobody has claimed that survival is compulsory. If the essential actions are accepted, then the Strategic Alignment Model provides a comprehensive and practical way of thinking about the issues and the Strategic Alignment Process provides a practical way of implementing the transformations (see Schein, 1987).

There are four ways in which the concepts of Strategic Alignment can be applied, as follows:

1. **Organizational reconnaissance**: this can be described as 'a quick canter around SAM'! Using the principle described in preceding sections, a rapid review can be undertaken to check the status of business strategy, the existence of formal descriptions of the organizational infrastructure and processes, the establishment of IS infrastructure and processes, and the status of an IT strategy. The extent to which the various relationships are understood gives a good measure of the alignment that exists, and this can be invaluable in planning and implementing the introduction of SAM and SAP to the organization.

2. **Developing a planning infrastructure**: either as part of the organizational reconnaissance or as a separate step, the availability and effectiveness of supporting processes can be assessed. If the processes exist, then any 'tuning' can be defined. If processes do not exist, then SAM and SAP together help to define what is needed, and to ensure that what is set up relates to real needs and not just a pointless bureaucracy.

3. **Progressive establishment of initial alignment**: if alignment is poor, then SAM provides a framework for building alignment and the SAP provides a roadmap for the journey. In this case, progress around the SAP triangles will be slow. Contributions from the domain anchor may be poor, initial definitions of the domain pivot may be weak, issues involved in confirming components of the domain pivot may be unknown, and potential response from the impacted domain may be unpredictable because the supporting processes are new. SAM and SAP provide a means of preserving the long-term goal of improved business effectiveness through improved organizational alignment in the midst of considerable information, organization and process confusion.

4. **Progressive improvement of alignment**: this is the process described in section 19.5. It is the mature application of SAM and SAP as a part of the organizational culture (Schein, 1985). In addition, experience with SAM leads to a style of thinking about organizational problems. Once SAM 'gets into the blood', it provides a useful framework for solving problems in many areas of business.

19.7 THE PRESCRIPTION IN CONTEXT

Strategic alignment is not a new concept: its desirability has been known for a long time. There are many approaches to achieving it, many well documented and available as 'services' from consulting organizations. Applied with intelligence, these processes or methodologies can be helpful, but:

the lack of involvement of management,
the assignment of the task to the IT department or external consultants,
the time involved if a linear process is used,
the loss of interest of management as the scale of the problem emerges,
the additional problems for management that appear,
and so on

all contribute to failures. Management's vision (including the role of IT), involvement and commitment are critical prerequisites for achieving alignment. Having the best process is not enough.

It may appear that there is no role for external consultants in building alignment. This is not correct. Consultants can contribute useful expertise that does not exist within the organization, particularly expertise relating to the processes that are being introduced. Their most important contribution is as independent process consultants or facilitators, without being associated with internal structural groupings and without long-term dependency on the organization. What is often missing is the enabling of the organization, through the development of its own experts, to continue the processes after the consultants have left. Unless effective knowledge transfer occurs, the consultants make no contribution to enhancing the capability of the organization.

It is essential that the organization's management 'owns' the commitment to alignment, the process being implemented and the obligations for action that derive from the process. If consultants are given the task of 'creating an IT strategy from our business strategy', this often means that management has delegated (and probably abdicated) **their** responsibilities. Organizational alignment is so important that it is not sufficient for management to assign the work to 'experts' and then 'bless' the results afterwards. They are unlikely to understand what they are 'blessing' and will, almost certainly, not feel the visceral commitment to implementing the range of changes in various parts of the organization that alignment implies.

In many organizations, the use of Information Technology is unrelated to the overall business strategies that the organization is pursuing. Cost reduction through labour substitution is the usual motivation for IT applications of this kind. Cost justification of these applications derives from the contribution that the applications make to **administrative expenses**. The management within the organization most concerned with these applications is usually the **Information Systems management**, with some involvement from the local administration management whose processes are being automated. The applications are **independent** of the strategic context of the organization as a whole.

As the vision of IT's contribution to the organization develops, the need to derive the applications of IT from business strategy develops. Cost justification may become more difficult as the applications relate to business effectiveness or quality issues. For this **dependent** approach to succeed, it requires that cost justification be based on **business expenses**, since the IT applications may relate to operational issues that are 'an essential cost of doing business'. **Business management** now needs to be involved in the decisions. These two 'styles' and their implied cost justification and required management involvement are shown in Figure 19.8.

As the vision of the contribution of IT develops further (to the point that IT extends the organization's strategies through enabling new ways of doing business, enabling new ways of managing relationships with suppliers or customers, or even creating new business opportunities), so an **interdependent** approach is needed. In this case, cost justification needs to be seen in terms of **business investment**. The expenditures now relate to the development of organizational capability, and not just businesscapability. Obviously, decisions now must involve **strategic or corporate management**. (See Venkatraman, 1991.)

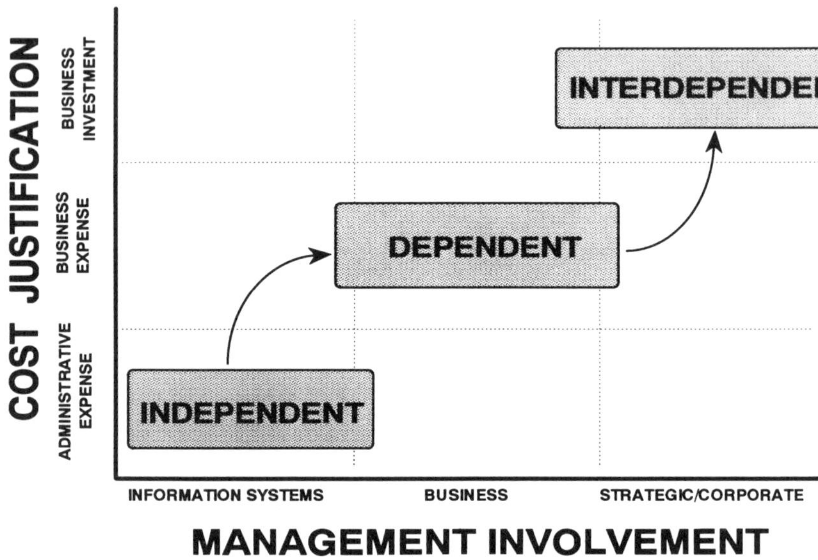

Figure 19.8. Implications of various forms of strategy/IT dependency

For an organization that is at the independent stage, it may be tempting to try to 'leap-frog' the dependent stage and go directly to the interdependent stage. This is a risky approach and there is no evidence of its successful achievement. A measured progression seems to be essential, with the dependent stage necessary to allow the organization to develop the understanding of IT capability and the realities of IT implementation, particularly the introduction of such techniques as structured methods, prototyping, Knowledge-based Systems, etc., before moving onto an interdependent stage.

The general management prerequisites for successful alignment, that have been repeated many times, apply to both progressions and to all three styles. There are many methodologies available that can help with progression from an Independent to a Dependent style. These methodologies can be applied to harmonizing the relationships between the organization's business strategies and the IT strategies. The Strategic Alignment Model and Process can also be used. However, as the organization progresses to an Interdependent style, so the importance of organizational alignment increases and the power of SAM and SAP is essential.

This paper has concentrated on the underlying principles of organizational alignment and the concepts of the Strategic Alignment Model, the need for supporting processes, and the Strategic Alignment Process. Many of the arguments can be illustrated by examples where various aspects of alignment have been tried and either failed or succeeded. To have added these cases would have meant that this document would have needed to be extended significantly. The reader will find many relevant examples in the references.

The basic concepts that have been described all derive from work at the Sloan School of Management at the Massachusetts Institute of Management during the Management in the 1990s '(MIT90s) research programme' (see Scott Morton, 1991 and ICL, 1990). This major programme ran from 1984 to 1989 and involved a partnership between the researchers at the Sloan School and the sponsors of the programme from government agencies and business. This work has been further developed by the author and by others in the ICL group, including the ICL management consulting subsidiary, IT Partners Limited.

REFERENCES

Henderson, J C and Venkatraman, N (1989) *Strategic Alignment: A Framework for Strategic Information Technology Management*, a 'Management in the 1990s' research programme working paper, ref. 90s:89-076, from the Sloan School of Management, Massachusetts Institute of Technology.

Henderson, J C and Venkatraman, N (1989) *Strategic Alignment: A Process Model for Integrating Information Technology and Business Strategy*, a 'Management in the 1990s' research program working paper, ref. 90s:89-077, from the Sloan School of Management, Massachusetts Institute of Technology.

Both these working papers are also available as Sloan working papers and as working papers from the Center for Information Systems Research, Sloan School, Massachusetts Institute of Technology.

ICL (1990) *A Window on the Future – An ICL Briefing for Management on the Findings of the Management in the 1990s Research Program*, ICL Publication Reference P3326 (36949). This gives a summary and an interpretation of the lessons from the MIT90s research programme.

Macdonald, K H (1991) Business Strategy Development, Alignment, and Redesign, in *The Corporation of the 1990s: Information Technology and Organizational Transformation* (ed Scott Morton, Michael S.) Oxford University Press, Oxford – see pp 159-163 in chapter 6 for an introduction to SAP, and pp 310-322, Appendix E, for a description of the process.

Porter, M E (1980) *Competitive Strategy: Techniques for Analyzing Industries and Competitors*, The Free Press, New York.

Porter, M E (1985) *Competitive Advantage: Creating and Sustaining Superior Performance*, The Free Press, New York. His competitive framework (industry rivals, suppliers, customers, new entrants and substitute suppliers), illustrates the breadth of view of the 'market' needed here. This applies to both the private and public sector.

Schein, E H (1985) *Organizational Culture and Leadership*, Jossey-Bass, San Francisco.

Schein, E H (1987) *Process Consultation Volume II – Lessons for Managers and Consultants*, Addison-Wesley Publishing Company, Reading, Massachusetts. This is a mine of useful ideas about facilitation and helping group working.

Scott Morton, M S (ed) (1991) *The Corporation of the 1990s: Information Technology and Organizational Transformation*, Oxford University Press, Oxford: this provides a synthesis of much that derived from the 'Management in the 1990s' research programme.

Venkatraman, N (1991) IT-Induced Business Reconfiguration, in T*he Corporation of the 1990s: Information Technology and Organizational Transformation* (ed Scott Morton, Michael S.) Oxford University Press, Oxford – see pp 122-126 of chapter 5, for the essential argument relating to IT as a strategic resource.

Ibid., see pp 151-154 of chapter 5 for an introduction to independence, dependence, (which Venkatraman refers to as 'Reactive to the Strategic Context'), and interdependence. The connection of these styles to cost justification and management involvement is mentioned in the text, but Figure 19.8 is from K H Macdonald.

Ibid., see pp 154-157 of chapter 5 for an introduction for an introduction to the underlying theory of the Strategic Alignment Model and the alignment patterns that relate to various domain pivots.

20 Formulating business strategy to exploit the new IT

D. Kaye
Independent Consultant

20.1 INFORMATION TECHNOLOGY'S NEW IMPACT ON STRATEGY

Strategy drives structure drives systems. The new power of IT is a reverse drive of systems onto strategies and structures. A strategy and structure that will make a business competitive should now be formulated with full recognition of what can be done with IT.

IT now has the capability to change the fundamentals of a business, its direction and its activities.

Therefore IT's new potential impact has to be appreciated very early in the process of defining strategy. And since strategy definition is the task of top management and strategic planners, it is they who must appreciate IT's potential. IT is changing management's game. But, paradoxically, as IT becomes more and more powerful in its effects on strategy, it becomes easier for top management to know enough about IT to put IT into strategy. It becomes less important for them to appreciate the details of what can and cannot be done. More and more, as time goes by, the technology will be able to handle the details.

20.2 OPEN INFORMATION CAPABILITY

What has been happening, and is continuing to happen at a very fast rate, is that the technical advances in computing, in data storage and in communication are all coming together to a point where it starts to make sense to assume that, if you put in enough effort and money, you can have an 'open information capability' (Kaye, 1989).

An 'open information capability' means the capability of ensuring that information which is available in *principle*, such as about past or present events, but from which potential users may have been barred by cost or technical limitations, can be made available in *practice*, to people authorized to use it. This means that 'user friendly' information about, for example, what is or has been happening, or about what people want or have wanted, can be made available, instantly, reliably, in the most convenient form for use, and relatively cheaply, no matter the apparent complexity of getting it from wherever in the system it may have been placed.

Furthermore, developments in ways of building software and designing systems are helping to contain costs by improving programmer productivity. Also they help systems builders to respond to changes in management requirements by reducing the elapsed time for developing a working system. Thus not only is an 'open information capability' becoming technically feasible for an organization to have within its planning horizon, it can also become economic if the scale of the organization and the potential benefits are right.

An 'open information capability's' strategic importance comes from the fact that opportunities for service or for competitive advantage may have been foregone in the past, because getting and processing the necessary information was too complex for the opportunities to be exploited economically. The capability of IT to handle complexity brings these opportunities back into play. And because it's becoming cheaper and quicker to develop an 'open information capability', and cheaper and easier to operate it, devising a strategy for sustained competitive advantage has to be done in the knowledge that it's likely that someone somewhere in the world will be developing an 'open information capability' and learning how to exploit it.

What matters for top management is *not* the details of IT, of what it can do and what has to be done to make it do it, but that an 'open information capability' is a prospect to be reckoned with. The prospect of an 'open information capability' means that it now makes sense to think what should be the ideal strategy and management arrangements to which a business should aspire, irrespective of where the information needed to make them work is going to come from.

20.3 OPEN INFORMATION PROCESSING

The process for creating an open information capability needs analysis and imagination. It requires sharp focusing on the critical success factors of the business; then thinking hard how they might be improved by liberating them from the existing constraints on information; and so to create a new target vision for the strategies and structures of the business.

'Open information visioning' is a phrase which describes the process. It's the first step to a new reality being opened up by what is in effect the IT revolution. Taking this step has to be top management's task. Only they have the perspective and understanding of the business and – crucially – the authority to bring to the process of creating for the post-IT revolution world an ideal but achievable vision of corporate strategy and structure.

Let us now imagine an example of what 'open information visioning' is about and of what its impact might be on the fortunes of a company.

20.4 AN EXAMPLE OF OPEN INFORMATION VISIONING

Imagine you are a resolute and ambitious manager taking over an ailing manufacturer of fitted kitchens, not in desperate trouble, but just not doing very well, and vulnerable to interest rates and competition.

What should you do? Fix things that have to be fixed in the short term? Yes, clearly, or you will go out of business some time in the medium term. Analyse the company's strengths and weaknesses and formulate a strategy for sustained competitive strength? Yes, certainly, you and your people have read the right management textbooks, and hired the right management consultants and you are determined to prosper in the medium and long term.

And when you have your strategy? Then doubtless you will work out how to organize the company to carry out the strategy. And you will see that someone works out all the details of how to track what is going on and how to get information to all the managers in their new positions, so that they don't have to drive blind, so that they can do their administration efficiently, and so that they can run their business effectively knowing what orders are coming from the wholesalers and how long it is taking to meet them, and what their stocks are, and how much it is all costing. Then the managers will be able to do their job and your strategy will be implemented. Maybe.

But what if someone else has a better strategy? What if someone else has a better product? What if someone else can offer better product variety to respond more closely to the peculiarities of the customer's vague vision of an ideal kitchen into a practical design which can be installed in only days from items which are known to be in stock? And what if that someone can keep his stock costs low and his administrative costs under control? Well, you reply, it sounds as if that someone would have found a way of squaring the circle. Maybe. But just suppose he has. Then your beautiful strategy will fail.

So could the circle be squared? Suppose for a moment you could have to hand all the information that is out there waiting to help you, if only you could get hold of it, and suppose you could do what you wanted to do with it. Suppose you could do this without it costing you much. Imagine. What would you do?

Maybe you would have a salesman sit with the customer, learning directly what is wanted, sketching ideas to match the customer's vision, perhaps making suggestions to extend that vision. Then you would have the salesman check the measurements of the kitchen and simultaneously check the availability of stock components, and how long it would take to produce special components, and what it would all cost. And then maybe you would have the salesman start over again and modify the design to fit the customer's budget better and to be ready when the customer needs it.

Well, you might say, that sounds like a very expensive service, and not realistic. And anyway, you say, you could never get the wholesalers to hold all the stocks that would be needed for what is starting to sound like a mass-customized market. And you couldn't get enough salesmen who could do the sketches; and those that could wouldn't do a good job of checking stocks and production schedules, and if you could get them, they would cost the earth. So forget it.

Well, you'd be wrong. Let's assume that information available in principle would be available in practice. What would you do? How about having the kitchen salesman sit with the customer, together with the salesman's computer. And how about having the computer connected directly to databases in the factory showing stocks and production schedules and delivery times and costs. Suppose the salesman types into the computer the data on the various components needed to match the customer's vision, and suppose the computer then draws a sketch of the kitchen, showing it from various aspects. Suppose also it checks the delivery times and cost, and that the salesman suggests new ideas and then makes some changes to the design until the customer is happy with price and delivery as well as design. And suppose that the computer does all the work passing the order for the kitchen components direct through to the factory and its manufacturing and stockholding systems. Suppose then the completed order is scheduled to the factory computer for dispatch to the retailer or customer.

The fantasy starts to appear realizable. The customer would get superior service for a product which would respond as well as possible to requirements. Administration and stock costs would be kept under control. And, if the manufacturer managed the retail outlets and worked direct to them without going through wholesalers, the manufacturer would keep end-to-end control of image, quality and service. The result, if everything is done properly, is likely to be a competitively superior strategy.

But note the implications on market strategy and product strategy, on manufacturing strategy and on the very frontiers of the company – now including retailers but excluding wholesalers, most of whom would be bypassed. And the strategy for the enabling information systems (how they should be developed, by when and for what cost) would be absolutely critical to the business strategy. But the strategy for the systems would follow the business strategy, and the business strategy would assume open information and be ideal in the sense that the critical success factors of the business (the product, the variety of product in the range needed to respond to the customer's vision, the effectiveness of customer communication, delivery time and reliability, quality, cost and image) should be achieved as well as is possible when liberated from information constraints.

20.5 TOP MANAGEMENT RESPONSIBILITY FOR OPEN INFORMATION VISIONING

Not only has top management the duty to do 'open information visioning', it has the knowledge to do it. To exploit the potential impact of IT on strategy and structure does not mean that top managers must themselves become expert in IT, nor that they need to become knowledgeable about the various offerings of computer manufacturers and software designers, and good and bad ways of putting them together into cost-effective systems. For most top managers this would be unrealistic.

To 'open information visioning' management need to bring just their experience and imagination. Their imagination must be enhanced by an understanding of IT only in the sense they should understand that IT developments are leading to the possibility of an 'open information capability' by changing the possibility of information supply, and thereby the possibilities for improving the critical success factors.

The IT revolution can make ‘competitive complexity’ critical to strategic success. By enabling people to handle greater complexity, IT brings into play opportunities for superior service or competitive advantage that were foregone in the past because they were too complex to exploit economically.

IT is strategic for top management not only when its developments are so large that its cost or disruption is a strategic matter but because it can change the business strategy itself. So top management ought to take its possibility into account when formulating strategy. And they can do this without being intimidated by the technology.

20.6 TRIGGERS FOR CHANGE

A key question of course is what will trigger the necessary change in the process of strategy formulation? What is it that will make managements take seriously all this impact of IT on strategy? What makes some managements change their game, while others wait to have their game changed? The answer depends on how urgent is the need for change, on where management is coming from, and who they are. What triggers management to make the change and what inhibits it.

Change is risky. It is risky because the more complex the system, then the greater is the chance that experts will underestimate the time and cost to get the system working and that it won’t do what it was intended to do. And it is risky because all change – however well planned – leads generally to surprises, some of which will be unpleasant, and some of which will be more important in their consequences than the problems or opportunities which provoked the change in the first place. ‘Beware the law of unintended consequences’ should be a text for all strategy formulators and change managers.

Change is heavy work. Change, particularly IT-induced change, is expensive and diverts management attention. So ‘don’t change unless you have to’ is a pretty good maxim. But recognize that long lead times are generally needed, not only to design and install new IT systems, but also to change the culture, structure and skills of the business so that the intended benefits of the systems can be achieved. So change may have to be anticipated a good while ahead of when it will be urgent to change, and undertaking to do something which is both risky and onerous requires special circumstances, or a special type of person with a special type of drive, or both.

Change, if it is going to happen, will be competitor-driven, or self-driven, or vision-driven. And without one of those drives, change will not happen as and when it should.

20.6.1 Competition

Consider first the stimulus of competition. All the time, developments in technology change what can be done and the value of doing it. Someone, somewhere will then, sooner or later, do what can advantageously be done, and, in so doing, will create for himself a competitive advantage and, for others, a competitive threat. To that threat, some of the others will react, provided they are rewarded with incentive or the promise of longer survival. And others will not react and will sooner or later lose their business. So, where there is the opportunity for economic advantage or survival to be achieved by reacting to competition, and management has the incentive to react, the burdens and risks of change will be undertaken.

But, reacting to someone else's successful initiative may be too late. The skills and resources needed to react may have been dispersed as a result of the competitor's success. The old market may have been lost. Indeed, especially where the competitor's success has been built on extensive development and use of information systems, barriers to entry by old or new competitors may have been built. So consider the other two varieties of change, self-driven change and vision-driven change.

20.6.2 Self-driven Change

Self-driven change occurs where an organization is imbued with the aspiration to excel and is motivated to make incremental changes to strategy, activity and management arrangements so as continually to improve the factors of cost and volume, quality and service which are critical to the success of the organization. Self-driven change enables the organization to build up its posture within the existing arrangements to react quickly to competition when it comes.

So the enterprise where change can be self-driven is on top of things, even if it's not ahead of the game, but it's ready for the game. Its culture is one where bit-by-bit improvement is expected, and management incentives support this expectation. But that may not be good enough if there can be substantial change in strategy based on substantive change in information systems.

20.6.3 Vision-driven Change

The management structure built up to drive and control a regime of incremental change is likely to present a barrier to the substantial change in information systems required to support substantial change in strategy and structure, with its implied changes in the power of significant people in the organization. That barrier to substantial change persists until a leader is appointed with vision and power; with a vision of new possibilities and with power to send the organization on a path towards it. When that happens, self-driven change moves into the more dangerous and sometimes more rewarding territory of vision-driven change.

From time to time, the difference between the strategies and structures which technology could support and what is actually done becomes so great that incremental change is too slow to bridge the gap. Indeed the new possibilities may be so different from present practice that deciding to change to them is impossible with the existing power structures. This is when change depends on whether the organization has a leader with the ability to commit to a vision of the technically possible strategy which is commercially or politically the best, and whether he has the power and sup-

port to achieve the vision. He needs to be able to visualize and effect what is sometimes referred to as a 'quantum change', or 'paradigm shift'.

Such a leader has to be something of a prophet, with perhaps the excess of enthusiasm of the prophet. If he also has the wisdom to balance enthusiasm for his vision with the prudence and realism of his organization's experience, then the dangers of innovation have a chance of giving way to its benefits.

20.7 THE REALITY

In the end, whether management takes up the challenge of engaging in 'open information visioning' to put IT into strategy depends on how vulnerable they are and whether they can afford to react to the initiatives of competitors, or whether being incrementally proactive is enough, or whether they recognize that complacency with past success may no longer be appropriate and they have the leadership which is rash or brave enough to go for quantum change.

REFERENCES

Kaye, D, (1989) *Game Change:The Impact of Information Technology on Corporate Strategies and Structures*, an Anderson Consulting Management Briefing, Heinemann Professional Publishing.

21 Future Information Technology strategies

H. Green
Hill Samuel Bank Ltd
and Kobler Unit, Imperial College of Science

21.1 INTRODUCTION

21.1.1 Background

In any field, scientific, business or otherwise, the absence of an established (and accepted) paradigm makes it possible to scan all knowledge and available facts with equal address. The essence of this philosophy has been considered by Kuhn (1962) in his work on the structure of scientific revolutions. Information Technology and/or Information Science seem to be open to development of the kind where all knowledge and available facts still need weighing and consideration. It is submitted that no single paradigm is as yet fully developed and accepted in connection with Information Technology (IT) and particularly with IT strategy.

The principal message of this chapter is that IT is continuing to evolve and change. The rate of change is such that the formulation of IT strategies require constant review and needs to remain tightly centred on business goals and commercial priorities. The historical account of IT strategies is interesting to note and the message is: IT strategies have by and large failed and with little if any impact on increasing shareholder value resulting. It has been well documented that some organizations have been technology driven to the point of commercial collapse. The responsibility to shareholders when this happens is very real and it is the responsibility of the main board. The literature review which follows documents the historical developments. The development of future IT strategies needs to be anticipated under the leadership and control of the main board. The stakes are higher than anyone recognizes.

As is well known the role of an IT director in organizations is central to formulating strategic IT planning and recommendations. The actual role and achievements of IT directors, however, remain disputed and as discussed by Grindley (1991) and in the cross-industry survey by Breen (1990), IT directors are not achieving the organizational impact and lead which might otherwise be expected or assumed. The indications are that in the future IT directors may be required at two levels: an operational director and a strategic planning director.

From the review of noted work in the field and as evidenced by recent research, there is still no basis by which to formally, as if from first principles, establish an IT strategy. In specific terms there is no agreed framework which any organization can use for developing an IT strategy.

We take the opportunity in this chapter to illustrate a number of concerns, requirements and ideas in connection with future IT strategies. Perhaps one principle has been established and that is that an IT strategy cannot be developed without a sound and concrete business strategy specifying and identifying requirements. Any IT strategy must bring value to an organization. The view represented here is that an IT strategy is secondary. However, some business strategies could arise from the reverse approach. In the chapter contributed by Kaye in this book, the subject of which strategies should or could follow from which is discussed at some length.

In summary the remaining sections of this chapter establish a conceptual model for the interaction between the CEO, the IT or MIS department and IT users. Some of the key implications for IT strategy creation are considered. The changing value and cost of technology and information over time are discussed including the idea of throw-away technology. In future there may be commercial justification to consider one-off expenditures without regard to the overall organizational needs. The last is presented with a view to the future shape of organizations. The IT centralization versus decentralization issues are highlighted for due consideration in the formulating of strategy. The concept of a core IT resource for organizations is presented and hence the suggestion is made for devolved IT resources to remain with end-users. The purpose and aim of this chapter is to outline thinking and new directions for the future and particularly the formulation of future IT strategies.

An account of historical developments is presented in sub-section 21.1.2, the purpose of which is to document some of the principal developments and lessons concerned with IT strategies.

21.1.2 Historical Review

An informative and extensive study of information and the implications for IT strategy can be reviewed in the thesis of Porat (1976) which systematically established the structure of an information economy. Since the middle part of the 1980s numerous monographs and research papers have been published concerned with the issues and requirements for devising effective IT strategy. Strassman (1985) argued that the pay-off in connection with IT would come from people and not the technology. In the work edited by Clark, Hayes and Lorenz (1985) the central theme was the transformations necessary within organizations to remain and become increasingly competitive. Improving efficiency and becoming technologically innovative were cited requirements.

Undertaking and managing change in organizations as a result of introducing new information and technology was reported on by Boddy and Buchanan (1986). At a more academic level, Boland and Hirschheim (1987) attempted to analyse the more important issues in planning and developing information systems. A view of IT as a competitive weapon was explored by Synott (1987) while Cross and Bawden (1987), Gibson and Jackson (1987), Willcocks and Mason (1987) and Blackler and Oborne (1987) presented work on managing and leveraging the value of IT within the workplace and the inter-relationships between IT and human resources. The general argument is that misalignment of IT, organizational needs and culture can result in a declining value of IT investments if IT investments are not managed in an overall organizational context.

Henderson and Venkatraman (1990) have developed a model for the strategic management of IT they call Strategic Alignment Management. An additional model based on the idea of 'partnership' as a strategy for managing IT user relationships has been proposed by Cooprider and Henderson (1990). They identify two basic dimensions to the partnership framework: partnership in context, the degree to which members of the partnership will be sustained over time; and partnership in action, the ability of members of the partnership to influence key policies and decisions of the partnership effectively.

Somogyi and Galliers (1987) edited numerous contributions on the subject of strategic information systems and the way in which IT developments tend to evolve in organizations. An interesting note is the number of papers that emphasized qualities and skills beyond technical competence as key to developing effective IT strategies. Tomlin (1988) presented a survey of issues and challenges facing management in connection with IT strategy, planning and utilizing the implemented resources. Laudon and Turner (1989) edited a collection of papers specifically concerned with the use of IT to bring about change in organizations; the contributions made emphasized the strategic role of IT in facilitating organizational innovation and business growth. Methods to improve and expand information systems research have been noted by Cash and Lawrence (1989) in connection with qualitative research methods and by Benbasat (1989) with reference to experimental research.

A number of specific industry reports and the role of IT in these have also been compiled. Most recently, for example, the importance and relevance of IT to the financial and securities industries have been reviewed by Lucas and Schwartz (1989) and the general impact of technology on global financial markets by Siegel (1990). An emphasis on discussions and presentation of issues concerned with managing information, the value of IT and strategic planning for information systems has been the subject of work by Knight and Silk (1990), Ward, Griffiths and Whitmore (1990), Strassmann (1990), Siegel, Madnick and Gupta (1991) and Green (1991). The last two have reported on the particular problems of connectivity of information systems and the strategic relevance of information systems connectivity to the overall achievement of increased IT utility and value. Strassmann (1990) provides an overall framework for decisions concerned with IT investments and argues strongly against traditional cost to revenue analysis; developing new measures of IT value are central to Strassmann's work.

21.1.3 Overview of Chapter

The remainder of this chapter is organized into four further sections. Section 21.2 presents a number of unresolved issues in connection with IT strategies. In section 21.3 the falling costs of technology are considered in relationship to alternative approaches to IT planning and expenditures. In section 21.4, a presentation is made of the anticipated future developments and how organizations should expect to benefit from these. Finally section 21.5 summarizes the more important concerns for the development of future IT strategies suggesting a considerable degree of change will be needed in organizations when it comes to aligning IT value with shareholder value.

21.2. UNRESOLVED ISSUES

21.2.1 Strategic Relationships

Strategic relationships are a cornerstone for developing successful IT strategies. At the core of the problem of defining effective IT strategy is the need to establish proper flows in relationships between different organizational groups. Articulate planning is a necessity. Figure 21.1 extends these ideas through the conceptual model illustrated. Once projects are set into motion the need for formal project management methods is paramount. The most effective project management approach would require an on-going MIS group and user partnership to remain involved and co-existing for the project life-cycle and beyond. It is not unusual for one to find an MIS group thinking in terms of: we have it, you should use it and you should pay for it. In contrast, users tend to think in terms of: who needs it, who wants it and how much will it cost?

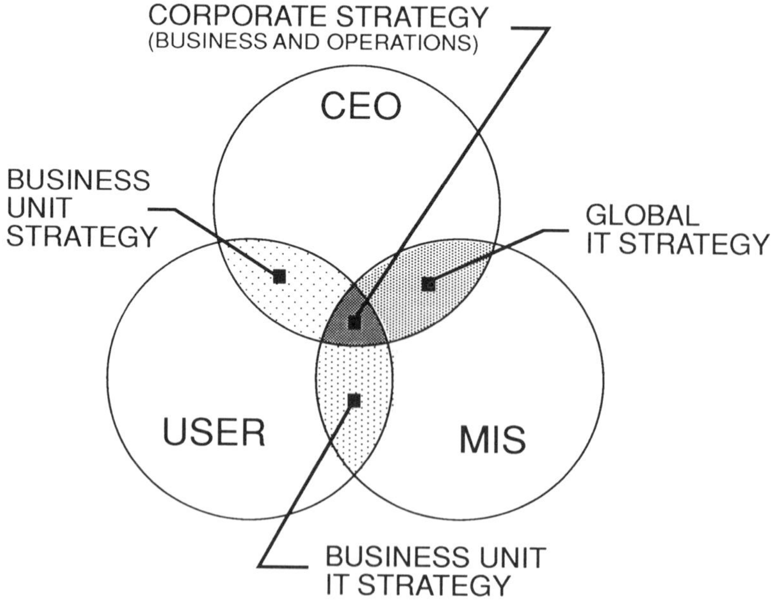

Figure 21.1. Conceptual relationship model between the CEO, MIS department and any single-user group/business unit

Figure 21.1 illustrates a conceptual relationship model between the CEO, the MIS department and any single-user group (e.g. business unit). Figure 21.1 can be interpreted as a Venn diagram where the intersection relationships are what is of interest to analyse. With reference to Figure 21.1 the intersection of all three groups as represented by the cross-patched area in the Figure can be interpreted as the central requirements for any organization. The central requirements are the overall definition and achievement of corporate strategy and goals and the intersection (or bringing together) of all resources needed to achieve these. This is true for any given user group (or business unit) as much as it would be if all user groups or all business units in the organization were involved. The other three intersecting boundaries suggest what key relationships may exist between the intersection of groups and their resources. For instance, between the CEO and the MIS group the corporate-wide standards and global strategy should be the key point of any discussions or planning involving IT. At the intersection between the MIS department and a user group, specific requirements or strategy need to be brought to the table, either in connection with a business strategy needing a certain MIS strategy or, when appropriate, an MIS strategy being made available which suggests to end-users how new business opportunities or strategies could be developed. Henderson and Venkatraman (1990) have considered similar organizational alignment and partnership challenges.

As it often happens what the MIS groups tend not to distinguish are the levels of strategy differentiations as represented by Figure 21.1 and that while it may be ideal to find some specific MIS strategies within a global strategy which could be handed out to users as specific requirements may merit, in the real world this is of very limited value. The reason that value is limited is because truly generic IT solutions rarely exist.

21.2.2 Dynamic Planning

Dynamic planning remains unresolved. Dynamic planning is needed in order to keep flexible and fluid the balance between current requirements and future uncertainties. As suggested by Figure 21.2, many organizations have reached a point where they have very good static models. A static model sets boundaries and is necessary to identify and undertake the development of IT strategies and the integration of these across the organization. Figure 21.2 represents a static model based on the assumption that the organization has a firm foundation or knowledge of requirements and inputs and that these are known to everyone who needs to know. The implicit assumption is that integration of human resources, technology and management requirements can be achieved by conceptually positioning these as pillars on the organization's foundation and with the roof over the top (the systems) holding it all together to represent the operating of the whole. To date there seems to have been little progress made in developing a dynamic model to account for effects as illustrated by Figure 21.3, where at any given time the mixture and degrees of achievement or capabilities between the human resources, the technology and the management of an organization can all differ. Arguably most IT strategies are approached with a static

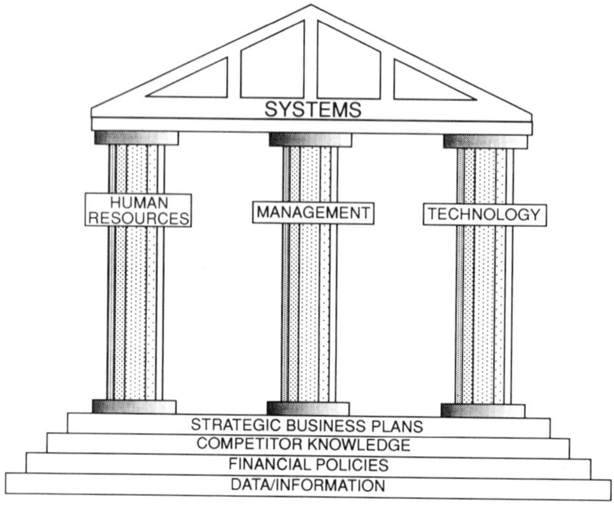

Figure 21.2 Static model of organizations used in developing IT strategies and planning

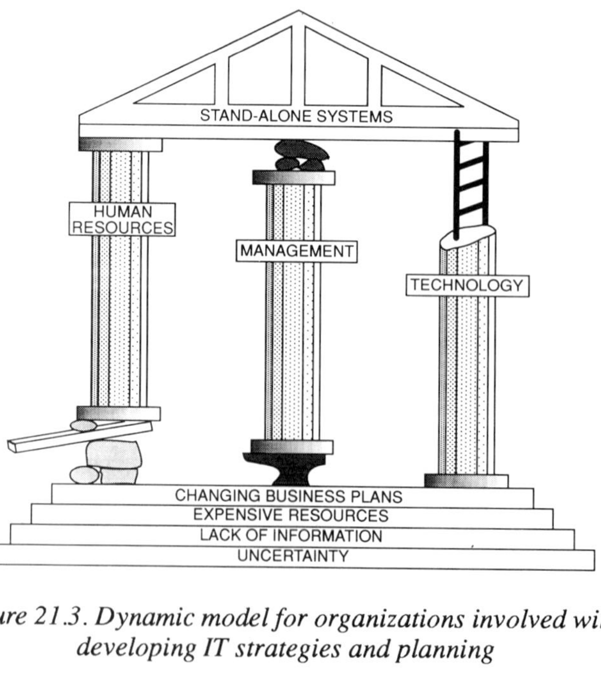

Figure 21.3. Dynamic model for organizations involved with developing IT strategies and planning

organizational view and have as yet to be able to take account of or provide for the real-world dynamics as represented by Figure 21.3.

21.2.3 Positioning of IT

The centralization versus decentralization of MIS and/or IT resources remains a fundamental and unresolved problem and conflict in the majority of organizations. The issue is with establishing what is required or optimum in support of a business need. Throwing away all forms of traditional thinking, the better approach may be to consider developing and managing a central core of information technology resources operated by experts who would maintain and deploy these to users as and when they were required. The shift towards decentralization is already a reality and is likely to continue to increase in the future. The central core resources need to be viewed as internal to the organization. The fact that organizations are increasingly utilizing external data services and other forms of information exchange (both in terms of producing and selling information etc.) lends credibility to the suggestion that a balance will need to be struck between an all-encompassing MIS group and one whose new role is curtailed.

As represented by Figure 21.4, one approach to the centralization versus decentralization issue could be to analyse within an organization the degree of external versus internal IT and IS resources which supply and/or are necessary for operating

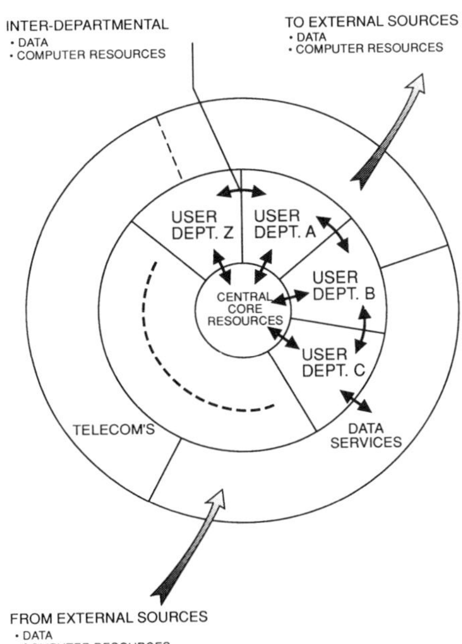

Figure 21.4. General relationship model to establish internal and external IT resources and the degree to which IT resources can be centralized or decentralized

any given department or business unit. Collecting the information would facilitate an analysis of what internal technology and sourcing balance is natural for any given user or business group within the organization.

The MIS and IT professionals will argue that lacking standards and proper control all user developments can end up a disaster. However, users who uphold themselves as wanting to be independent of an IT or MIS department must be made responsible and bear the cost and any consequences of their failings in managing IT and MIS resources. This implies that it may thus make sense to place dedicated personnel in user areas, who are MIS or IT professionals who are loyal firstly to the department they work for but would equally be responsible for managing the deployment and utility of central technology resources in and out of their area. This approach is already being practised in some organizations and when properly planned and committed, it works.

In so far as the issue of standards goes it is very unlikely that for a long time to come there will be any such thing as industry-wide IT standards. Standards often make a peg for very sophisticated-sounding arguments against decentralization, particularly by the MIS and IT professionals. See, for instance, the recent work by Gray (1991). The issue of centralization versus decentralization of MIS and IT will remain around for some time. Centralization versus decentralization must, however, be considered in the overall context of things. The overall context should include considering centralization versus decentralization issues as part of the relationship and strategy interactions already discussed and as represented by the Figure 21.1. Centralization and decentralization are believed to also involve less tangible issues and those are the conflicting policies and politics that naturally exist within organizations.

We have already discussed in the preceding paragraphs the concept of utilizing the central core IT resource approach as one step towards devolving tthe end-user from central resources and providing for his own requirements. What can be expected in the future? The key will be with sophisticated technology and expected increases in user computer skills. The subject of core IT resources is of growing importance and becoming central in many IT strategy plans. Grindley (1991) comments on and refers to the principal benefits and detriments.

21.2.4 Removing Technology Barriers

To date, technology has been a barrier to achieving high-value IT strategies. Real business performance and benefits should be seen almost directly after any new strategy has been agreed and implemented. The recent work by Scott Morton (1991), outlines various developments and issues which bring into perspective the achievements of the 1980s and the challenges for the 1990s as far as information technology management and strategic developments are concerned. The contrast between what has been the historical approach and what might be considered the future approach is that technology has been a barrier in the past but that it should not be expected to remain a barrier. Achieving any and all integration of information required in an organization will be a cornerstone of the future.

21.2.5 Changing Role of IT Directors

The implications for a centralized core IT resource are significant in connection with the future role of IT directors. What sort of background should future IT directors be expected to have? Where will they come from? Will an IT director be needed at all? These are straightforward questions but the answers are not and some of those provided by some companies are not expected to please everyone.

Perhaps the strongest view in support of the need for an IT director for the future is that the role will continue to attract people who are attracted to business and vice versa. The indications are, however, that the most suitable future IT directors may be professional business managers and who have had nothing, or very little, to do with information technology at the technical level; see also, Grindley (1991) and Breen (1990). The immediate senior staff should be comprised of a team of technical experts who are there to achieve the development of identified requirements; either as approached through an interaction relationship as illustrated by the concepts in Figure 21.1 or by analysis and development of centralized core IT resources as illustrated by Figure 21.4.

Arguably, the future IT director will be a corporate operations manager and rightly would be someone who remains at the board level and hopefully speaking a language which would be absent of all technical terms. The technical background IT director will not be necessary in the future. The problem of what to do with existing IT directors who have come up from the data processing or other technical ranks will be one of considerable pain for some and a necessary consideration for all commercial organizations to deal with in the future.

21.3 FALLING INCREMENTAL COSTS

From the main board's perspective the question in any IT spend decision should be: is it worth spending the money?

It should be expected that over any period of time there will be an on-going change in the value of IT investments that organizations make. There should also be a reduction in costs associated with the acquisition of new technology and the maintenance of existing technology. Figure 21.5 qualitatively illustrates a number of concepts. Ideally, investments in IT should be prompted by increasing shareholder value. Translated in terms of Figure 21.5, this means that for any initial IT investment made the value of information generated and the resulting contribution to shareholder value should increase over time and not otherwise. Likewise the cost of technology to achieve increased shareholder value should not be sustained but rather be expected to decrease. Initial costs should eventually be expected to be written off save for the ongoing costs of necessary maintenance. The need to balance and prioritize costs should remain pragmatic.

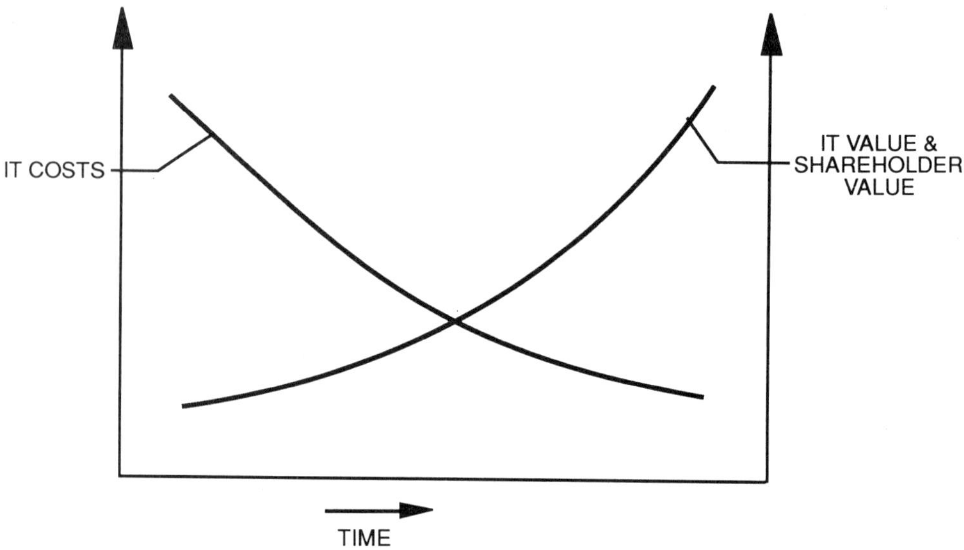

Figure 21.5 Qualitative relationships between IT costs and value, shareholder value

Sometimes it may even be preferred to consider buying in IT to gain rapid market share or achieve high value even if the technology would be of no use elsewhere in the organization and may indeed have to be thrown away after some specific shareholder value benefits are achieved. An ultimate goal should be to achieve connectivity with information systems in such a way that maximizes the transfer of information, assists in the gathering and retention of knowledge in the organization and in parallel serve to increase the value of the business. There is little justification for all IT developments to be handed over to the MIS department or that all key developments need to be undertaken by internal MIS resources. In simple terms, the MIS department is and will always remain (in the majority of organizations) a cost centre.

Consider this situation: a business opportunity presents itself. Software and hardware is commercially available off the shelf to satisfy the business needs. It is likely that within two years' time or less such a software or hardware product as identified in connection with business development and planning may no longer be viable to maintain. The long-term viability of any technology must be continuously questioned. Why then expend the resources, time and effort in developing in-house solutions when the alternative of purchasing solutions and using them to the extent needed is already an achievable reality? Some of the issues outlined here have a lot to do with decisions about centralized versus decentralized IT and MIS resources as already discussed in section 21.2.3.

21.4 WHAT IS ANTICIPATED

Increasing shareholder value must remain and be expected to remain the central point for all future IT strategies. Commercial reality requires this.

The current developments in technology allude to a future where the mechanical constraints known to all who have been or are involved with IT, will have just about disappeared. This may be true of the long term, in the medium term there is still a transition to go through. That transition will require careful management and a significant part of future IT strategies will require to undertake management firstly of the identification and subsequently the management of such transitions. Developing an IT strategy for the organization of the future should be a simpler task than at present. The key will be with identifying what is needed, when it's needed, who should supply it, and being able to account for how the resulting implementations will contribute to increasing shareholder value.

In essence, the sophistication of technology should be expected to continue to increase and at a fairly significant rate. This should be of substantial benefit in that the skills required of non-technical personnel should be much less than historically needed to make more sophisticated and increasingly valuable use of the technological resources which should or could be made available to them. Hence, facilitating the identification of IT responsibility which users should be given.

Until now the emphasis behind most IT strategies and systems planning has been upon providing computer resources to move components of information from the point of entry to the point of utility. Computing in its classical sense makes use of some form of input data into a computer program of sorts and then some form of data processing is carried out. The usual output is in the form of reports or computer-printed ledgers familiar to most. This form of so-called information processing has reached its capacity in terms of useful value. Data and information input and output processing as described will continue to be a part of the future. However, the future of computing will be primarily concerned with the overall process of work flow. Work flow is conceptually and fundamentally different from information flow. It will be necessary in order to achieve any degree of work flow in the organization of the future to have technology which appears to the user seamless and painless at any level. In brief, work flow will be concerned with the integration of an organization's data and information without regard to the source or user of such. By anticipating the seamless integration of technological, information and human resources, work and knowledge flow will be seen as a priority to be achieved by any future IT strategy.

IT planning and strategy must be expected to shift from one of technology 'limited' to one concerned with what needs to be done. This shift requires abandoning the issue of how technology could be used and moving onto creative thinking, designating opportunities and solving user requirements in such a way that there is no regard given to 'how are we going to do this?' The doing should be taken for granted. Having a central core technology resource would facilitate executing set-up of user requirements because it then becomes a real balance between corporate-wide technology standards and new specific user needs. User needs being provided for at an interactive level between users and the MIS personnel.

The enabling technologies necessary to support future developments as described here have already been identified and reviewed in a series of working papers by Siegel et al. (1991) and Green (1991). Organizations should anticipate finally standing at ease with technology. The stakes are very high and as noted by Strassmann (1990) organizations should be expected to get what they need when they need it and how they need it in the sense of the information systems required to run the organization and to maintain positive growth in shareholder value. The management and leadership of future organizations, will thus be able to remain accountable for their successes or failures due to their business and industry expertise and not technology expertise.

There is no doubt that significant changes in organizational structures and traditional thinking of the role of IT are ahead. The implications as to the role of IT directors and their identity are considerable. In a recent survey, sourcing out of computing operations and data management was researched. The principal message was that outsourcing saves money (up to 30%) on measures based on annual IT spend on telecommunications and data management and that outsourcing is a real part of the future.

21.5 REMARKS ABOUT THE FUTURE

In a chapter such as this where a free hand has been taken, noting ideas of potential, one cannot draw absolute conclusions. This chapter has hopefully motivated thinking across a range of issues and tried to visualize how these could be integrated. Creating, developing and seeing through to implementation IT strategies in the future will require radical and articulate re-thinking of established outlooks and concepts.

History has shown some significant lessons in the failings of IT, and the impact on organizational survival when things have gone wrong. Technology, like the ocean, needs to be respected. It is not to be tampered with unless necessary and only then with considerable care and expertise if there is any hope of achieving quality and value with the implementation and subsequent use of technology.

In summary, the future development of IT strategies in organizations at the board level should be able to focus on the creative use of IT and systems utility generally. Little if any emphasis should be placed on the technology.

BIBLIOGRAPHY

Benbasat, I (ed) (1989) *The Information Systems Research Challenge: Experimental Research Methods*, Harvard Business School.

Blackler, F and Oborne, D (eds) (1987) *Information Technology and People*, The British Psychological Society, Leicester.

Boddy, D and Buchanan, D A (1986) *Managing New Technology*, Basil Blackwell, New York.

Boland, R J and Hirschheim, R A (eds) (1987) *Critical Issues in Information Systems Research*, John Wiley & Sons, New York.

Breen, P (1990) *The Emergence of the Main Board IT Director*, Heidrick and Struggles, London.

Cash, J I and Lawrence, P R (eds) (1989) *The Information Systems Research Challenge: Qualitative Research Methods*, Harvard Business School.

Clark, K B, Hayes, R H and Lorenz, C (eds) (1985) *The Uneasy Alliance*, Harvard Business School Press.

Cooprider, J G and Henderson, J C (1990) *Partnership between Line and I/S Managers: A Management Model*, Boston Univ. Working Paper 90-71.

Cross, R and Bawden, D (1987) Information Technology: Human and Organizational Factors, *Journal of Information Science*, 13, pp. 277-284.

Gibson, C F and Jackson, B B (1987) *The Information Management Imperative*, Lexington Books, Lexington, Mass.

Gray, P (1991) *Open Systems*, McGraw-Hill, New York.

Green, H G (1991) *Connectivity: The Strategic and Planning Issues, Departmental Report*, Kobler Unit, Imperial College of Science, Technology and Medicine, London.

Grindley, K (ed) (1991) *Information, Technology Review 1991/1992*, Price Waterhouse Special Report, London. (See also, Grindley's chapter in this book.)

Henderson, J C and Venkatraman, N (1990) *Strategic Alignment: A Model for Organizational Transformation via Information Technology*, Boston Univ., Working Paper 90-70.

Keen, P G W (1986) *Competing in Time*, Ballinger Publishing, Cambridge, Mass.

Knight, A V and Silk, D J (1990) *Managing Information*, McGraw-Hill, U.K.

Kuhn, T (1962) *The Structure of Scientific Revolutions*, vol. II, no. 2, University of Chicago Press, pp. 15-27.

Laudon, K C and Turner, J (eds) (1989) *Information Technology and Management Strategy*, Prentice-Hall, New Jersey.

Lucas, H C and Schwartz, R A (eds) (1989) *The Challenge of Information Technology for the Securities Markets*, Dow Jones-Irwin, Homewood, Illinois.

Porat, M U (1976) The Information Economy, PhD Thesis, Stanford University, Calif.

Scott Morton, M S (1991) *The Corporation of the 1990s, IT and Organizational Transformation*, Oxford Univ. Press, U.K.

Siegel, D R (ed) (1990) *Innovation and Technology in the Markets*, McGraw-Hill, New York.

Siegel, M, Madnick, E S and Gupta, A (1991) *Composite Information Systems: Resolving Semantic Heterogeneities*, Working Paper no. CIS-91-02, Sloan School of Management, MIT.

Somogyi, E K and Galliers, R D (eds) (1987) *Towards Strategic Information Systems*, Abacus Press, Cambridge, Mass.

Strassmann, P A (1985) *Information Payoff*, The Free Press, New York.

Strassmann, P A (1990) *The Business Value of Computers*, The Information Economics Press, New Canaan, Conn.

Synott, W R (1987) *The Information Weapon*, John Wiley & Sons, New York.

Tomlin, R (1988) *Information Technology Strategies for Tomorrow*, Amdahl Executive Inst. Research Report, Hampshire, U.K.

Ward, J, Griffiths, P and Whitmore, P (1990) *Strategic Planning for Information Systems*, John Wiley & Sons, New York.

Willcocks, L and Mason, D (1987) *Computerising Work*, Paradigm Publishing, London.

22 Reconfiguring for lean supremacy

D. Norman
DNA Management Group

Mass production is obsolete, rudely pushed aside by the staggeringly competitive lean enterprise. The reconfigured, customer-obsessed, lean and learning organization is here, now. Rivalling the industrial revolution in importance, lean firms (Womack et al., 1990) are already pulverizing ill-prepared adversaries. Most attempts at lean reconfiguration are paradoxically flawed by myopic thinking, an oversight compounded by management's failure to challenge profoundly wrong, yet long-cherished assumptions about cost behaviour and customer value.

Unassailable global leadership by lean firms such as Nissan, Komatsu and Mitsubishi are scorching flat-footed competition in two fundamental ways. Premier customer value is consistently delivered through highly differentiated products and services produced at extremely low cost, whilst pushing customer expectations beyond the reach of many competitors.

The supremacy of lean economics is awesome. It is applicable to manufacturing and service (Quinn, Doorley and Paquette, 1990) firms alike. The cornerstone of lean practice is the incredibly low-cost base constantly reinforced by rising productivity of world-class 'benchmark' resource utilization in which half the floor space, people, machines, time for NPD, inventory and money, all together are used. Quality rises inexorably, time-to-market collapses, risks diminish and defects plummet, whilst margins are bolstered by higher prices.

The enduring advantages of massive productivity gains and customer adaptability fundamentally distinguish these firms from the corpulent, disadvantaged and uncompetitive majority of firms. These companies are entrenched in Japan, and grossly misunderstood everywhere else. Well intentioned though myopic attempts at hollowing-out, JIT or process management (see value chain in Figure 22.1.) will fail to stem the rising tide of impending national economic deprivation, spiralling unemployment and corporate slaughter.

The lean enterprise is achieved by a holistic approach to the firm's business. IT is an important tool in this attempt but would remain of little value without a clear focus on the firm's strengths, close attention to business process, the development of the 'learning organization'.

There are five ways to reconfigure business value activities: core, hollow, process; and the revolutionary enterprise reinventions and close cousins of, time and lean.

22.1 THE CORE BUSINESS OR BACK TO BASICS

A retreat back to the core business at the corporate portfolio level, is often precipitated by escalating globalization, intensified competition or predatory financial practices. It involves the deliberate shedding and strengthening of business units or whole firms. Examples include BAT's exit from retail (and other) businesses to selectively refocus on tobacco and financial services, and Philips' divestment of their loss-making data processing division to DEC in order to reposition on consumer electronics. This is distinguished from the notion of core competencies which is an important feature of leanness.

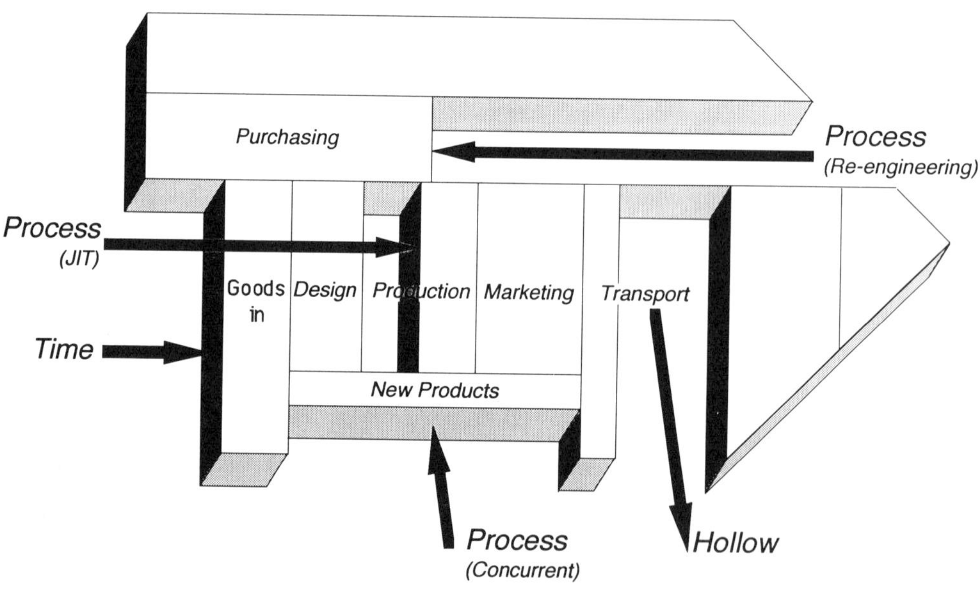

Figure 22.1

22.2 HOLLOW

The hollow corporation is a fundamental reconceptualization of the firm. Sometimes called an 'intellectual holding company', it is characterized by outsourced overheads, strong coordination capabilities and a skeletal value chain of distinctive service competencies. Firms like LA Gear, Benetton and First Direct bank reconceived the business at formation, whereas other specific business process activities, like Amstrad's production in the Far East or BT's £400m transport division, are, or could be, sub-contracted, divested or 'hollowed-out'.

22.3 PROCESS

This comprises process management, just-in-time (JIT), re-engineering and concurrent engineering.

• Process management
This is an approach to work simplification of specific business areas, activities or processes. Motorola (*Fortune*, 1991) evaluates departments like a factory: materials, labour, products, customers and cycle time. It applied the concept to internal auditing and achieved a ten times improvement in cycle time, reduced staff by a third and saved on external audit fees, whilst sales doubled. The hardest part is figuring out where the process begins and ends. Supporters include Corning Glass, Amoco, IBM and the 1991 Laura Ashley SFA-Simplify, Focus and Act programme to cut complexity, duplication and staff.

• Just-in-time
A recent convert to JIT, Havelock Europa (Buxton 1991) a Nottingham storefitting firm discovered that only 22 production steps out of 116 actually added value in the factory, and process time was only four hours out the seven weeks spent in the plant. Lead times were cut from 25 to five days, stock reduced by £2m and more are reported. The principles are well understood by many firms.

• Re-engineering
This is the re-conceptualizing of business activity analysis around the capability of computer technology. Ford (Hammer, 1990) undertook to reduce costs in the accounts-payable department, through automation and paring the headcount of 500 by 20%. They were astonished to learn that Mazda only had five people doing the same job. After adjusting for firm size, Ford should have had a workforce nearer 100. Conventional productivity improvement approaches were jettisoned to accommodate a radical rethink. Analysis showed that most effort was spent matching (and mismatching) purchase orders, receiving documents, invoices and making payments. The new system called 'invoiceless processing' is organized around a computer database reducing staffing by 75%. Batterymarch (Scott Morton, 1991) is a USA financial investment firm with $12bn of pension funds under management who redesigned its business processes around IT and halved professionals from 36 to 18, and support staff from 108 to 17.

• Concurrent
Like most firms, NCR (Port et al., 1990) used to develop new products in steps, largely independent of each other. They now use a collaborative team approach called concurrent engineering, where specialists from design, hardware, software, purchasing, manufacturing and field support work together. Development for a new supermarket checkout terminal was recently completed in half the normal time, had 85% fewer parts and assembled in one quarter of the time. Facilitated by Computer Aided Design (CAD), new products incorporated quality, ease of maintenance and

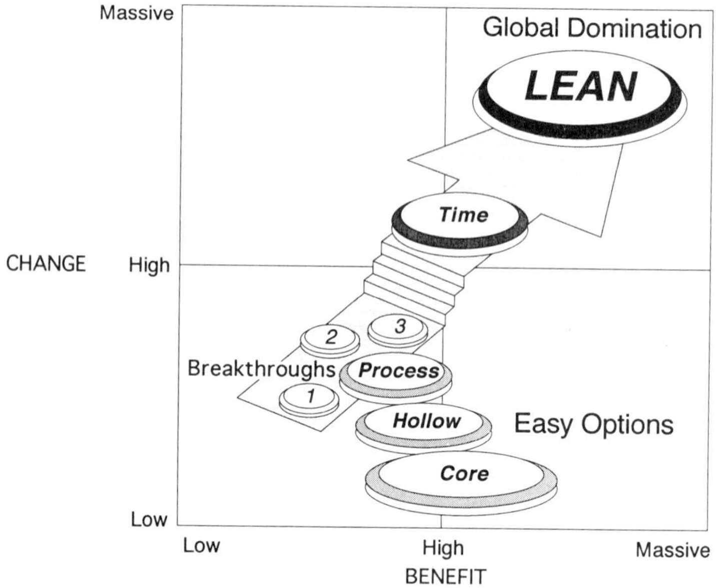

Figure 22.2

manufacturability from the start. Development time cut by 30-70%, quality improved by 200-600% and return on assets 20-120% higher. Also called 'simultaneous' engineering, users include: AT&T, Westinghouse and Kodak.

22.4 TIME

Reconfiguring value activities around time (Stalk and Hout, 1990) rather than costs or assets will surface powerful new insights. Citicorp, Wal-mart and Sun have secured leadership positions by focusing on time compression as the critical management and strategic parameter. Much vaunted by BCG with a decade of experience, and other respected consultancies. A close relation of leanness, economies of speed drives higher productivity, better quality, less inventory, less space, lowered risk, faster throughput and NPD, whilst offering greater variety, price premiums, lower production volumes and better customer service.

22.5 LEAN

The lean enterprises (Womack, 1990) command the strategic high ground. Their immense global economic and business superiority will simply obliterate all Western firms who fail to rapidly reinvent themselves. Stepping onto the lean fast-track will require radical 'breakthrough' approaches (see Figure 22.2), making the value chain

in Figure 22.1 resemble a wedge of Swiss cheese. Reconfiguration demands a holistic systems and paradoxical synthesis perspective, with a focus on knowledge-intense value activities and flexible service networked linkages (Kieretsu). Organizational redesign must be underpinned by learning capabilities which accelerate continuous improvement (Keizen), broaden skills development and instil effective teamwork.

For those firms with lean competitors in the frame, only 'breakthrough' strategies which deliver massive and on-going improvements in performance will ensure survival. Further, any investment in Information Technology which aggressively supports, enables or facilitates a lean strategy of ultra-low cost, vastly superior quality and enormous flexibility must be vigorously pursued.

Evidence to date, in the automobile industry for example, suggests that lean manufacturers (exclusively Japanese) are the most automation intense. This investment yields productivity advantages three times better than US and five times better than European manufacturers. This productivity lead is virtually independent of the degree to which the European and US manufacturers have themselves automated. To capture the benefits of information technology mandates a coherent and co-ordinated approach which effectively accommodates the business strategy, people issues and information management.

Severe obstacles to leanness are rooted in Western mindsets predisposed to problem decomposition and myopic solutions, analytical left brain and sequential mass production reasoning, crippling either/or thinking, quick-fix preferences and vested interests which support problem resolution not elimination. The customer-obsessed, lean and learning organization has placed industrial economic paradigms in turmoil by unleashing a groundswell of industrial and commercial dislocation resembling the displacement of craft methods nearly a century ago.

REFERENCES

Buxton, *Financial Times*, Havelock: Running Counter to Tradition, 26 June 1991.

Fortune, 25 February 1991.

Hammer M, Re-engineering Work, *Harvard Bus. Rev.* J/A 1990.

Port et al., *Business Week*, A Smarter Way to Manufacture, 30 April 1990.

Quinn, Doorley and Paquette, Technology in Services. *Sloan Mgmt Rev.* W.1990.

Scott Morton M (ed), *The Corporation of the 1990s,* OUP. 1991.

Stalk G and Hout T, Competing against Time, The Free Press 1990.

Womack J et al., The Machine that Changed the World, Rawson 1990.